PRESENTS

CLAPTON BECK PAGE

✦ ✦ ✦ ✦ ✦ ✦

GuitarPlayer PRESENTS

CLAPTON BECK PAGE

✦ ✦ ✦ ✦ ✦ ✦

**Backbeat
Books**

An Imprint of Hal Leonard Corporation
New York

Portions of this book are adapted from articles that originally appeared in *Guitar Player* magazine, 1968–2010.

Published in cooperation with Music Player Network, New Bay Media, LLC, and *Guitar Player* magazine. *Guitar Player* magazine is a registered trademark of New Bay Media, LLC.

Published in 2010 by Backbeat Books
An Imprint of Hal Leonard Corporation
7777 West Bluemound Road
Milwaukee, WI 53213

Trade Book Division Editorial Offices
33 Plymouth St., Montclair, NJ 07042

All text content courtesy of *Guitar Player* magazine/New Bay Media, except those articles listed below.

"I Don't Feel I Have to Prove Anything, and I Still Enjoy the Work," p. 53, © 1988 Dan Forte; "Emotion Rules Everything I Do," p. 95, © 1973 Steven Rosen; "My Vocation Is More in Composition Than in Anything Else—Orchestrating the Guitar Like an Army," p. 193, © 1977 Steven Rosen; "There's Always Something in the Guitar That Never Ceases to Amaze Me—Some Sick Sound That I Never Heard Before," p. 147, © 1999 Lisa Sharken; all rights reserved. Reproduction or transmission of any part, in any media, without the author's written consent, is strictly prohibited.

Photo credits: pp. 8, 51, and 207 © Michael Putland/Retna Ltd.; p. 55 by Terry O'Neill/courtesy of *Guitar Player* magazine; p. 66 © Luciano Viti/Retna Ltd.; pp. 81 and 133 © Robb D. Cohen/Retna Ltd.; pp. 92–93 © Baron Wolman/Retna Ltd.; p. 105 © Gijsbert Hanekroot/Sunshine/Retna Ltd.; p. 113 © Andrew Kent/Retna Ltd.; p. 174 © Brian Hineline/Retna Ltd.; p. 197 © Philip Townsend/Camera Press/Retna Ltd.; pp. 198–99 and 210 © Jorgen Angel/Retna Ltd. All other images courtesy of *Guitar Player* magazine.

Printed in the United States of America

Book design by Damien Castaneda

Library of Congress Cataloging-in-Publication Data is available upon request.

ISBN 978-0-87930-975-6

www.backbeatbooks.com

CONTENTS

+ + + + + +

PREFACE

✦ ✦ ✦ ✦ ✦ ✦

The future of rock music was unwritten back in the swinging London of the early 1960s, when three skinny, guitar-obsessed young punks started gigging in the city's clubs and studios. In some ways, Eric Clapton, Jeff Beck, and Jimmy Page weren't much different from the scores of other kids who were turned on by the blues and rock and roll LPs brought over by American servicemen and British sailors who had traveled to the States. But there was something magical burning in that trio—something that transformed them from mere fans or rote copyists into sonic alchemists who twisted the foundations of electric and acoustic blues into a thrilling blues-rock hybrid that forever changed popular music.

It's also interesting, although all three were members of the wildly inventive British band the Yardbirds—and each derived considerable inspiration from the blues—that they took different paths towards evolving the lexicon of rock guitar.

Clapton was the blues purist—so pure, in fact, that he exited the Yardbirds in 1965, as soon as the band started charting pop hits ("For Your Love" was the last straw). But when he joined John Mayall and the Bluesbreakers for the recording of *Bluesbreakers with Eric Clapton*, his experimental side kicked in. In the studio, Clapton cranked up a Marshall amp to unprecedented volume levels, plugged in a Gibson Les Paul, and unleashed some of the most searing blues-based lines ever recorded at the time. Soon, "Clapton Is God" graffiti was painted on walls all over England. A year later, Clapton formed Cream, and his soaring, improvisatory approach to the guitar expanded basic blues into blues-rock, psychedelic blues, and even jazz-rock and pop-rock.

Jeff Beck was the shaman of the trio. *His* blues often sounded as if they were filtered through psychedelic alien radio waves. His playing could be simultaneously feral and otherworldly, and his experiments with Eastern motifs, fuzz, and feedback helped transform the Yardbirds into a much stranger and more exotic group than the typical blues ravers or pop rockers. Beck provided a great foil and counterpoint for Page when both served in the Yardbirds together, although, sadly, few recordings exist of them playing dual lead guitar. Beck's restless creative spirit served to greatly influence heavy metal (with his 1968 solo album, *Truth*), and, later, pretty much invent rock fusion (with 1975's *Blow by Blow* and 1976's *Wired*). To this day, he remains one of the galaxy's most imaginative and original guitarists.

Like Beck, Jimmy Page was also a facile amalgamator of styles, but he was also a gifted songwriter and producer whose pop-music smarts were forged through countless sessions as a studio musician. (Page's successful studio career was one reason he declined to join the Yardbirds when first asked in 1965, and instead recommended his buddy Jeff Beck.) Page's powerful combination of talents attained critical mass in 1968, when he transitioned the faltering Yardbirds into a little group called Led Zeppelin. Through the cultural and musical juggernaut that was Zeppelin from 1968 to 1980, Page simultaneously rewrote all the rules regarding rock audio production, rock bands, rock tours, acoustic rock, and rock guitar. Not surprisingly, he ultimately became one of the most influential, emulated, and revered rock guitarists in history.

As this trio of transcendent guitarists exploded across the musical vistas of the '60s, '70s, and beyond, *Guitar Player* was there to detail each player's tones, gear, techniques, and creative concepts. Clapton and Beck tended to make themselves available quite readily throughout the years, and we have a fair number of interviews to show for it. Page, however, could be private and mysterious, and, as a result, we only have his 1977 interview. But that article is a solid-gold smash—it's the only comprehensive guitar interview Page gave while he was still a member of Led Zeppelin in the band's heyday.

The Beatles' appearance on *The Ed Sullivan Show* in 1964 may have stirred millions of boys and girls to pick up guitars and start garage bands, but one could argue quite convincingly that it was Clapton, Beck, and Page who elevated rock guitar playing to the level of guitar heroism.

This thrilling collection of *Guitar Player* interviews provides essential clues to each player's mastery of the instrument—clues that everyone at *Guitar Player* and Hal Leonard Publishing hope you will use to unlock your own inner guitar hero. Rock on!

Michael Molenda
Editor in Chief, *Guitar Player*

It's always a pleasure to be asked to edit books on guitar heroes and guitar lore, and I'd like to dedicate this one to my mom and dad (who always encouraged my love of rock guitar, even as they feared what that love would do to me), Kirk Griffin (who kick-started my life of musical bliss by dragging me into my first "pro" band), Neal Breitbarth (who was generous and crazy enough to let me be his musical and studio partner during our formative years), Cheryl Muñoz (whose beauty inspires me daily), and the fabulous editors and readers of Guitar Player *(who never fail to educate and exhilarate me).—MM*

·CLAPTON·

1.
"THERE'S NO REASON WHY ANYONE SHOULD LISTEN TO ME, WHEN THEY CAN LISTEN TO THE MASTERS"

✦ ✦ ✦ ✦ ✦ ✦

BY FRED STUCKEY
JUNE 1970

Sitting in bare feet on the edge of a massive bed with a carved wood headboard, Eric Clapton talked with *Guitar Player*. His soft-spoken manner made it difficult to hear his words clearly over the noise of conga drums and tourist chatter rising from Sausalito's main street. Eric's hotel room overlooked the park where so many of San Francisco's freaks and hip types spend pleasant Marin County afternoons watching the tourists watch them.

With thin, sculptured fingers and fine, collar-length hair parted in the middle, Eric has the reserved bearing common to most Englishmen. He was born a quarter of a century ago to a working-class family in a small town 30 miles south of London. Soon after his short-lived art school education, he was playing lead guitar for the Yardbirds. That was the beginning of a career that has netted Eric Clapton fame, fortune, and—strangely enough—humility. In the midst of the whirlwind madness of first-line appearances at San Francisco's Fillmore West and elsewhere, Eric has preserved a quiet dignity.

Eric left the Yardbirds to join John Mayall, England's foremost patron of American blues. He stayed with Mayall for two years. During that period, he mastered the blues idiom, and that training has been the cornerstone of the Clapton sound ever since. After the Mayall band, Eric got together with Jack Bruce and Ginger Baker. The result was the phenomenal Cream. Particularly for underground audiences, the Cream was a dynasty of sound. Through four unbelievable record albums and as many

Clapton in 1967, noodling on his 1964 Gibson SG Standard, famously painted with psychedelic designs by Dutch artists "the Fool."

tours, no rock group had more charisma with audiences than the Cream. Cream followers were cultish in their enthusiasm. Eric's entrancingly sustained notes were an apex of rock-guitar solos.

Since the Cream, Eric formed and toured with Blind Faith, and has played guitar behind Delaney and Bonnie and the Beatles. He sings, plays guitar, and has written most of the tunes on an album, *Eric Clapton Sings*, recorded in Los Angeles on the Atlantic label.

"I don't really like to try and play jazz when I'm not really a jazz guitarist."

✦ ✦ ✦ ✦ ✦ ✦

When I saw you recently with Delaney and Bonnie, I noticed you weren't using the Les Paul you used with the Cream.

I still play a Les Paul. But with Delaney and Bonnie, I used an old Stratocaster I'd acquired. It's really, really good—a great sound. It's just right for the kind of bag I was playing with them.

Have you done anything to the Stratocaster—like modify the pickups, or have the frets shaved?

No. I just set the switch between the first and middle pickups. There is a little place where you can catch it so that you get a special sound somehow. I get much more rhythm and blues or rock kind of sound that way.

With the Cream you used big Marshall amps, right? Lately you've been using smaller Fender amps.

With Delaney and Bonnie, I used a Dual Showman—a big Fender amp. But I hardly ever jack it right up, you know. I'm not getting the sustain or hold-over sound I used to get. It's still there a bit, but that's the Stratocaster.

When you played through those big Marshall amps with the Cream, would you turn them up to get that distorted, hold-over sound?

Yeah. I'd turn the amp and the guitar up all the way. It seems I'm known as a guitar player for that sustain sound—you know, holding notes for a long time.

What kind of strings do you use on the Stratocaster?
Ernie Ball Super Slinky.

How about the strings you used on the Les Paul, on the live side of *Wheels of Fire*?

♦ Fender Rock and Roll strings.

With the Cream, did you use more than one Marshall?

I had the option. I always had two Marshalls set up to play through. But I think it was just so I could have one as a spare. I usually used only one 100-watt amp. I tried to use them in series several times—connected with a split lead—but it didn't work out too well. I would have one end of the cord going into the guitar and separating into the two amps. It was very hard to control and too loud, really.

What kind of wah-wah pedal do you use, like on the "White Room" track on *Wheels of Fire*?

Vox.

How do you typically set the volume and tone controls on your guitar and amp?

That depends on the guitar and amp. When I use the Stratocaster and Dual Showman, I have the pickup switch set between the first and middle pickups—which is a very bright sound, but not completely trebly. I take a little of the treble off, and I put on all of the bass and the middle. And I set the volume at about half.

Do you have a pick preference?

Yeah. Fender—the heavy ones. When I pick, I rest the butt or palm of my hand on the bridge of the guitar, and use it as a hinge or lever. When I stretch strings, I hook my thumb around the neck of the guitar. A lot of guitarists stretch strings with just their hand free. The only way I can do it is if I have my whole hand around the neck—actually gripping onto it with my thumb. That somehow gives me more of a rocking action with my hand and wrist.

Have you gotten into jazz chording much? Are you a theory man?

No, not at all. The way I learned to play was, I picked up the guitar and pieced together a chord out of the sounds without knowing they were chords that had names like *E* and *A*. I was inventing those things when I first started to play. I did a lot of listening—particularly to blues. I never took lessons, but I always wanted to jam a lot. That's a good way to learn to play.

Who were some of the blues people you listened to?

Oh, Robert Johnson for one. Of course, the way Robert Johnson played is very hard to accommodate into an electric-guitar style. The way

Robert Johnson played was sort of a solo trip—it was an acoustic-guitar style. You can't really adapt it to the electric guitar very well without over-simplifying it. For guitar playing alone, there are a lot of people I like who didn't necessarily make it as solo blues artists. There was a guy called Tampa Red who was great, and there's Blind Willie Johnson, who played slide guitar. He was fantastic—he played with a penknife. Most of them are dead and gone now.

From listening to your style of lead guitar, you must have listened to B. B. King quite a bit, too.

Yeah, I met him. We played the same gig quite recently in Philadelphia. He got up and jammed with us, and I sat through both of his sets. He just blew our minds. He's better than he ever was. He has always been good, but right now, having acquired a little success, it has obviously given him a lot more confidence in being able to play up to a white audience. He's really just playing his ass off.

Were you listening to blues when you were playing with the Yardbirds?

Sure, the Yardbirds was rock music, but it was very psychedelic, too. We played long kinds of build-up things—climaxes, up and down things, dynamics with a lot of blues things going on, too. Listening to blues was the only thing interesting to me.

On the *Goodbye* album with the Cream you played on three tracks—"Doing That Scrapyard Thing," "What a Bringdown," and "Badge"—where you got a sound that was distinct from the other guitar sounds you put down on the album. Did you do anything different for those cuts?

We did those cuts after we decided to break up. That was after the last tour—the farewell tour. We were told by Atlantic that we didn't really have enough live stuff to release on the *Goodbye* album that was acceptable. So we had to go into the studio and cut some tracks after the tour. We all had bits of songs, so we went into the studio in L.A. and cut them—all in the space of three or four days. That's why they're really the same sound. And they really are a lot better than any of the things we had done before, because we were relieved of the pressure of the tour. We were all feeling a lot happier about things, because we knew we could do what we wanted.

Did you do anything different with your guitar or amp for those three tracks?

I discovered a Leslie speaker that had been adapted for the guitar. You've got the Leslie speaker and a little preamp that looks like a foot

Clapton at Cream's first major gig during the Sixth National Jazz and Blues Festival, Royal Windsor Racecourse, July 31, 1966.

pedal, and you plug the guitar into that. The Leslie has two speeds on it, and the sound is kind of like an organ.

Why did the Cream break up? It was the biggest group at the time. Who made that decision?

It was felt rather than decided. The tour before the last one was such a harrowing experience that we split from one another during it. We would hang out on our own with friends we had acquired in the cities we were in. We weren't living as a group at all. There was a lot of conflict.

That split manifested itself in the music the Cream was playing, right? At times, the Cream gave the impression that you, Jack Bruce, and Ginger Baker were battling each other onstage.

Not all the time, but it could easily get into that. We were playing the right kind of things to be able to express ourselves in that way.

How did the success of the Cream—all the hype and publicity—affect your attitude about things?

It made me very bitter indeed about being successful. When we first came here to play, that was when our egos really broke loose. Up until then, we were just an ordinary English, provincial group. We came to America, and the bubble burst. We thought we were God's gift. Then, we started to get put down by the press and so on, and I came down overnight. I think we all came down in the period of the tour preceding the farewell tour. It was just a question of working out the dates and getting back home so we could break it up.

Were you affected at all by playing as intensely and loudly with the Cream as you did?

I actually went deaf for a period of time. When we were playing at the Fillmore for a while, I was wearing specially designed earplugs. I had to, because I couldn't hear anything anymore. I was playing full volume in a kind of weird, traumatic state—knowing that I had to play, and not really wanting to. I was deaf, and I couldn't hear anything. I was wearing these earplugs, and I couldn't hear through them. I was really brought down.

Have you played in front of a Marshall turned up full volume without earplugs?

Yeah. I don't think I'll ever be the same. I think one ear is stronger than the other. One ear is at least half deaf—I don't know which one. When I'm onstage, I have to stand a certain way to be able to hear everything. Otherwise, I can only hear half of what's going on.

When you played with Delaney and Bonnie, the total sound was not as loud as the Cream.

But it was still very loud. It was loud because of my influence. Before I guested with them, they were a lot less loud. I'm still coming down from playing extremely loud. It takes a long time to be able to feel comfortable that what you're playing is going to make it even if you're playing quietly, you know.

Playing live with Delaney and Bonnie, I noticed that sometimes your leads weren't on top of everything at times.

It's hard to work out the balance when you're playing with that many people. Unless someone comes around the back and says to turn up, as far as I'm concerned, everything is fine. Some of the times I wasn't loud enough, but I didn't want to be up front anyway. I just wanted to complement what they were doing. I didn't want to change their sound. It was very difficult for me to just slosh myself in there, and please some of the people who came to see me without changing the sound of the group.

How did the Delaney and Bonnie thing start?

It started on the Blind Faith tour. We had three or four days off at one time, and everybody from our group went home because they were homesick. I stayed, because I wanted to get into things here. I had no one else to hang out with, so I hung out with Delaney. He was very keen and everything. We started writing songs. And that was essentially more of a groove than it was to play with my own band. Blind Faith was going through all that hype stuff at the time. After the tour, I decided it would be nice to get together with them, and expose them a little more, and see if I could be of any help. Delaney gave me a lot of confidence to be able to sing.

Yeah. You do a good job on "Crossroads." You close your ear with your finger when you sing. Why?

Because I can hear myself singing in my head. Otherwise, I've got to go on what I hear through the monitor, or what's coming out of my mouth. If you put your finger in your ear, you can hear yourself singing in your head, and that helps you get better pitch.

Were you having a little trouble singing and playing guitar follow-up runs with the Cream and Delaney and Bonnie?

It's kind of awkward. I'd like to get more into that. I think that's really the essence of what I should have been doing all along. With some of the songs I've done onstage, they are not mathematically proportioned. When you play a 12-bar, you can know it by heart and play around it. But other songs have a different form, so I'm not sure what to play, or when to play. If it's blues—like "Crossroads"—it's a lot easier.

After the Cream, you got together with Ginger Baker and

**Steve Winwood. With that band, Blind Faith, you cut one album,
and did one tour here in America. The album did very well. What
happened to Blind Faith?**

Well, I left. I mean, after the tour we sort of had a holiday. And I
decided during that time that I was going to fetch Delaney and Bonnie
over to do a tour of England and Europe. They really wanted to come.
So we set it up. Blind Faith—that particular group name is now
defunct—that was really just an album or a tour. The rest of the group
have augmented themselves—acquired more drummers and a great big
horn section—and replaced me with another guitarist. They are called
the Air Force, and it's like Ginger's band.

How about Steve Winwood? Is he with Air Force?

Yeah. He's with them. It's Ginger, Rick—the Blind Faith bass player—Steve, and about five other guys.

When did you first meet Winwood?

I first met him in Birmingham. I was either with the Yardbirds or with
John Mayall. He was with Spencer Davis, and it was the first time I had
ever seen the group. They hadn't had a hit record yet, and they were doing
"Boom Boom"—you know, John Lee Hooker stuff. He was really, really
young. He still is—he just turned 21. He is brilliant at whatever he does.

What did you think of the Blind Faith experience?

It wasn't quite what Steve and I had hoped it would be. We started out
with very big ideas about it, and gradually it started to lose the original kind
of concept of what we were going to do. Finally, we were just living up to
our commitments—just doing the tour and playing the album. It didn't
come off as well as we had intended. Our names got in the way—you know,
all that supergroup hype. The best stuff we did was when we were just jamming at Steve's place, or at my house. We have tapes of that, which are just
hours of instrumental, fun-type jazz things. That's what Blind Faith was all
about, but it was never exposed to the public. When we came to do the tour,
we were so nervous about playing in front of that many people—with all that
hype going down—that we just tried to be as professional as possible. We
played the album, and tried to do an act. We didn't make it on that level.

**Do you have to perform in a loose, free situation in order to
be an effective guitar player?**

Yeah. It has to start from that kind of basis. It can evolve into something later, but you've got to be able to stretch out.

**As rock music goes, the Blind Faith album was pretty sophis-
ticated. Do you think it went over people's heads?**

Maybe, but I think that some of the songs—and the treatment of some of the songs—was just right. I think that in about a year's time, it would be easier to appreciate that record. I still like it. It was one of the nicest things I ever did. There are only a couple of tracks on it that don't really please me. "Sea of Joy" was one. It wasn't really as good as when we had written and rehearsed it. And "Do What You Like," because it was really against my musical principles. I don't really like to try and play jazz when I'm not really a jazz guitarist. I don't really like to play in a group that's playing jazz too much. "Do What You Like" was in a jazz time, and it sounded kind of like the *Mission Impossible* theme, you know. I really couldn't get it together. On the solo on that track, I was trying to be something I wasn't. I was trying to be a jazzman. I've never really listened to jazz, so therefore, I really wouldn't pretend to play it. I've listened some of it, and I like it. It's not necessarily above my head—I can dig it and understand it—but it's not my main thing.

You know, quite a few American musicians are trying to break into the rock market with not overly spectacular results.

They are probably more adept at being able to make the transition from jazz to rock, though. It's easier for a jazz musician to simplify his style, than it is for a rock musician to complicate his.

One of the problems with the jazzmen is that once they get into the kind of lyrical complexity of jazz they have trouble being funky.

You're probably right.

To get back to your guitar playing, you spent the two years before the Cream playing a fairly pure form of blues behind John Mayall. You stayed with the blues scale during those days. Did you make a conscious change of lead style when you began playing with the Cream?

Yeah. A lot of the time, I did try new things because the songs were different. The leads had to be different. I tried to play more things—like hillbilly music and rock and roll stuff.

Did you plan your leads, or, for that matter, do you plan them now?

No. The only planning I do is about a minute before I play. I desperately try to think of something that will be effective, but I never sit down and work it out note for note.

You usually don't build your solos around a theme riff.

I might, say, if the song is a very popular one. Like when I played "Sunshine of Your Love" with the Cream, I'd play something like what I laid down on the record. I'd hint at it, but not necessarily repeat it.

Have you heard other guitarists around playing what are obviously your runs?

I do sometimes think that, but it's probably just conceit on my part. There's no reason why I should think that—seeing as how I copied most of my runs from B. B. or Albert King or Freddie King. There's no reason why they should listen to me, when they can listen to the masters—you know, the source.

What do you think of American rock guitarists these days?

They're great. They're getting better all the time. There's not one I've heard lately that I wouldn't say isn't great. I've yet to hear any lately that are really bad. There was a lot of bad guitar going down earlier, but now it's really rounded itself off. Everybody seems to be playing their asses off.

By the way, was that you playing the lead guitar part on "While My Guitar Gently Weeps" on the Beatles album? There were some rumors that you took George Harrison's place on that track.

That was me. George and I were doing something the day he was to record that track. He had to go down to the studio that day, and cut the track with the rest of the group. They were all waiting for him, and he wanted me to play the guitar on the cut because he thought he couldn't do it the way he wanted to hear it. I didn't agree with him. I thought he should have played guitar on it, but it was great for me to do it. We agreed that I wouldn't get paid for it, or have my name mentioned.

Did you use your Les Paul on that track?

Yeah, the Les Paul through a Marshall amp.

You've played with the Beatles since, right? The famous Plastic Ono Band.

That was Lennon's freedom thing. He has this band—the Plastic Ono Band—which is anybody who shows up and can do it. It's as simple as that. Lennon asked me to do it when they were in Toronto, and we did another thing in London when Delaney and Bonnie were there. Lennon is a beautiful man, really very far-out.

You know, it surprises me in a way that you've kept your head together after having played for so long with so many heavy, heavy bands.

Well, I've lost a lot of it. I've lost a lot of the peace of mind I used to have. It can be acquired again, but it takes a concentrated effort at being still and staying at home. I'm not too keen on too much more touring. I'd like to take a holiday.

2.
"I THINK JAMMING IS PRETTY MUCH A WASTE OF TIME"

✦ ✦ ✦ ✦ ✦ ✦

BY DAN FORTE
AUGUST 1976

Eric Clapton is now 31 years old. For more than a decade, he has been *the* rock guitarist.

Doubtless there are "better known" guitarists—such as George Harrison—and rock's creative genius on the instrument remains the late Jimi Hendrix, but it would be hard to find anyone to match Clapton's longevity and consistency as a lead guitarist in the rock field.

When Hendrix's future manager, Chas Chandler, first approached Jimi with the idea of moving to England, one of the young guitarist's first questions was, "Will I get to meet Eric Clapton?"

In past *Guitar Player* readers' polls, Eric has always placed high, winning Best Rock Guitarist four consecutive years, from 1971 to 1974, then taking a surprise first place in the blues category as a write-in candidate last year. He was also voted Overall Best Guitarist in 1973.

Beginning guitar at around age 17, Clapton—born March 30, 1945 in Ripley, England—was a charter member of the Yardbirds, a band whose influence is still strongly felt by many hard-rock units. Here his gutsy, aggressive, improvised blues licks established Clapton as one of the first *noticeable* lead guitarists of that era. Like the American blues bands they emulated, the Yardbirds put the guitar leads and fills into the forefront of their overall sound.

Their first recording. *Five Live Yardbirds*, was released in England in 1964, when "Slowhand," as he was once known, was 19 years old. Just as the group was beginning to realize a degree of international pop notoriety, Eric quit to concentrate on the blues—to be replaced on lead guitar by Jeff Beck, and later Jimmy Page. Though the Yardbirds' first LP released in the U.S. [*For Your Love*] pictured only Beck on the cover, it was, in fact, Clapton's guitar that highlighted eight of the album's eleven tracks.

"You always know when you come to a dead end. Then you have to make up your mind about what you're going to do."

✦ ✦ ✦ ✦ ✦ ✦

Already heavily into country blues artists like Big Bill Broonzy, Blind Boy Fuller, and Robert Johnson, Clapton then joined John Mayall's Bluesbreakers, and totally immersed himself in Chicago blues. It was during this period that the name Eric Clapton took on a somewhat mythical, cult-figure status in Britain. Like the "Bird Lives" syndrome that swept through bebop havens after the death of Charlie "Yardbird" Parker, the slogan "Clapton is God" could be found scrawled on signposts, sides of buildings, and even rocks across England's countryside.

Within days after leaving the Bluesbreakers, Cream was formed. Consisting of three virtuoso soloists—drummer Ginger Baker, bassist Jack Bruce, and "E. C." on guitar—Cream was perhaps the first rock band to successfully combine a free-form musical concept with mass appeal. They were also one of the first rock groups to earn a large following based on their *instrumental* abilities rather than catchy "hits," extravagant stage acts, or personality promotion. They were simply very creative musicians and widely accepted as such.

When Cream made its *Farewell* tour in 1969, barely two years and four albums after its inception, the veteran guitarist had just turned 24. This super-trio was succeeded by an even shorter-lived quartet, Blind Faith—with keyboardist Steve Winwood, bassist Rick Grech, Baker, and Clapton. After an extended hiatus from performing live, Clapton emerged in the role of sideman to Delaney and Bonnie and Friends, his first American group. Here he met and played with what later became the nucleus of Derek and the Dominos—which also included co-guitar great Duane Allman on their premier album, *Layla*.

With the Dominos' breakup and another three-year absence from the music scene, Eric's current lineup was formed, piece-by-piece, while recording *461 Ocean Boulevard* at Miami's Criteria Studios.

The following exclusive interview took place on May 7, 1976, in Los Angeles, where Clapton was putting the final overdubs on his upcoming album, to be released later this year. Along with Eric's electric, acoustic,

Clapton during the recording of *Layla and Other Assorted Love Songs* with Derek and the Dominos, 1970.

slide, and Dobro work, the LP features Ron Wood, Jesse Ed Davis, and Eric's second guitarist George Terry, plus a duet with Bob Dylan on "Sign Language."

After Derek and the Dominos, you had sort of a layoff from performing live. How did you get back into playing guitar?

It was nothing sudden. I don't think I've ever really stopped for very long. You just develop a different set of chops for concerts than you do for recording or just sitting around writing. In the last two years, they've been getting better and better onstage, and then they kind of wear down when I'm off. When you're in the studio, you can't really stretch out much. You have more license to experiment onstage.

That seems the opposite policy of guitarists who say they'll only try new licks in the studio, where they can go back and erase or redo any mistakes.

Well, in the studio what always affects me is the fact that I know I'm going to hear it back. So I don't want to make *any* kind of mistake if I know there's a chance I might hear it on the tape.

Do you still ever practice—sit down and run scales?

I never have done that, but I do sort of play around quite a lot. I can't play just to silence, though. I have to be prompted into it by listening to something or hearing something on the radio.

In an interview, Paul Kossoff said that in 1974 you were better on guitar than ever before. Do you think you're still improving?

I think I'm improving all the time—in my own particular fashion. The chances are that I'm probably slipping behind the times in my tastes or my direction. But when it comes down to my personal approach and playing the guitar, I'm still learning and kind of progressing. I'm pretty sure of that. You always know when you come to a dead end. Then you have to make up your mind about what you're going to do. I haven't felt that too many times yet.

When you get into a new style, like reggae, do you have to alter your technique much?

I don't have to adapt much for anything like that. It's not difficult to play that way. What I always find the most difficult is keeping up my technique of just playing lead in any situation. What I would find hardest of all would be to be featured in a jazz composition of some kind, and have to play a solo over strange chords. But things like reggae and popular songs of any kind are always pretty simple.

Have you ever gotten into jazz?

Well, the one thing that hung me up straightaway was that technique they have of double picking, up and down. I use both down strokes and up strokes, but I've never been able to do that fast thing. Any of those guys seem to be able to do that.

What about jazz chording?

Well, that's another situation. Watch any of those guys, like George Benson or someone. The amount of fret positions they can get out of, say, three or four chords—you know, I just don't know about that stuff [*laughs*].

Being self-taught, where did your chord background come from?

I just listened to records, and I tried to figure out which strings they were hitting at the same time.

Instead of barre chords, you seem to play down at the nut a lot.

Those were the chords I learned. I also think when you're using light strings, you tend to become a bit insecure about going up the neck too far with big, full chords. Because what will sound right at the bottom of the neck with light strings, by the time you've taken out 12 frets it could be out of tune.

You've played blues right from the beginning, but only recently got into playing slide, which is an integral part of blues.

I always used to play slide just on the acoustic guitar, and that was never employed onstage, and consequently it never got on record, either. I think what really got me interested in it as an electric approach was seeing Duane Allman take it to another place. There were very few people playing electric slide that were doing anything new. It was just the Elmore James licks, and everyone knows those. No one was opening it up until Duane showed up and played it a completely different way. That sort of made me think about taking it up.

Are there any similarities between your electric slide technique and Duane's?

No, not a great amount, because I approach it more like George Harrison. Duane would play strictly blues lines. They were always innovative, but they were always in the blues vein. I'm somewhere in between him and George, who invents melodic lines, often using scales.

What do you use for a slide?

A glass tube about the width of the neck of the guitar, so I can get all the strings covered. It's a thick one [*an Isis medium*].

Do you have any special guitar setup for slide?

Yes, a Gibson ES-335. But it hasn't got a high nut. I just raise it at the bridge. I don't play it down at the bottom much. I usually keep it up near the top [*high*] frets. I use the same strings as I do normally on the other guitars: Ernie Ball Super Slinky, gauged .009, .011, .016, .024, .032, .042. [*Ed. Note: Eric's road manager, Willy Spears, says that the last time the strings were changed on this guitar was mid-1974. Normally, Clapton's strings are changed only when they break—except for the high three, which Spears sometimes changes when he feels they're going dead. Willy says, "He won't even let me buff them."*]

Do you play slide in standard tuning or open chords?

I use open G [*D, G, D, G, B, D*] most of the time. I prefer G, because you get more of a country sound. It's more melodic.

Do you ever use open tunings when not playing slide?

Yes, on "Tell the Truth" [*Layla* and *Derek and the Dominos in Concert*]. That's tuned in open E [*E, B, E, G♯, B, E*]. But I wasn't playing slide—I was just making chords in open tuning. If you tried to transpose them onto a straight guitar, it would be very difficult. It's like a barre *A* on the fifth fret. I'm holding down the fifth and third strings in a sort of *E7* shape—holding it on and taking it off. That comes directly from Keith Richards. Some of the Stones' things—like "Street Fighting Man" where he has all these great guitar sounds—he just tunes it to an open chord and invents fingerings.

After Cream, where you were the only guitarist, how did you come to form bands that always included a second lead guitarist?

I wanted a variety of performance styles, and I didn't think I could do those things as well as those guys do theirs. There were certain songs that I felt required their technique. I didn't want to just attempt it and get a second best by doing it myself.

Is there anything in particular that you look for in another guitarist?

No, it depends more on their personalities—if they're well-composed musicians who don't have to show off. I like to have someone in the band who's stable, you know, who can play and get on with people. I don't like to play with people who've got to prove themselves.

Did it get tiring playing in bands, like Cream, where you had to solo constantly?

Absolutely—it really did. Sometimes, you just end up playing every lick you know before the end of the set, and then you're f**ked, you know, because you're just repeating yourself over and over again. I've really become more devoted to the song itself and the presentation of the actual music. I think jamming—unless it has a goal at the end of it—is pretty much a waste of time. It's just like exercising or something. If you're jamming, and something comes out of it, and you make something that you can stand hearing again, and that has a form and turns people on, okay. I think musicians, as they grow older, usually become interested in doing something more lasting. It's a very youthful thing to go around and jam with everyone who's known—kind of like sowing wild oats. Then you've just got to settle down and make everything count, and make sure that it's worthy of being heard again—not just a throwaway.

When you play with another guitarist, rather than straight rhythm chording, you often throw in little riffs and counter melodies.

As a rule, I actually *prefer* to play rhythm, or let whoever else I'm playing with take the stage. But there are times when I just can't resist joining in.

In the beginning, was it hard for you to coordinate singing and playing at the same time?

Well, for as long as I've been playing the guitar I've been singing and playing. Not anything difficult, you know—I couldn't play a lead line and sing a different line independently, like what Hendrix could do.

You were one of the first people Jimi Hendrix jammed with when he went to England. What was he playing like at that stage?

He did the whole show. He did two songs and pulled out every stop. He did everything that he did for the rest of his career in those two songs. It just blew the audience away. They'd never seen anything like it before. He wasn't into his clothes scene at that point. I think he was just wearing jeans and a jacket of some kind. But his technique and his vibrato were just as strong.

Being a British bandleader with an all-American group, does this create any musical conflicts?

I don't think so, because we cut our teeth on the same kind of music—the blues and R&B. We were listening to the same stuff at approximately the same time—just in two different places. The only real difference is in the lifestyles.

What causes you to switch guitars over the years?

It's a fad, I think. Like, at the Concert for Bangladesh, I was playing a Gibson Byrdland. If you remember, Chuck Berry had a lot of publicity photographs taken with a Byrdland, and that looked like a very delicious guitar. I couldn't get hold of an old one with the black pickups, so I got one with humbuckers instead.

Were there any feedback problems using a full-box guitar?

Yes—that's one thing I never accounted for. You have to really be careful—especially on the low, bass strings.

What other guitars do you own?

Let's just say I have a selection of Gibsons and Fenders and a few Martins. The Stratocaster is my basic stage guitar. I've also got a Switchmaster—the old Carl Perkins type—a lot of good old acoustics, and an old mandolin-guitar.

Do you have any specially-made guitars?

I've got a wood-body Dobro with a Martin-type neck, reworked by Randy Wood. I got it at George Gruhn's shop in Nashville. I also have a 12-string made by a guitar maker in England called Zemaitis. It's reputed to be the biggest 12-string in the world. It's about the same dimensions as a mariachi bass. He really did a beautiful job.

What's your main acoustic guitar?

A Martin D-28. It has a pickup built into the bridge called a Barcus-Berry Hot Dot, and they're really good. I don't know the pros and cons about miking an acoustic live, but all the sound people I've worked with have said it's a hassle, because the microphone will pick up wind and leakage from the other instruments. The dynamics just go mad if you back off three or four inches.

Do you always use a flatpick?

Yes. I use a heavy pick made by Ernie Ball. I think it's the exact same thickness and gauge as a Fender heavy. I've never kept the fingerpicking up long enough. I do play around like that for my own pleasure at home sometimes, but I wouldn't be able to cut it professionally.

What about your changes in amplifiers over the years?

Music Man is my favorite now—a HD 130 Reverb—because they have dual volume controls. You can use them in the studio at low volume, and still get a fair amount of distortion—just as if it were a really big amp. I also like their sound. They're just like Fenders—in fact, I think Leo Fender had a big part in designing them. [*Ed. Note: Actually, Tom Walker who worked for the Fender company from 1948 until 1969 was Music Man's main designer, although many of the ideas were passed on from Leo Fender during their association in Fender's pre-CBS days.*]

Were the amps you used previously more suited to your sound at that time?

The Music Mans could have been used with Cream. You can get exactly the same sound as you would with a Marshall, but then you can take it down to the same volume as a Champ. It really has a wide range. [*Ed. Note: Roadie Willie Spears reports that Eric's amps are beefed up, with the bias up all the way, by Walker at Music Man. This HD 130 Reverb has special open-back cabinets, as opposed to the folded horn type, with JBL 120 speakers. Eric also uses a Leslie cabinet, with JBL components, for which he has had a special footswitch devised by Keyboard Products and modified by Fred Meyers, soundman for Santana. This switch has fast/slow and on/off positions, so that the guitar can go either straight through the amp, through both the amp and the Leslie, or through just the Leslie at either fast or slow speeds. The only other effects pedal Clapton uses is a Cry Baby wah.*]

Why do you record at such low volumes?

There's less interference, less noise. I like to record a lot of tracks as live as possible, including voice. So if you've got a really loud amp, you're going to leak onto everyone else's track, and you won't be able to sing either. I also like to record tracks without headphones. I like to hear the sound the room is making itself, rather than the balance coming through the board and into the cans. I recorded "Motherless Children" [*461 Ocean Boulevard*] with just a Pignose mini amp.

Do you plan on presenting any more older bluesmen, like the records you did with Howlin' Wolf [*The London Howlin' Wolf Sessions*] and Freddie King [*Burglar*]?

It would probably come up. Those kinds of things are usually on the spur of the moment—like within a week's notice. There's no one I can think of right now that I would go out of my way to do. With Wolf, on "Red Rooster," he was very, very vehement about it being done right. Because he considered us to be English and foreigners, and therefore we wouldn't have heard the song, right? So he just got his guitar out and said, "This is how it goes." It's not on the album, unfortunately, but he played it all the way through once on his own with us just sitting there listening. He was playing slide Dobro, and it was just bloody amazing! And he said, "Okay, you try it." So we all tried playing it like him, but it didn't really sound right, so I said, "Well, why don't you do it with us?" And that's the bit that got on the record.

Do you think those sessions—mixing a blues stalwart with several rock greats—come off well?

That one came off. But I am actually biased against those things. My ego told me to listen to the one I did with Howlin' Wolf, and I liked that, because I like The Wolf anyway, whatever he did. He never could go wrong, because you could put him in with, oh, Buddy Rich or someone, and he'd still dominate the show. The other reason I did that session was that, for a long time, I'd really wanted to meet his guitarist, Hubert Sumlin, because he did some things that freaked me out when I was picking up the guitar—that stuff on "Goin' Down Slow," for example, is just the weirdest playing. He's truly amazing!

In last year's *GP* readers' poll you won Best Blues Guitarist as a write-in, so obviously people still think of you as a "blues guitarist." Is that how you think of yourself?

Yes—that's what I do best. That is really my personal style. If I'm put into any other kind of situation, I'd have to fly blind. In the blues format, I can just almost lose consciousness—it's like seeing in the dark.

3.

"I AM VERY MUCH A CHAMELEON. I CAN BE ALTERED AND CHANGED BEYOND RECOGNITION BY SOMETHING THAT NO ONE ELSE CAN UNDERSTAND"

✦ ✦ ✦ ✦ ✦ ✦

BY DAN FORTE
JULY 1985

Few figures in pop music arouse the public's curiosity as does Eric Clapton. Guitarists, in particular, are interested not only in his instruments, his recordings, his sources of inspiration, but in his outlook on life, as well. What are Eric Clapton's views? What is the man like?

For someone whose ever-changing career has been dissected time and again, Clapton remains a mysterious persona, an enigma. Even specifics about his various bands, records, and stylistic stages are often confused.

Interviews with Clapton are very rare. He is, by nature, somewhat shy and withdrawn, and often extremely self-effacing. He sometimes insists that what he has to say probably wouldn't interest anyone.

The following interview was conducted April 13, in Pensacola, Florida, on the morning of the third date of his current tour. Having turned 40 two weeks earlier, Eric was somewhat philosophical and introspective, but not at all introverted. Looking very healthy, he talked openly and articulately for hours, welcoming queries about every aspect of his playing, his various bands, and his often-tumultuous lifestyle.

At the tour's opening concert in Dallas, Clapton was in perhaps the best mood he has *ever* been in onstage. In fact, his fingers were still a bit tender from the experience several days later.

"I couldn't stop playing," he smiled, recalling the show.

That spirit carried over to the Pensacola stage, with his current group: guitarist Tim Renwick, bassist Donald "Duck" Dunn, drummer Jamie Oldaker, singers Marcy Levy and Shaun Murphy, and keyboardist Chris Stainton.

E. C.'s two-hour-plus concert encompassed most of his 20-some years as a guitar icon—from Cream's lyrical "Badge" to blues such as "Double Trouble," hits such as "I Shot the Sheriff" and "Lay Down, Sally," and new material from his chart-climbing *Behind the Sun*. As bandleader, singer, and, of course, guitarist, Clapton was clearly in command. The identity crisis he discusses here, which lasted for most of the '70s, seems to be behind him at last.

Stylistically, do you see *Behind the Sun* as a departure?

Very much so. Yeah. And, also, it's not truly me, either. "Forever Man" and two other songs on the album were something I did to appease the Warner Bros. heads. The difference between the Phil Collins-produced project and the cuts with producers Lenny Waronker and Ted Templeman was chalk and cheese, to me. To the outsider, it probably seems like they're blended very well, but, to me, the feel is totally different. Really, what I was trying to do with "Forever Man" and the other two was get a feel that I heard on the demos. That's songwriter Jerry Williams from Fort Worth, Texas. He is, to me, the best white person in the States, but he can't get a record deal because his personality is larger than life, to put it mildly. He wrote "Forever Man," "See What Love Can Do," and "Something's Happening." I've got a cassette with 19 of his songs, and all of them are blinders.

Why the division between the Phil Collins productions and the songs produced in L.A. by Waronker and Templeman?

Well, Phil and I completed an album in a month and mixed it in a month. And it had three tracks on it that are gone now—which were definitely not viable to the Warner Bros. picture of having a complete album of hit singles. They wanted a very "up" rock and roll album from me. They expected that, without having to say anything. And they *didn't* get that. They got kind of a rounder picture—a couple of ballads and a slow blues with just an acoustic guitar. I thought, and I still do, that a lot of people would have liked to hear that side of me.

As it happened, it wasn't what the heads of the company wanted, and they made this clear to me. I said, "Well, why don't you tell me what you would like it to be, and I'll see if I can go with that." They sent me these Jerry Williams songs, and I really was knocked out. He has been around a long time, but he hasn't got a record deal, mainly because he doesn't make compromises—*at all*. Of course, the demos are what he considers to be finished product. He doesn't like to refine them, or clean them up. And, in actual fact, he's right [*laughs*].

Anyway, I said, "Yeah, I'd love to record these." I got Lenny and Ted to produce them with musicians of their choice because Phil was unavailable, and I thought if they were going to produce it, they would probably want to use their people—the L.A. "A Team." If I'd taken my band, there would have definitely been a "camp" feeling. My band would only listen to what I say, so there would have been an "us and them" situation straightaway. Whereas, with the session people, it was really only a question of me fitting in.

Did you feel like *they* had a camp, so it was you and them?

Not at all. They were great. There may have been that from me, because after getting to L.A., I felt a little alien about the whole project. I started to wonder if I was selling myself down the river, or selling myself short. But they soon got rid of that feeling. They're very good people, and very quick. Of course, I was immediately put into the studio with Steve Lukather and his fantastic box of gizmos, and I was very intimidated by that for a little while. Then he crossed the bridge. He made the first move to make me feel welcome.

He was probably even more intimidated by you.

This is what everyone kept saying to me. But it's a little different. I really admire those guys, and I respect them for the way they treated me.

The new album sounds quite a bit more high-tech than what you've done in the past. Did you have to adapt to the technology much?

No. In fact, I wrote most of the songs for the album on synthesizers. I'd run out of ideas on the guitar. And I can't play the piano, you see, so it's the same old thing as when you first buy a guitar—you think you're inventing all this stuff. You become an instant composer, really. You think they're brand-new chords—until you meet people who *really* play, who tell you what you're doing is the same old stuff. But it sounds so great, I write easier. I got a Sequential Circuits Prophet 5 because it has such a nice memory bank, so it's easy to write on it. Put a claw shape down [*laughs*], and you've got this nice sound.

How did you record the guitar parts?

I played on the tracks and overdubbed most of the solos. It was great with Phil, because he's a real fan. I was saying, "Well, what do you think of that one?" He'd go, "It's dynamite, man. Dynamite!" I'd say, "No, it isn't." I felt like I could have played anything, and he'd love it. That's great from a producer. So I'd do three or four solos on a song, and say, "*You* sort it out." And I knew that he could be more enthusiastic about it than I. I'd probably listen to a solo three or four times and get fed up with hearing it, whereas in the same situation, he could work for two days picking which parts of each solo. Some solos—for instance, on "Just Like a Prisoner"—he edited down from quite a length.

Had you done that with producers in the past?

Yeah, yeah.

When you take three passes at a solo section, how similar is one take to the next?

They would all be identical in every way, except that the high points would be in different places. If I was to spend a day in the studio recording the same solo for the same song, each one would have its high points. It would be up to me or the producer to say, "We can either have a solo of all high points, or we can leave one as it is." I mean, I would prefer to be able to go in and play the solo, and just leave it, but you never do that in the studio. As much as everyone wants to leave it alone, they all want to actually make something of it. "It's great, but wouldn't it be that much greater?" And they're right—for the finished product. You can't do that in a live situation, so why *not* do it in the studio? It's just taking creativity that one step further.

Of the producers you've worked with, does anyone stand out as your favorite?

I think Tommy Dowd is always the number-one man for me. Phil is a different kettle of fish. I love him, and he's a great musician, so he has another angle. If I could get the two of them to produce a record together [*laughs*], that would be *it* for me. They're my ideal producers.

Before going in to overdub a solo, do you ever plot in advance what you're going to play?

Yes, and it never fails to come off as miserable. If I start, I'll compose the whole solo, and it will turn into a symphony. It's that whole Leonard Bernstein thing: If we start with a little motif and play it three times, and the third time we introduce a coda, and that coda becomes—well, sud-

29

"I AM VERY MUCH A CHAMELEON. I CAN BE ALTERED AND CHANGED BEYOND
RECOGNITION BY SOMETHING THAT NO ONE ELSE CAN UNDERSTAND"

denly, you've got a symphony on your hands, which everyone can spot straightaway as being boring. And I'm not recognized for that. People don't like me to do that.

After you've played a spontaneous solo that's a keeper, do you then follow it pretty much note for note onstage?

Sometimes. It's just a question of familiarity—finding a reference point to come back to that you've established, so you can go out and come back to that place again.

"I really don't like [Cream's live version of 'Crossroads']. I think there's something wrong with it."

✦ ✦ ✦ ✦ ✦ ✦

Cream's live version of "Crossroads" [on *Wheels of Fire*] is often cited as one of the best live cuts—and live guitar solos—ever recorded. Was that edited from a longer jam?

I can't remember. I really haven't heard that in so long—and I really don't like it, actually. I think there's something wrong with it. I wouldn't be at all surprised if we weren't lost at that point in the song, because *that* used to happen a lot. I'd forget where the I was, and I'd be playing the 1 on the 4, or the 1 on the 2—that used to happen a lot. Somehow or another, it would make this crazy new hybrid thing—which I never liked, because it's not what it was supposed to be. What I'm saying is, if I hear the solo, and think, "God, I'm on the 2 and I should be on the 1," then I can never really enjoy it. And I *think* that's what happened with "Crossroads." It is interesting, and everyone can pat themselves on the back that we all got out of it at the same time. But it rankles me a little bit.

"Forever Man" has a fatter guitar sound than you've gotten in a long time.

I used a different Strat, and I put heavy strings on it, and I tuned it down two frets to *D*. Not an open *D*—just straight, but a whole-step down from concert pitch, so I could play the riff as if I were in *E*.

Do you think your guitar playing is distinctly British?

Not at all. I think all of the members of my band, myself included, are American, musically. I can see it much better in some ways than Americans can, because I'm over there in England, looking at it from a distance. I have a lot of inbred stuff that I heard as a kid, which I wouldn't have heard in America. English folk music is very much kind of in the back of my head, subconsciously. So, I suppose that comes out every now and then in terms of meter and length.

But it was your arrival—along with Beck and Page—that helped launch the concept of "English guitar playing."

It's that same thing about being able to listen from a distance. Perhaps the audience needed to hear it coming from a long way away, although it's identical to what's in their backyard, really. For instance, Stevie Ray Vaughan is exactly what I wanted to be when I was 16 years old. He's doing it right here, you see.

Stevie Ray has an abundance of that sort of youthful, aggressive one-upmanship.

Yes, I would imagine I'd be up against it if we got together. We just missed down in Texas—we were trying to connect. But I know if we'd gotten together, it would have definitely taken on those proportions.

Have you found yourself in those situations?

Oh yeah. See, what he has picked up is a genuine black attitude—which is great—like Albert King. Buddy Guy is the same, but he's much more humanitarian, let's say [*laughs*]. Not Albert or Freddie King. Freddie could be pretty mean, but subtle with it. He'd make you feel at home, and then tear you to pieces.

Obviously, your early playing was largely defined by how aggressive and forceful it was, but did you have that killer instinct, also?

Absolutely. And it's still there. I just don't get into a jamming situation very much these days. But if I do, yeah, it *has* to be there. What else are you going to do? You can't just sort of walk off. But there is a way of approaching it. There would always be a loudmouth in these situations—just like in samurai films. If you ever saw *The Seven Samurai*, the best swordsman of all gets into a situation where he doesn't want to fight, but he's up against this real bull of a man who's saying he's the best. The samurai finally says, "No, I won, but if you insist, you can say that you won." That's what I do: I let the loudmouth, or the villain, mouth off, get it all out of the way, and then I just come in very quietly—like B. B. King. Just one note or something that will shut *everyone* up—if you can find it [*laughs*]. It doesn't always work.

In the movie *Moscow on the Hudson*, Robin Williams plays a Russian saxophonist who gets blown off the stage by his idol of the

31

"I AM VERY MUCH A CHAMELEON. I CAN BE ALTERED AND CHANGED BEYOND
RECOGNITION BY SOMETHING THAT NO ONE ELSE CAN UNDERSTAND"

sax. **Did you ever have an experience like that?**

I think I've had that several times, and every time it has been healthy, as well as very heartbreaking. When it's done to you by someone who you really hero-worship, the first thing you feel is real betrayal. The bottom line of all these relationships should be a colleague-type feeling, and if that is taken away, you really feel like your father has just kicked you out or insulted you. That's very painful. At the same time, it teaches you to grow up very quickly and become self-reliant.

It must also feel weird to jam with your idols and smoke them.

Oh, yeah. That has also been possible. There have been times I've played with, for instance, B. B. or Freddie, where the main contingent in the audience was my followers who hadn't heard of Freddie King. So it would be possible for me to win in that situation just by being me—even if what I played wasn't better. You have to be aware of that and not allow it to happen.

Did any of the ARMS [1983's Action and Research into Multiple Sclerosis concert] shows get into all-out shootouts between you, Jeff Beck, and Jimmy Page?

It was very much there between me and Jeff, and I think it was also there between Jeff and Jimmy. But because I'm not familiar with Jimmy's playing—I never worked with him—we had no time to develop a rapport. So, as a three-part thing, it couldn't happen. I also think Jimmy was pretty much under pressure as it was, and to have thrown him more of that would have been unfair. He was very nervous about going out there. He needed to be supported, and not attacked from every angle. He was very frail.

Beck seemed to be the most blatant gunslinger.

I think he is. And at that time, and for many months after that, I began to think of Jeff as probably being the finest guitar player that I'd ever seen. And I've been around. I still think that way, if I really sit down and mull it over. Carlos Santana, of course, is very high on my list. For pure spirituality and emotion, that man is number one. But there's something cool and mean about Becky that beats everyone else. I have to hand it to him in that respect. Although he was involved in that ARMS thing, he was pretty detached. He could have been any-where. He was just going to play, and that was it—never mind what the whole thing was about. He does actually have that love for Ronnie Lane, as well, but when it came to playing, forget everyone else. For some reason, on that show, I couldn't do that. I felt like I was almost an organizer of the thing, so I couldn't actually get off the ground very much.

As a member of the Yardbirds, your role was basically to solo. Is it hard to carry over that gunslinger attitude when you've got bigger responsibilities in your own group?

Of course it is. As a sideman, up until the point where you come in for your solo, there has been no light on you, so you come in absolutely fresh, and that's your big moment. Whereas when you're in the front all the time, and you're singing one of your songs, it's all you. And when you play the solo, it's *still* you [*laughs*]. There are no dynamics to it, in that respect, and that's a bit tough sometimes.

Do you think it actually affects what you play?

Yeah. I don't deliberately change the solos, but I think of devices—or ways of playing the solo—to make it more interesting. I went through a period of trying to minimize everything—to take shorter solos—and it was very badly received. My idea at the time was that by minimizing it, I would make it more potent, but I didn't succeed at that. The audience was right in many ways. I was trying to look at it like I was B. B. King or J. J. Cale, but B. B. is B. B., and I'm me. It's no good adopting someone else's personality or philosophy.

Is there any one blues player who you think you're most similar to in terms of attitude?

I think Buddy Guy.

But he's a lot wilder. He sometimes bends up to God-knows-what pitch.

Yeah, that's where I stop [*laughs*]. I've seen him do some mad stuff, which is fantastic. But I take what I like, and then I stop there.

Who was the most stimulating guitarist you ever played with?

[*Long pause.*] I think of all the people I've ever played with, the most stimulating in an onstage situation was Freddie King. That would closely be followed by Carlos Santana. Because, in both of those situations, we had time to get to know one another—to know when to stop and let the other one play, or when to push or not to push. That takes time—the length of a tour. In a working band, I think Albert Lee and myself were the most stimulating pairing, but in a very different way—more camaraderie.

What about musicians other than guitar players?

I think Steve Winwood is very high on the list. Also, harmonica players, like the guy that used to play with Muddy Waters—Jerry Portnoy. Saxophone players, as well. I once worked with King Curtis, and that was

33

"I AM VERY MUCH A CHAMELEON. I CAN BE ALTERED AND CHANGED BEYOND
RECOGNITION BY SOMETHING THAT NO ONE ELSE CAN UNDERSTAND"

frighteningly good—something I wanted to repeat forever. He had exactly the same idea about what lines to play as I did. It was like another instrument with the same person playing it.

You've become a model for a whole generation of blues and rock guitarists. You must hear a lot of your own style in other work of other guitar players.

I do, and the funny part is, the parts I recognize as being directly taken from my playing are the parts about my playing that I don't like. Funny enough, what I like about my playing are still the parts that I copied. Like, if I'm building a solo, I'll start with a line that I know is definitely a Freddie King line, and then I'll—I'm not saying this happens consciously [*laughs*]—go on to a B. B. King line. I'll do something to join them up. So that'll be me—that part. And those are the parts that I recognize when I hear something on the radio that sounds like me. Of course, it's not my favorite bit. My favorite bit is still the B. B. or Freddie lines.

When you say you were copying various blues guys, you were still adding quite a bit of your own. For instance, your version of "Hideaway" [on *Bluesbreakers*] differs quite a bit from Freddie King's original.

Exactly. I was copying feel, I think, by that time, or atmosphere.

That's a hard concept for a lot of players to grasp.

I started working on what the guy would *live* like. I would picture what kind of car he drove, and what it would smell like inside. Me and Jeff Beck had this ideal of one day owning a black Cadillac or a black Stingray that smelled of sex inside and had tinted windows and a great sound system. That's how I visualized these players living. That's what feel is all about. If I wanted to emulate somebody, I would try to picture what they would live like, and try to live that way. You develop this kind of image.

So even if your image isn't completely accurate . . .

It helps you get to *somewhere*—which is another thing altogether.

Do you continually go back to the same sources when you need inspiration? Can you always get inspired by hearing Freddie King or Robert Johnson?

Or Otis Rush or Buddy Guy. Yeah. And it's not so much technique that I listen for—it's content, really, and the feeling and the tone.

Is that what set Robert Johnson apart from the rest of the Delta bluesmen?

Yes. Absolutely. It was so intense. It was difficult for me to take it when I first heard *King of the Delta Blues Singers*. A friend and I were both blues fanatics, and he was always a little bit ahead of me in discovering things. We went through Blind Blake and Blind Willie Johnson—working our way backwards, to the root of it—and he finally came up with Robert Johnson. He played that album for me, and I couldn't take it. I thought it was really non-musical—very raw. Then I went back to it, later, and got into it. First hearing it, it was just too much anguish to take on.

It's like hearing an exorcism or something.

Exactly.

Cream has been credited as the fathers of heavy metal, progressive rock, acid rock . . .

This is what I'm beginning to find out [*laughs*]. Someone threw this at me two months ago, and it honestly never occurred to me until then. I always assumed that Zeppelin was the beginning of it. I think you could actually say that there was a concept there that was picked up on maybe more than the music.

You did sort of legitimize jamming onstage.

Right. That's probably what it's all about—the lengthy guitar solos and improvisation. That may have been a stepping-stone for a lot of the heavy metal things that happened.

Do you think the faster-is-better trend of younger players misses the point that you see as the purpose of guitar soloing?

Well, it's not the way I would approach it, but it's hard to form a judgment on it when you don't know what it will turn into in the end. It may be that they're developing a whole new frame of reference. See, what may happen from that is a kind of rebellion in five or ten years' time that may take it back to where *we* recognize it. Or it may just become brand new. I would hate to say, though, that they're all missing the point.

Do you feel that there's a bond tying you with the generation of lead guitarists that followed you, such as Eddie Van Halen?

If Eddie Van Halen likes the way I play, then assumedly, he must like what I liked. But if he can recognize all of that and still do what he does, then we have to accept that he's on to something that we're not really clear about. Because he couldn't be doing what he does and recognize Robert Johnson without there being something valid going on. He *is* very fast, and, to my ears, a lot of the time he kind of goes over the top. But that's because I'm a more simple player. Maybe I would play like

35

"I AM VERY MUCH A CHAMELEON. I CAN BE ALTERED AND CHANGED BEYOND
RECOGNITION BY SOMETHING THAT NO ONE ELSE CAN UNDERSTAND"

that if I had the technique. I've heard that he slowed down records of mine to learn the solos. That's dedication! I don't know quite how to respond to that.

Did you ever slow down records to learn solos?

Not slow them down. Well, early on, I did that with Duane Eddy's records—singles like "Cannonball."

All of the guitarists who've played in your band have differed enormously. Is there a common prerequisite you look for?

With players, again, technique isn't as important as personality and feel. I can hang out with a guitar player for a very short time and either get a feeling from being with that person, or not. I may get a feeling from being with *that player*, but I may not want to hang out with him. He may be dynamite—very aggressive and very to-the-front—to the point where I think, "I can't handle this more than twice a week." Every night would just be too much. It would be too demanding. Constantly having to prove yourself is not very relaxing—it frays your nerves. I always end up with people in my band who I can really get on with as people, and that is what they play like, as well.

Playing with someone as extroverted as Jack Bruce must have pushed you night after night.

Night after night—to the point where it was really a question of just a battle, a war. I don't think he did it deliberately—it's just the way he is as a musician and as a guy. I mean, he has to clear a space around him, and you can't get very close a lot of the time.

In the video of the ARMS show in London, you switched to your Explorer when you did the slow blues. Do you still see the Gibson as your blues guitar?

In some respects, yeah. When I get up there onstage, I often go through a great deal of indecision—even while I'm playing. If I've got the black Stratocaster on, and I'm in the middle of a blues, I'm kind of going, "Aw, I wish I had the Les Paul." Then again, if I were playing the Les Paul, the sound would be great, but I'd be going, "Man, I wish I had the Stratocaster *neck*." I'm always caught in the middle of those two guitars. I've always liked the Freddie King/B. B. King rich tone. At the same time, I like the manic Buddy Guy/Otis Rush Strat tone. You can get somewhere in the middle, and that's usually what I end up doing—trying to find a happy medium. But it's bloody anguish.

Is there any consistent setup that you try to have all your guitars conform to?

"You can only really do exactly what you want when there is no pressure to be what you've become popular for."

✦ ✦ ✦ ✦ ✦ ✦

Yes. All of them need to be about 1/8" in the action, and I like it to be constant all the way down. I can't stand it if the nut is low, and the action gets higher as you go up the neck. I always take the wang bar off, and have five springs, and just tighten the whole thing right up. I like frets to be generally somewhere between a Strat and a Les Paul. Les Pauls' frets are too thick, and Fender frets are sometimes too thin. The Fender Elite is very nice because it has a blend. The neck on Blackie—the Strat I play all the time—is probably my favorite shape. It's almost triangular on the back—V-shaped—with a slightly curved fingerboard, as opposed to the flat one. That, to me, is the best.

Is the Strat you use for slide set up differently than Blackie?

Yes. It has a very high action with a higher nut and thicker strings. I always use Ernie Ball strings.

What year is Blackie?

I don't know, because it's made up of about three different guitars. I was in Nashville in 1970 with Derek and the Dominos, and I went into the Sho-Bud shop, and in the back they had a rack of Stratocasters and Telecasters and various Fenders—all going for $100 each. No one was playing them then. Everyone was going for Gibsons . . .

Because of you, largely.

Yeah, maybe [*laughs*]. Well, I wasn't alone. But Steve Winwood had kind of gotten me interested in them, because he was playing a blond-necked Strat. It sounded great. Then I thought, "Well, yeah, Buddy Guy used to play one," and I remembered a great picture of Johnny Guitar Watson playing one on the *Gangster of Love* album. So I just bought a handful of them, and took them all back to England. I gave one to George Harrison, one to Steve Winwood, and one to Pete Townshend. I kept three, and out of them, I made one—which is Blackie. I just took the body from one, the neck from another, and so on. I have no idea what

37

"I AM VERY MUCH A CHAMELEON. I CAN BE ALTERED AND CHANGED BEYOND
RECOGNITION BY SOMETHING THAT NO ONE ELSE CAN UNDERSTAND"

year the various parts are, so it's actually not a good collector's guitar at all. Well, it is now [*laughs*].

I feel that that guitar has become part of me. I get offered guitars, and endorsements come along every now and then. Strings & Things from Memphis tried to get me interested in a fairly revolutionary-looking guitar, the St. Blues. I tried it, and I liked it, and I played it onstage. I liked it a lot. But, while I was doing that, I was thinking, "Well, Blackie is back there. If I get into this new guitar too deeply, it's tricky, because then I won't be able to go back to Blackie. And what will happen to *that*?" This all happens in my head while I'm actually playing [*laughs*]. I can be miles away thinking about this stuff, and, suddenly, I shut down, and say, "This is enough. No more. Nice new guitar. Sorry. You're very nice, but. . ." That's when I drag the old one back on, and suddenly it's just like jumping into a pool of warm water.

If you come across a creative block, and you've had Blackie in your hands for a week, can you pick up another guitar and come up with a new idea?

Yes, it will happen like that. Usually, it happens with an acoustic guitar or a gut-string or, as was the case with the album, the Roland GR-700 guitar synthesizer. I got the pedalboard and the memory bank—the guitar is interchangeable. I bought the new model guitar, and I couldn't play it, because it kept sliding off my lap. So, I got one with the old Strat shape, and the electronics are more or less identical. And that inspired me—just picking it up and playing a chord. But, generally, see, I don't play the electric much at home. I usually play this acoustic—I got it from Santa Cruz Guitars—because it has a nice sound.

Even though you have Blackie, do you still have the temptation to shop around and collect guitars?

Yes, and there are still guitars that I want. They're like the Holy Grail for me. There's the fat-bodied guitar that Chuck Berry played in all the publicity photographs of him duck walking—a Gibson ES-350. It has those black P-90 pickups. I'm always on the lookout for a good one of those. They're actually very rare. I know of a couple, but the people won't part with them. Or if they do want to part with them, they'll quote such a high price that you say, "Well, no, that's actually silly." Because I won't play it—I only want it because it looks good. On the other hand, there will come a time when someone will walk into the dressing room with *the* guitar, and you don't know why—it just *is* magnificent—and then you have to buy it. It could be a Les Paul, an Explorer, a Stratocaster—but it's just so perfect. You can tell by the way it feels that it has been played. If you can pick up the guitar and tell that someone great has played it— you can actually tell that—then you want to take it and endow yourself with what the *guitar's* got.

Do you still have a basement full of guitars?

I've still got them all, but I turned the basement into a recording studio. So, all the guitars were sort of delegated to people to look after for me, and there's a warehouse where we keep most of our equipment. Some are with friends, or with my manager, or in my house, or with my roadie Lee Dickson, and [Who roadie] Alan Rogan has some that have drifted through his hands. They're scattered about. I actually don't know how many are out there, but I know I've got a good few. I love them all. The best Les Paul I ever had was stolen during rehearsals for Cream's first gig. It was the one I had with John Mayall—just a regular sunburst Les Paul that I bought in one of the shops in London right after I'd seen Freddie King's album cover of *Let's Hide Away* and *Dance Away*, where he's playing a goldtop. It had humbuckers, and it was almost brand new—original case with that lovely purple velvet lining. Just magnificent. I never really found one as good as that. I do miss that one.

Judging by the sound you achieved on the *Bluesbreakers* album, you must have been turned up to 10 on your amp.

Maybe it was. We'd gotten used to it, obviously. I remember reading an interview with [engineer] Gus Dudgeon where he said that I put my amp in a certain place, and he went over and put a mic in front of it, and I said, "No, put the microphone over there on the other side of the room because I'm going to play loud." I think that sounds like it would be true. We all had a definite idea of what they were doing in Chicago when those blues records were being made. John Mayall had ascertained that you could tell by the sound—the compression that was evident on the Little Walter records, for instance—that maybe they were recording the whole bloody thing through his vocal mic. Because when he took his mic away from his face, the band would get louder—which was a great sympathetic thing to happen. Then, when he'd start singing, they would die down. We had definite ways of thinking about how we wanted to be recorded. That still appeals to me a great deal—having one mic in the room and everyone arranging themselves around it to their satisfaction. So, yeah, I was probably playing full volume to get that sound, and then I'd place myself in a way that it would be a good mix for the band. I was playing a Marshall 60 watt.

39

"I AM VERY MUCH A CHAMELEON. I CAN BE ALTERED AND CHANGED BEYOND
RECOGNITION BY SOMETHING THAT NO ONE ELSE CAN UNDERSTAND"

**Your tone changed between the *Bluesbreakers* album and
Fresh Cream.**

Yeah, we were using bigger Marshalls by then—100 watts. And we
used the stacks in the studio. *Fresh Cream* was done in England, and
Robert Stigwood produced it. I don't know who the engineer was. Then
we went to America to do the Murray The K show, and while we were
there, they invited us into the Atlantic studio, and I played with Tom
Dowd, and Felix Pappalardi became our producer. So Tom Dowd was
the one getting the sound on *Disraeli Gears*.

**It sounds like you're using a fuzz on tunes like "Outside
Woman Blues" and "Swlabr."**

There may have been. What we used to do was trip down to Manny's
every day and pick up whatever was new. That's how I got my first wah-
wah. Jimi was knocking around New York then, too, and we used to trade
things. I have no idea how many gadgets were passing through the studio then. But it may have just been straight, with the Marshall full up. In
those days, it would get that quality.

**Did you go straight from the Marshall amps you used with
Cream to the Music Mans you used in the '70s?**

No, I was on Fenders for quite a while. The Fender Showman was
my number-one amp during Derek and the Dominos. When I got the
Tulsa boys together, [bassist] Carl Radle came up with a Music Man,
and I really got into them. The first ones were really great, but then I
started blowing them up a lot, and they started sounding very thin. So I
went back to Marshall recently. On the ARMS tour, I was using a little
old blonde Fender Twin.

**You've recently started using a chorus effect—for instance, on
"Same Old Blues" [from *Behind the Sun*].**

I'm a funny person like that. If I like it, I'll forget it's there. I've got
a pedalboard that was built for me by the man who works with Steve
Lukather [Bob Bradshaw]. It has a bank of presets, but I just use the one
chorus, and then a deeper chorus. I sometimes put it on the minimal one
and forget that it's on—I just leave it. Then, if I go back to normal, I
think, "God, that sounds so straight." Very rarely now do I just play completely straight.

**The story goes that between the time you left the Yardbirds
and when you joined John Mayall, you locked yourself in a room
in the country with nothing but your guitar. Is that true?**

Yeah, that's true, but they're missing something there. I actually stayed with a friend whose ideas had always interested me—Ben Palmer. His approach and philosophy of music—and life, too—were such that I regarded him as a bit of a guru. Through the Yardbirds, I was starting to feel very lost and alone. I was being made to feel I was a freak, and I started wondering if I was a freak. They all wanted the simple things of success and the charts, and what was wrong with that? "What's the matter with you? Why don't you want this?" And I began to think that I was really crazy. So I went off to see Ben Palmer, and it was just like, "Oh, yeah. Of course you've done the right thing." He immediately made me feel human again.

So the improvement in your playing was more a function of clearing your head than just woodshedding.

Clearing my head and playing the guitar, as well. He made me feel normal again, and I wanted us to form a band together, but he was off the music scene [*Ed. Note: Palmer later played piano on the* Eric Clapton & The Powerhouse *sessions, and became Cream's roadie*]. He didn't want to get involved again. So I just hung out for about three or four weeks with him, and we played together, and I got strong again. Strong in my ideas, and my feelings, and my self-confidence in what I was doing.

Once you eventually did achieve enormous success, with all its attendant problems, did you long to be just a sideman again?

Yeah. I'm still not absolutely sure about this, but it feels to me like you can only really do exactly what you want when there is no pressure to be what you've become popular for. When you play a concert, there's so much pressure on you to do old things, new things, and what the audience wants. When you become successful, you've got to bow to that to a certain extent. That cuts off a lot of your creative energy. It's quite limiting.

When you first got interested in blues, what was the scene like in London?

Alexis Korner and Cyril Davies were already going before I played guitar—or while I was doodling. I'd go see them, and the Stones were forming. It was very stimulating. There was something about seeing a band play live what you'd only heard on records. It was fantastic. The first person I ever heard in England bend notes was called Bernie Watson. He was in the original Cyril Davies band. Their hit was "Country Line Special." The story on Bernie Watson was that he was a classical guitar player who liked to do this for fun. He was the original one who sat down with his back to the audience. Never stood up. And he was the first one I saw play a twin-cutaway Gibson semi-acoustic. He

41

"I AM VERY MUCH A CHAMELEON. I CAN BE ALTERED AND CHANGED BEYOND
RECOGNITION BY SOMETHING THAT NO ONE ELSE CAN UNDERSTAND"

was really a bit of a cult hero. He was a very mysterious man. I never
spoke to him.

**Were there any seminal inspirational records you heard in
your formative years?**

Both of the Robert Johnson albums [*King of the Delta Blues Singers,
Volumes 1 and 2*] actually cover all of my desires musically. Every angle of
expression and every emotion are expressed on both of those albums.
Then the *Ray Charles Live At Newport* album, B. B. King's *Live at the
Regal*, *The Best of Muddy Waters*, the Howlin' Wolf album with the rock-
ing chair on the cover—hasn't got a title—Jimmy Reed's *Rockin' with
Reed*, *One Dozen Berries* by Chuck Berry, the Freddie King album with
"I Love the Woman," *Freddie King Sings*. Those were the formative ones.

When you need to be inspired, do you still turn to old records?

I can get stimulated by new things, too, but to retap the root of
what I'm doing it for, and what started me off, then I would need to go
back to an old record. The first thing I'd think of then would be something like the Blind Willie Johnson album [*Blind Willie Johnson—His
Story*] where the interview is on one side, and then him playing
"Nobody's Fault but Mine." That's probably the finest slide guitar
playing you'll ever hear. And to think that he did it with a penknife, as
well [*sighs*]. Of course, if I come up to date, Stevie Wonder or Carlos
Santana are always great. We had a funny confrontation. When Carlos
was Devadip, and I was heavily into the booze, we met up in Chicago,
and he said that he would like to get me interested in his guru, Sri
Chinmoy. He took me to his room, and he had this whole assembly for
the prayer—a little shrine and candles and incense. I said, "Well, I can
go for all this, if you'll do my trip with me—which is we'll drink a bot-
tle of tequila together." He agreed. So I went in and meditated, and I
thoroughly enjoyed it, because of the way Carlos presented it as truly
spiritual—not a cloak or an act. I got a lot from it. And I almost felt
funny about having to then take him the other way. But he went for it.
We sat and listened to Little Walter and a bunch of blues records, and
we drank tequila all night—got smashed and very silly. To this day, I've
heard reports that he enjoyed that part of it more than he did the med-
itation [*laughs*]. The spiritual thing never overcame him, or converted
him into anything other than what he already was—a very sweet, beautiful man.

**On the first Yardbirds album released in America, *For Your
Love*, which cuts did you play on, and which featured Jeff Beck?**

I'll have to think. I'm on "Sweet Music"—which was produced by Manfred Mann—"Got to Hurry," "I Ain't Got You," the middle of "For Your Love, "I Wish You Would," "A Certain Girl," and "Good Morning Little Schoolgirl." I'm not sure about "I'm Not Talking" or "My Girl Sloopy." That's Jeff on "Putty," and he's also playing slide on "I Ain't Done Wrong."

You're quoted as telling Paul Samwell-Smith to promise never to play lead guitar again after the first time you saw him onstage with the Yardbirds.

[*Laughs.*] Well, I'll tell you one thing—to give you an idea of how different we were. I remember him arriving at rehearsal one day saying, "I heard a great record today." I said, "What's that, Paul?" "It's called 'The Elusive Butterfly of Love.'" Does that give you an idea of how different we were [*laughs*]? He was pure folk-rock. They approached me to play on the *Box of Frogs* album [reuniting several former Yardbirds], and I would have done it if I hadn't been working. I was in the studio myself. But I'd love to guest with them.

On "I Feel Free" [from *Fresh Cream*], are you playing in the same key as the rest of the band? I don't mean that to sound critical . . .

[*Laughs.*] I know what you're saying. I think I was inspired by Jack's kind of Dadaist way of thinking. That was a really weird song to do. But he wanted to have a double standard going. He wanted the band to sound straight, but with a kind of weird twist to it. So he wanted to make a pop single that was just not quite what it seemed to be. When I got to my solo, I thought, "Well, I'll play a solo that sounds a little off the wall, as well." So I chose the lines to be a sort of third harmony.

Was it the personalities of the three of you that made Cream so much different than just a blues band?

I think it was the sense of humor—it didn't allow us to be any one particular thing. If it got too much into a straight rendition of anything, one of the members would have to sort of elevate it from just being repetitious or stereotyped. One ingredient would become parody, and then it would become something original. We were also very, very image conscious. We were *trying* to do something totally original.

Your image now is pretty laid-back. But even the existence of Cream would suggest a much cockier side.

The cockier side is still there—and always has been—under a disguise. It's just that if you put yourself up for trouble all the time, it's

"I AM VERY MUCH A CHAMELEON. I CAN BE ALTERED AND CHANGED BEYOND
RECOGNITION BY SOMETHING THAT NO ONE ELSE CAN UNDERSTAND"

The "cool suit" era of
Eric Clapton, 1985.

easy to see what your moves are—if you've got a potential enemy, where he can hit you. My whole thing has been to be aggressive with my playing underneath a disguise of being laid-back. So when it comes, they're not expecting it.

During the Beatles' *White Album* period, you and George Harrison were obviously influencing each other, and he made great strides as a guitarist.

Well, he was very much held down by the others. When we met up, I was trying to boost his confidence a lot, and tell him that he was great, because he was great. It was just that he was in a powerhouse band where everyone was fighting to get to the front—and they really did fight. There were the most cruel confrontations going on all the time. Then he got outside the group and came across Delaney & Bonnie, and they really wanted to hang out with him—not just because he was a Beatle, but because he had great musical ideas. A real mutual admiration society built up between us.

How did the slow coda at the end of "Layla" come about?

Jim Gordon wrote that. He had been secretly going back into the studio and recording his own album without any of us knowing it. They were all love songs composed on the piano. And we caught him playing this one day, and we said, "Come on, man. Can we have that?" So he was happy to give us that part. And we made the two pieces into one song. That's Duane Allman on slide on the ending.

Is he playing the high melody in the head fretted or on slide?

Both. Well, he played in standard tuning, so he could do both whenever he felt like it. He could start a line fretting it, and end it on slide. I can't play slide in standard tuning. I'd really like to be able to. I use open *A*—like open *G* a step up [*E, A, E, A, C♯, E*].

When you perform "Layla" onstage, you sometimes play the high part, and sometimes play the low part. Who did which on the record?

Well, Duane and I played all of it together. We found that whenever we were going to do an overdub, neither of us would do it alone. We'd either do it in unison or in harmony. So we did all of it together.

All artists aspire to really make a statement—a masterpiece. Having done that with "Layla," what sort of pressure does that create?

Within, a great deal. But that's pressure mainly caused by fans or managers or record producers. It's always so subtle that you begin to

45

"I AM VERY MUCH A CHAMELEON. I CAN BE ALTERED AND CHANGED BEYOND
RECOGNITION BY SOMETHING THAT NO ONE ELSE CAN UNDERSTAND"

wonder if it is just you who is making it that way. The greatest things you do are always done by mistake—accidentally. I had no idea what "Layla" was going to be. It was just a ditty. When you get near to the end of it, that's when your enthusiasm starts building, and you know you've got something really wonderful. You can be so-so about it as you're making the track—singing the vocals—but if as you start to add stuff and mix it, then you really are in charge of something powerful. What I'm saying is, when I started to do that, it didn't feel like anything special to me. If you try to write something that's already got all of that, it's impossible. You just try to write something that's pleasing, and then try to get it to that.

Your fans' image of you as a guitar hero has often almost eclipsed their perception of what made you a guitar hero—your talent. Did that ever cause an identity crisis?

Yes. Quite a lot. I fall for the same thing. What they base that on is very much a kind of western—I mean, Wild West—gunslinger image. And that appeals to me, as well. The crisis comes when I find that I'm not the fastest—or that, in fact, that isn't the important part. When the crisis comes, you have to sit down and think about it seriously—if your music is suffering because of how potent your image is.

How do you focus back on the essence?

You just have to stop, really. It's like doing anything over and over again. It becomes meaningless. It's just repetition, until you deliberately make yourself stop because you're fed up, and it's making you depressed. You go away from it, have a breather, and come back. I find that if I ban myself from playing guitar for about a week—and that's the longest I think I could ever do it—when I pick it up again, I'll get an idea. You do something completely different that you had no idea you were going to do. Something inside you that is uncontrolled wishes to express itself, and that's where you begin. You look at *that*. Then, of course, the minute you start to polish it and hone it and take a look at it too much, it's gone again. You need to—*I* need to, anyway—stop and let the thing express itself without controlling it. It's all that outside influence and self-conscious approach to your playing that actually ends up destroying it.

Do you often surprise yourself with something you've played?

Yeah. It usually is when you've made a mistake, or you're not concentrating, or when you're just having too much fun. You try something—or you just go to the wrong fret—and you suddenly are doing something that you didn't want to do, but you like it. Then you try to repeat it, and you get back into that polishing syndrome again, and it will become boring. It's usually when you're making mistakes that you find out there are other places to go that you hadn't planned out.

A lot of guitarists talk about this sort of zone they get into on their best nights when the guitar almost seems to be playing itself. When does that take place?

For me, it comes from outside as much as inside. I'm very, very influenced by the band. If everyone is playing really well, you can't help being inspired by that. It drives you on, and suddenly you get to this point where you know that everyone—including you—is having a great time, and you're at the front of it having the greatest time of all. You get to what seems like a peak. But suddenly you start *thinking* about what a great time you're having, and then it's gone. Or what I always do, without fail, is hit a bum note. I'll really be out there flying—I think, "God, I'm flying!"—then [*hums a sour note*], and it's all over. [*Laughs.*] Everyone in the band just goes, "Aw, man!" You look around, and they're all smiling. But if you can get to that, you can get back up there within the space of a few minutes.

Did those nights happen more often when you were a certain age or with a certain band?

I think with Mayall's band, it was always very easy. With all the bands I've been with, I've found that time and place where you could just fly. Blind Faith was so short-lived that we didn't ever really groove. When we were rehearsing and hanging out before we ever toured, we did a lot of great stuff.

What's your objective when soloing?

It's almost like a samurai, again, in the pacing. I really want to hit everybody, but it has a lot to do with timing and space. The objective is to make everyone feel like they have just been struck by a bolt of lightning. And that's very difficult to do [*laughs*], time after time. It's the whole thing of construction and pacing, and maybe making them wait—which I don't do enough. I really would like to perfect that. Make them all wait for the first note of the solo, and then hit exactly the right note so they're all satisfied. You only do that every now and then—I do, anyway. I see guitar players who seem to know exactly what they're doing, and set it all right. For myself, one night a week I may get all of them like that, and then the rest of the nights, I may get one solo exactly right. It all depends on how you start the solo. If you start it wrong, you've really got no chance.

47

"I AM VERY MUCH A CHAMELEON. I CAN BE ALTERED AND CHANGED BEYOND
RECOGNITION BY SOMETHING THAT NO ONE ELSE CAN UNDERSTAND"

If you're not getting the tone you want, it must be hard to overcome that.

That's the hardest one of all—if the guitar doesn't sound good. I've got a lot of problems at the moment, because the guy who mixes the sound and I have to make a compromise. He puts delay or reverb or whatever on the board, because if I put it up onstage, he has problems, and it gets very "washy." So I'm standing on the stage hearing it dry—I have to live with that—and I want to hear that ambience. That dry tone can be uninspiring, so you have to be double-positive about what you're feeling.

Are there physical or technical things that you used to be able to do at, say, 22 that you find harder now?

No, because I was never involved in pyrotechnics or gymnastics. I'm very lucky in that way. I never set myself too high a goal. It was always tone and feeling for me. Now, sometimes I can find it difficult to reach that because you can get jaded a lot easier as you get older. A lot of the fire is gone, so you have to stop and take a breather—even when you're onstage. But because I never really went full-out for technique, I never set myself up for something too hard to keep up.

What, if anything, would you like guitarists to have learned from you?

I think exactly that—the economy. There's a certain construction that's based upon the feeling controlling the technique. I think that has to be the case—not the other way around. If you really want to do something tricky, just do that once—don't keep repeating it. It has to be an expression of feeling.

At what point did you feel that you'd graduated from being a disciple of the American blues greats to being a peer?

I've never really felt that. It's almost like a generation gap. Those guys are my heroes, and they'll never stop being my heroes. They'll always be ahead of me, because they were to begin with, and you can't change that. I'll never overtake them.

Does that have anything to do with the sociological functions of blues—their being black Americans and your being a white Englishman?

Yeah. It's absolutely real. You're saying that the music should be able to transcend that? I think there's a happy medium somewhere that can be worked out, but to forget all the sociological things is a mistake.

But at some point, did you feel that you were transcending the process of pulling influences from different blues players and

creating a personality of your own on guitar?

I don't think I started to feel like that until I was with Derek and the Dominos. All through John Mayall, I was actually copying—consciously copying—although sometimes it doesn't sound like it. All through Cream, I was lost, really, *trying* to find an identity, but not really knowing whether I had one or not. It wasn't until I formed Derek and the Dominos—and we played live—that I was aware of being able to do exactly what I wanted and was happy with it.

With each band, did you have a change in musical philosophy?

Yeah, I think so. Even now, I get flashes—or upheavals—and in the mid '70s, I was having them quite a lot. The end of the Dominos came too soon, and that left me very high and dry as to what I was supposed to be. I'd been this anonymous person up until that time. It was difficult for me to come to terms with the fact that it was *me*—that I was on my own again.

After the Dominos, you went on the road billed simply as Eric Clapton. Was that a big step?

I think it was a massive step, and it really shook me. Because, then, I had to come to terms with the fact that I was also regarded as a pop musician, as well as a rock and roll musician, as well as a blues musician. So I had to present—and contrive in some way—an image that suited all of these categories without disowning any part of my audience. My ego wants to please all these areas. At first, I actually went onstage starting with an acoustic set—I did three or four songs with a Martin—and then got into some rock and roll and a few blues. All the '70s were like that in one way or another—trying to find my way. Later, I went through a period of thinking maybe I'd just do blues and R&B all night. But you can't ever satisfy everybody, or even yourself. Because if you do all blues, then you'd *like* to do "Let It Rain" or "Badge" because they're lighter and fun to play. So now I'm coming to terms with the fact that I've got enough material under my belt to do exactly what I'd like— maybe one or two blues a night, a few more on some nights.

Your stage shows have always been completely devoid of theatrics, yet you've openly admired people like Jimi Hendrix and Pete Townshend, who are just the opposite.

I think that was very shrewd on my part to choose a role that I could be fulfilling at the age of 60 [*laughs*]. I was reading where Sting said that he was going into films because he didn't want to be like Mick Jagger, cavorting around the stage at 40. Well, I've never done that, so I don't

49

"I AM VERY MUCH A CHAMELEON. I CAN BE ALTERED AND CHANGED BEYOND RECOGNITION BY SOMETHING THAT NO ONE ELSE CAN UNDERSTAND"

have to worry. I can do what I've been doing all my life.

What do you see yourself doing ten years from now?

More or less the same thing. Turning 40 was the nicest thing to happen to me in ten years. I had a great time in my 20s, but I was very serious. Anyone who knew me then will tell you I was the straightest person that ever lived. Because of my attitude towards playing music, getting high was out—no time for that whatsoever. When I turned 30, I did *all* of that, as much as I could. It got me into a pretty bad way. By the end of my 30s, I was really fed up. When I turned 40, I felt a lot more relaxed—because I didn't think I was going to live through my 30s. Drugs, music, religion—everything was tugging and pulling me in different directions. Whatever I got into, I was desperate to be the best—to get it right. Now, that kind of need isn't there.

Did your drug period and your religious period overlap?

Yeah, they did. They were all kind of caused by the same thing—which was a desperate need to transcend *something*, or to become something other than what I was. I find I'm not so manic about that now. I'm a lot happier with what I am, even though I don't know what that is. But I can accept it more. I don't want to *be* somebody else.

Do you feel like you now know where you're at spiritually?

Yeah, I do know where I'm at. I suppose I'm kind of a casual Christian. I believe that if I pray for something, then it may come along. If I don't, then I don't get it. You know, it's just good to be good—if you *can* be good.

You've always been perceived as a mysterious, enigmatic figure. Do you see yourself as a paradox?

I *am* that. Very much so. I've had a long time to get used to it, and I am very much a chameleon. I can be altered and changed beyond recognition by something that no one else can understand. It's very difficult to live with me because of that. My moods change a lot because of something I've imagined has happened. Yeah, I really don't understand myself very well at all, but I'm not unhappy with that. I'm quite used to it, and I accept it, and I know the warning signs, so I can avoid head-on collisions. As far as the changes in my appearance, they were gradual, actually. It's only when you see pictures side-by-side that they look shockingly contrasted. They coincide with gradual shifts from one way of thinking to another. But my deepest wishes to play are basically still motivated the same way. The music or the playing at the bottom stays the same.

4.
"BLACKIE IS SIMPLY WORN OUT"

✦ ✦ ✦ ✦ ✦ ✦

BY TOM WHEELER
JULY 1987

What would it take for Eric Clapton to part with his beloved Blackie—the black Stratocaster whose playability he once described as "like jumping into a big pool of warm water"?

"Blackie is simply worn out," reports Eric. "It's unplayable. The problem is in the neck. The rest of the guitar is okay, but the neck is worn out. The frets are almost down to the wood, and it has already been refretted once, and it couldn't take another refret. I've played it so much that even the sides of the neck—running along the length of the fingerboard—are wearing down. The neck is actually getting thinner. It's not even wide enough anymore to support the six strings, so I simply had to go with something else. Dan Smith and I came up with some ideas, and the guitars I'm playing now are the result."

Clapton performing with Blackie in 1974.

Fender designer/executive Dan Smith explains that Eric's guitars—the silver-grey one and the red one he's now using on tour—are the first two Eric Clapton model Stratocasters ever made, and are the prototypes for the forthcoming stock Eric Clapton model. Eric's guitars (as well as the forthcoming stock model) incorporate an active circuit and stacked-coil pickups with Alnico II magnets.

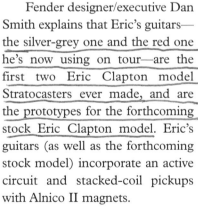

"We wanted to wind the pickups so that they would sound very close to a vintage Strat," says Dan, "but because pickups incorporating Alnico II magnets usually have so little output, we wound them to the same specs as if they were Alnico V. From the pickups the signal goes to the active circuitry, which does a couple of different things. First, it boosts the gain back up so that it's actually a little hotter than a regular Strat. You usually lose a little low-end response when two coils are stacked, so the active circuit also adds the bottom end back in."

The first knob (nearest the tailpiece) is a master volume control. The middle knob is Fender's patented Master TBX passive tone control, with a detent at the 5 position. From 0 to 5, it operates as a normal tone control for all three pickups. Between 5 and 10, the effect is minimal, but at 10, the tone control is completely shut out of the circuit, removing the guitar's one passive control.

"When you remove that passive control," elaborates Smith, "you get slightly more output, and more resonant peaks. It's a bit of a high-end boost, but it doesn't have that harsh sound of some active circuits. It's just a very natural sound of letting the pickups breathe."

The control nearest the output jack is a midrange boost. At 0, it has no effect on the sound, and when dialed in all the way up to 10, it adds 15dB of midrange boost and rolls off a bit of high end. Smith explains: "It's the same high end as you get from a humbucker. Eric calls it a 'compressed' sound, although it's not technically compression. It just has that beefy, slightly distorted sound—like his old Gibson SG that he played with Cream. The range is boosted from 200Hz to about 1,100Hz, and it peaks at 740Hz."

Smith and Clapton met in Dallas a little over two years ago, when Eric was already thinking of replacing Blackie. He had Dan play the guitar, and explained that he liked necks with an extreme V-shaped back. Dan agreed to make him a guitar that played like Blackie. He made about six necks, from a soft to an extremely pointed V. The most extreme V of all is now on the red Strat, and will be offered as a custom option on factory models.

"Eric's favorite neck is the one on the silver guitar," says Smith, "and that's the neck that is going on the stock Eric Clapton model from Fender. It's a little less radical—more like a U than a sharp V—like what you'd find on a late-'56 or early-'57 Stratocaster. It might not be for everybody, but it's the one Eric Clapton likes. So from now on, people are going to know that when they buy an Eric Clapton model, it's *exactly* what Eric is using himself."

5.
"I DON'T FEEL I HAVE TO PROVE ANYTHING, AND I STILL ENJOY THE WORK"

✦ ✦ ✦ ✦ ✦ ✦

BY DAN FORTE
AUGUST 1988

Myth and mystery have always surrounded the legend of Robert Johnson, the great Delta blues singer/guitarist. Perhaps they always will. For years, collectors and guitar players listened to the 30-odd songs he cut for Columbia in the '30s and tried to figure out who the "second guitar player" was, when, in fact, it was all coming from one man. Until recently, no documented photo of Johnson was known to exist. When one was finally unearthed, enthusiasts looked upon it as the blues equivalent of the Shroud of Turin.

As the story goes, Johnson used to follow mentors Son House and Willie Brown to roadhouse gigs and ask to sit in, only to be laughed at and ridiculed for his feeble attempts at slide guitar. He then disappeared for several months, and returned such a master that stories of voodoo and pacts with the devil were the only logical "explanations" for the transformation. The handful of tunes he cut in San Antonio and Dallas in 1936 and '37—tortured songs of anguish such as "Stones in My Passway," "Hellhound on My Trail," "Me and the Devil," and "Crossroads Blues"— only reinforced the notion that he was a man possessed.

Legend and mystery have also surrounded guitar hero Eric Clapton. Like Robert Johnson, he is one of a handful of guitar virtuosos for whom the term genius is inarguable. But in his formative days, playing with England's Yardbirds in the early '60s, Eric "Slowhand" Clapton was impressive and flashy, but he was still struggling—first to break through the sped-up rock interpretations of the blues that the Yardbirds specialized in, second to tap into his own soul. Legend has it that when Clapton left the Yardbirds in 1965, he locked himself in a room with nothing but his guitar. That may be a bit romanticized, but he did leave for the seclusion of a friend's house in the country, with the aim of clearing his head and concentrating on the blues. A month later, he joined John Mayall's Bluesbreakers. With Mayall's purist blues stance as his vehicle, Clapton immediately rose above the standard of his British R&B contemporaries, and most of his American counterparts, as well. He remained true to the idiom's ground rules and spirit, while pushing the form to its outer limits, and, occasionally, beyond. Most of all, he was able to express the full range of his emotions through his guitar as few players ever have. Had the time been 1935 instead of 1965, some people would have no doubt assumed that Clapton, too, had sold his soul to the devil. As it was, his worshipers declared him a god.

In his 25 years—chronicled in the six-LP boxed retrospective aptly titled *Crossroads*—Eric Clapton has had numerous personal and musical upheavals and abrupt changes in direction, often marked by radical changes in appearance. Much of his career—from the Yardbirds to Mayall to Cream to Blind Faith to Derek and the Dominos to solo projects—has also been punctuated by personal crises, including bouts with heroin and alcohol, a spiritual rebirth, and his well-known affair with the wife of his close friend George Harrison, Patti Harrison. He married Harrison in 1979, and was divorced earlier this year, after it was disclosed that he had fathered a child by an Italian actress.

Throughout, Clapton's reclusive nature has only added to his mystique. But in the July '85 issue of *Guitar Player*, devoted entirely to him, E. C. broke the silence and spoke candidly about matters both musical and personal. Since that time, Clapton has been more visible and outgoing than ever before. A couple of months after that interview, his rendition of his classic "Layla" was one of the LiveAid concert's most stirring highlights. He has recently lent his name to a new model of Fender Stratocaster, appeared in magazine and TV ads for Guild acoustics and Michelob beer, made videos (for "After Midnight," "Forever Man," and "It's in the Way That You Use It" from the movie *The Color of Money*), and served as house guitarist for the star-studded Prince's Trust concerts. He also jammed onstage with Buddy Guy, Robert Cray, Roomful of Blues, and others; recruited Dire Straits' Mark Knopfler and drummer Phil Collins for his own tours; and gotten into soundtrack work—beginning with his award-winning score for the 1985 British TV series *Edge of Darkness* and the film *Lethal Weapon*.

But the most obvious change in attitude has been in his onstage

Clapton with one
of his signature
model Fender
Stratocasters.

demeanor. Though Clapton concerts have always been virtually devoid
of theatrics, his 1987 shows were a far cry from the stoic, motionless Eric
of old. Instead, he roamed the stage with the aid of a wireless transmit-
ter and hammed it up with bassist Nathan East and keyboardist Greg
Phillinganes—occasionally even mounting the drum riser or sprinting
across the stage. The guitarist who always seemed oblivious to anything
but the licks streaming out of his amp was now playing to the audience
and obviously enjoying it.

Clapton attributes his new positive outlook to the fact that in 1985
he turned 40, and whatever demons or burdens he once endured were
lifted, if not removed. And though critics have repeatedly tried to count

him and the notion of guitar heroes out, he now commands perhaps his biggest audience ever. His 1986 *August* is one of the biggest selling of his 13 solo LPs, and *Crossroads* hit number one on the *Billboard* compact disc chart in only its second week on the charts—an unprecedented feat for a four-CD retrospective. (Meanwhile, the LP version of *Crossroads* entered *Billboard's* Hot 100 at number 80, and jumped 44 places to number 36 in its second week.) In 1987, Eric Clapton won the BBI Lifetime Achievement Award (England's equivalent of America's Grammy).

The following interview was conducted in May, the very week the *Crossroads* CD reached number one. At the time, rumors of a Cream reunion for Atlantic Records' anniversary concert were flying—rumors he dispels here. Articulate, philosophical, and candid, he looks back on the ground that *Crossroads* retraces, and gives some clues as to what's in store in the near future.

Have you listened to the *Crossroads* set, or read through the booklet?

Over a period of about two or three weeks, I've been dabbling with it. I kind of listen to a few tracks, and I get either embarrassed or kind of fed up or something, and then I stop. But I've read it all. I listen to it in bits and pieces, you know.

From an outsider's standpoint it's very dramatic to look at 25 years of a career that has had so many changes in direction. What's it like from the inside, looking back on things you probably haven't paid a lot of attention to in recent years?

Well, I do tend to like to leave the past where it is, usually. I mean, it's very nice to be aware that I've done all those things, but to have to examine them or live with them is going to be quite difficult for a while.

With it doing so well on the charts, and there being so much interest in it, does it create a situation where you're, in essence, competing with your past?

In a way, but I always was. Ever since I got through the *Layla* period, I was always aware that I had a lot of ground to cover—to make up for the vitality that was there in those days. So I've always had that problem in certain degrees, but no, I think it's great. You know what the best thing is about the whole thing? I haven't put out an album since *August.* So without lifting a finger, *The Cream of Clapton* did well, and this one's going to do well, so it's kind of like a great stopgap, because it keeps me in a fairly high profile, and without me really doing much work [*laughs*].

Did PolyGram just whip together the *Crossroads* concept and present it to you, or did you give them any input?

None whatsoever. In fact, the whole thing was very hush-hush, and I didn't know much about it until almost the beginning of this year. I knew there was going to be a boxed set, but I didn't know what form it would take, and I didn't know who was doing it, or what kind of research they were doing. So I just stood by and let them get on with it. And I think it was better that I did that, because I think [executive producer] Bill Levenson might have been a little bit too distracted if I had gotten involved.

"There was something very magical for me on [Hendrix's] albums. I always went for the more dreamy things."

✦ ✦ ✦ ✦ ✦ ✦

Were there any particular cuts you wish had been included or omitted?

Well, no. Actually there are lots of outtakes still existing that could always go on, I think, and they'll probably come out sometime in the distant future. But I don't know if they deserved to be on the album any more than what is there. Also—was it David Fricke at *Rolling Stone*?—he pointed out something that I didn't really become aware of until he said it, which was, he thought it was a little strange that it should end with a new version of "After Midnight." But, apart from that, I think the whole thing is great.

This month's Soundpage is a live cut of the Dominos doing "Little Wing" in 1970. Of all the Hendrix songs, why did you choose to cover "Little Wing"?

It just had such a powerful atmosphere. There was something very magical for me on his albums. I always went for the more dreamy things—as opposed to the more bluesy or heavy R&B or rock things. I found that his lyricism when he was writing ballads, like "Wind Cries Mary" or "Little Wing," was so different, in a way, that it was powerfully attractive to me. And I realized that those songs could be done by other people, too. You didn't need to be the wizard that he was in order to play the song itself. Those songs, in fact, were much more structured than some of his other things, and more melodic, too. As you know, Sting did "Little Wing," as well. The song itself, because of the way it was written, stands up so well that anyone could do it. In a way, the song was more important to me than who did it, actually. I think that was what it was.

After Hendrix died, was it different performing that song live?

It's pretty hard for me to remember how I was feeling, but knowing the way my attitude was—I mean, I shut off my emotions towards Jimi, in a way, because it was such a devastation for me after he died. If I was doing the song now, I imagine I would try to detach from the memory of it, because it would simply be too over-emotional to perform with Jimi's image in my head at the time. There are times when that can just distract you beyond belief. So I was probably doing it in as objective a way as I could. But that's not to say that it wasn't an emotional experience.

MTV and various other sources have reported that for the Atlantic Records anniversary show, there will be a Cream reunion. Is that just a rumor?

That is a rumor. Because I was asked just recently if I'd go out there, and I said I didn't really know if I could make it, because I've got a very heavy work schedule in London. On that day, in fact, I shall be in the studio recording music for a TV documentary about the beginning of the Second World War. That is something I cannot get out of. I'm locked in now. A lot of that Cream reunion stuff took off without me saying "yes" or "no." I sat on the fence for a while, and then I definitely said "no" a while back. So that is a rumor, unfortunately.

If the situation were right, and you were available, would there be anything holding you back from doing a Cream show at some point?

You know, that kind of thing has to be born from within the band— from within the people who were involved. If, by some quirk of fate, the three of us sat down and talked about it, or were in the same place coincidentally and we got on well, it could happen. There's no reason why not. But it's not going to happen through outside influences because of someone *else* thinking it's a good idea.

You've gotten very involved in film work recently, and you had just started to dabble in it at the time of the 1985 interview. Is adapting to another person's work as a collaboration a completely different sort of creative outlet, as opposed to performing or recording "Eric Clapton material"?

It is. It's very different, and there's a lot of pressure taken off because you're not worried about the music selling. You don't have to make a structured song, and, as you say, you're reflecting a visual aspect, and trying to enhance what's already there. So half the work is almost done for you. What you're really doing is bolstering up the whole thing. It gives me a great deal of freedom without the pressure, and I enjoy it for that reason.

A number of rockers have crossed that boundary in the past few years and have really flourished—particularly Ry Cooder and Mark Knopfler.

Yeah. I think they're both very tasteful at it, too.

What is your next project?

A studio album. I'm starting to work on it at the end of the year.

Will it be another abrupt change in style? *August* **seemed to have a lot more soul and funk influences than you'd had in the past.**

Yeah—it'll be slightly more progressive than that, I think. I don't really know what form it will take. It depends on what material I amass by that time. I'm compiling stuff now, and I'll be writing for the rest of the year. I don't really know who's going to produce it yet. I don't think Phil Collins is going to be producing—although he wants to play on some of it. So that always puts a big hinge on it—whoever's going to be behind the glass will make a lot of difference as to how it sounds. But I do want to make it just a straight rock album—if I can.

On the *August* **tour you went back to being the only guitarist in the group. What prompted the return to the solitary guitarist role?**

Well, I find that sometimes I get very uptight around other guitar players. If they're younger than me, they're either in awe, or they have an attitude before they start, you know, which I have to try to break down. Sometimes, it means that they're going to be flying all my old licks at me—or kind of making me too aware of my past—and we get stuck with that. The only time this hasn't happened has been when I've worked with Mark Knopfler. Although he's very appreciative of what I've done, he's kind of a forward-looking guy, and we're about the same age, so there's no competitiveness or anything like that. We work very well together, and I think he'll probably be very much involved with what I'm doing from here on in—up to a point, anyway.

Have you thought of having him produce you?

I have, yeah. That's a favorite idea of mine. I haven't actually asked him, you know. I don't know what he would say, so we're going to kind of leave it at that for the time being.

Will you be using basically the same band from the *August* sessions on your next LP?

It will be—except for Greg Phillinganes, because he's tied into the Michael Jackson tour until January, I think. It's a sad thing, because he's really a key member of the band, and I'm going to miss him, but we've replaced him so far with Alan Clark from Dire Straits. With any luck, we'll keep Alan until Mark wants him back, or Greg can come back to me.

Is there a tour slated for this year?

Well, yeah. I was just talking to my manager, Roger Forrester, about this. We're planning to be included on some of the Amnesty International tour, and we figured to get warmed up for that, it would be nice to do a little tour of America in September, to kind of kick it off. So you can expect to see us somewhere out there then.

Judging by your last tour of the States—and just in terms of you dealing with the public—you seem to have become much more animated and less reclusive lately. Is that something you're aware of?

Yes, I think so. I think I'm beginning to be able to relax more at what I do. Since I got in my 40s, the pressure has, for some reason, been lifted off a great deal. I don't feel I have to prove anything, and I really still do enjoy the work. There's no one reason, I don't think, but because of the guys I work with these days, because they're so good and are so supportive, I feel a lot less inhibited about what I'm doing.

You've definitely been much more visible—doing videos and TV commercials—even serving as "house guitarist" at the Prince's Trust concerts.

Well, you know, it has been great, the last couple of years. Everything that has been coming my way has been almost impossible to turn down because of the rewards and satisfaction I would get from doing them. I really have enjoyed doing all these things. It has not been something I would want to hide from. So I'm very satisfied with the ways things have gone so far.

Did you decide to retire your old Stratocaster, Blackie? Was that the reason for the switch to the Eric Clapton Signature Model Strat?

Yes. I was worried that if something happened to Blackie, I'd be out on a limb, you know. I mean, it's still playable—although not comfortably so. It has a great character—the guitar itself is really a character—and it worried me, taking it around on the road. It just seemed to be unfair. It's like taking a very old man and expecting him to do the impossible every night [*laughs*]. So it was Dan Smith's idea at Fender to copy Blackie as closely as we could, and update it with a little bit of electronic work—to give it a fatter sound, if I wanted it. Which is what one of the knobs does—it gives you a kind of graduation in compression. They duplicated the way Blackie felt, so I would have two or three Blackies, in effect.

The guitar that came to be called Blackie was pieced together from various Strats, right?

Yeah—a very kind of mongrel thing. I bought about five Strats in Nashville, in about 1969 or 1970, and I built Blackie out of all the best components of each guitar. So Blackie, in itself, was a hybrid, and now these new ones are copies of that hybrid.

After so many years with Blackie, does it feel comfortable playing the new models onstage?

Yeah. You just pick one up, and it's exactly right. For me, it's exactly the way I would want a guitar to be. I'm very, very happy with it. And someone else that I know, who's very into guitars, came along and gave me an objective point of view. He said it was the best guitar he'd ever played, all around. I mean, it's hard for *me* to say that—about my guitar that I've kind of put my name to—but for someone else to say it, I was very impressed.

Aside from having recorded the song "Crossroads," that theme—being at the crossroads—is something that has occurred numerous times in your career. Do you still feel like you're at a crossroads?

Well, it's definitely not behind me. It's something I can see on the horizon all the time. There's always an option for me that's very tempting to take—whether it's shall I go on touring, or shall I go into films? Or shall I get married, or shall I run around? There's always kind of different avenues that are very tempting to me, and I don't think I'll ever get across the crossroads. It's always standing right there in front of me, you know.

But at this point—now that you're in your 40s, and having gone through so many doors—do you now view it as nice to have options, instead of as a burden? In the past, the different avenues seemed to be something hanging over your head.

Yeah. I think that part of the crossroads is gone—all my apprehension about having to do it. I feel much happier about making decisions these days. Maybe that's a sign of growing old. I don't know. I just feel much lighter in my attitude towards it, you know.

6.
"IT TAKES A GREAT DEAL OF STUDYING AND DISCIPLINE FOR ME TO SING THE BLUES"

✤ ✤ ✤ ✤ ✤ ✤

BY MIKE BAKER AND JOHN PIDGEON
NOVEMBER 1994

Though Eric Clapton's first whiff of fame was with the Yardbirds, it was as a member of John Mayall's Bluesbreakers that he began to establish his legend. On Blues Breakers with Eric Clapton, *recorded in London in 1965, Slowhand's gutsy phrasing and searing "woman" tone created a new rock-guitar style. Despite the emotive musicianship that has been a hallmark of Eric's subsequent career, there are those who still wish the man would return to the sheer fire of his Bluesbreakers-era playing.*

Fast-forward to London, 1994. It has taken three decades, but Clapton is finally ready to grant that wish. His new all-blues album for Warner Bros., From the Cradle, *is a definite labor of love. The LP features seven original songs done in blues-approved fashion, and three faithfully rendered classics. Armed with a vintage Gibson ES-335, and abetted by a crack band featuring drummer Jim Keltner and keyboardist Chris Stainton, Clapton weaves howling leads that recapture the fat, horn-like tone of his Bluesbreakers performances. His gruff, sinewy vocals are far more seasoned than those on his early-to-mid-'60s tracks.*

Recording in London, Clapton set up a veritable arsenal of axes for the new sessions. We spotted several Strats, a silverface Fender Deluxe, a blond Showman head, and dozens of Ovations, Guilds, and other acoustics. He burned hottest, however, with his dot-neck 335 in hand, pumping the signal straight through a Soldano head. Guitarist Andy Fairweather Low chopped out rhythms on a fat Gibson archtop, while bassist Dave Bronze held down the low end on a Fender Precision. A black dog wandering through the studio contributed to the authentic blues vibe.

The old-school flavor of the proceedings was further enhanced by the fact that Slowhand and company recorded live, without isolation booths. The tunes we've heard jump with a spirit and joy rarely found on modern major-label releases, and Clapton's playing sounds heartfelt and purposeful. As E. C. has said many times, he's at his best when playing the blues, and his 30-year detour has only enriched his return to the idiom.

Our interview was conducted by John Pidgeon while filming Eric in the studio. The tape begins with Eric quoting one of his songs. —Mike Baker

"All along this path I tread,
My heart betrays my weary head,
With nothing but my soul to save,
From the cradle to the grave."

It's one of those things. You wake up in the middle of the night, run downstairs, and write it down. I didn't know what it meant, and I thought I would abbreviate it to "From the Cradle" for the title. What it means, I think, is that this music I'm making here has been my motivation. It's the thing I've turned to—the thing that has given me inspiration and relief. In all of the trials and tribulations of my life, I've always had this incredibly secure place to go to with the blues, and this is the first testament to that that I've ever made, really, on my own. And it's a bit scary, but at the same time, it's about time. It's long overdue.

When any kind of soul music was rare, the merest glimpse of a Bo Diddley or a Chuck Berry would send me into frenzies of delight, so when I heard what was behind that . . . I mean, that was like the front scenery of what I was later to discover when I found what was behind it, what made that come into being—you know, Muddy Waters, and behind that, Robert Johnson, and behind that the work song. It did something to me emotionally, for sure, but there was something much deeper going on, which I cannot define at all, and probably never will be able to.

What's given you the confidence to think that this is what you really want, and that you'll get away with it?

I think *Unplugged* helped a great deal. Age. A certain amount of rediscovered security in myself. But, I think, no matter how I feel about me, I still need to see some kind of exterior proof. *Unplugged* was definitely that. So when it went well—phenomenally well—I was very surprised, and, of course, very pleased. And it freed me up to a certain extent. I'm not saying that I'm completely different and changed by this experience, but I'm willing to take the gamble, based on that evidence, of saying "that was me, in one respect, but this is really, really me." To make this record about my blues influences and my upbringing is much more me than *Unplugged* was.

It has taken a lot of courage for me to go back. I mean, I'm really retracing my steps back to John Mayall and the Bluesbreakers. And then, when I was leaving John Mayall, in my head, I was going to an even more hardcore blues situation, which backfired. Although Cream became a great hybrid, it wasn't my intention to go that way. And now I'm going back to that jumping-off point. It's almost like I'm just leaving John Mayall, and I'm producing my own blues band. It took me 30 years of meandering around the backstreets to get there, and I don't know why. I just always felt very afraid of being true to myself, and I think that's quite normal in a way. I think everybody is—I'm not unique in that. But right now I want to do it, and I have this funny feeling I don't know how long it will last.

We've been making this album on and off for quite a few months. Today, I was listening in the car to Steve Winwood's *Back in the High Life*, and thinking, "This is great, but I'm kind of stuck in this blues thing and I've got to see it through, and I wonder how long I can do it." It may be that I'll just stay here. Maybe it's all right for me to keep doing this, because it's what I do best.

The bones of the thing is coming from inside me, and my need to pay tribute to all those people that I heard from day one—from the cradle to the grave, really—that I want to emulate and pay back and say "thank you" to. I'm actually trying as hard as I can to replicate what they did, but it still comes out as me—which is the beauty of the whole exercise. I used to think that pure imitation was no good, but, of course, there is no such thing, and I'm finding that out. As close as I try and get to the original, it still sounds like me doing it.

Sounds like you're covering some great blues songs.

We did Eddie Boyd's "Third Degree," which just blew everyone away for a little while. Some of them have been so accessible! We listened to his recording of it, and we went out and did it in two takes. It was just easy. I've always loved "Reconsider Baby"—the Lowell Fulson song— and that was the same. Yesterday, we did the Ray Charles song "Sinner's Prayer," and I didn't think I could ever do this song, because vocally it's very, very dynamic, but we did it very quickly. It's a wonderful process of working. We do everything live, so if one person makes a mistake, we all have to do it again, or we accept the mistake.

What happens to me when I listen to these songs is that I go away, and I still like going away to music, and these things do it to me better

Clapton goes for a stinging bend during a 1997 concert performance.

than anything else. It is still a fix for me to come here—to have a band of musicians. I walk through that door on the other side of the room, pick up my guitar, and we'll start work.

Is it easy for you to sing the blues?

For me, it takes a great deal of studying and discipline to sing the blues. And for a black guy from Mississippi, it seems to be what they do when they open their mouth—without even thinking. I know we go back to that thing about "I'm qualified to sing the blues because of what has happened to me," but I still don't think I'll ever do it as good as a black man.

Muddy's songs have been the hardest. He meant a great deal to me, and his music means more to me than anybody else's. I don't know why. It was the first that got to me, and the music of Muddy Waters is still the most important music in my life today. It has been the hardest. When I've approached Muddy's repertoire, I've always gone for the less well-known songs. I've done "Blow Wind Blow," and I've done "Standing Around Crying"—things that are not necessarily that well known to his audience. "Hoochie Coochie Man" is like the crown jewel. I mean, don't go near this song. Don't anybody go near this song! It's like into the lion's den with this one. We've done it dozens of times, and, to most people, it probably sounds all right, but, to me, it's just not good enough. So we do it again and again and again, and I don't know what it is. It's some kind of perfectionism in me—in that I love this man so much—that I want to do it absolutely perfectly. Of course that's not possible.

There are a lot of other musicians who can touch on other areas. I can't. I've tried to play folk, country, jazz, and a lot of pop music, but I do blues best, and that's been given to me to do. As much as I've questioned it and railed against it and been stubborn about my path, I'm back on it. This is me. In terms of my musical identity, it's where I come from and what I mean. Wherever I go in the future will be as a result of the blues.

7.
"MOST OF MY DEVELOPMENT HAS BEEN THE REALIZATION THAT I DON'T NEED TO BE A GENIUS"

✦ ✦ ✦ ✦ ✦ ✦

BY DARRIN FOX
JUNE 2001

Meeting Eric Clapton is like meeting the president of the United States. Although you may not agree with everything he does, you'd be hard pressed to find a more powerful and influential figure. Clapton has always been rock-guitar royalty—from his early days with John Mayall's Bluesbreakers (where he virtually rewrote blues/rock guitar) to his latter-day chart successes. On his new record, *Reptile*, Clapton revisits a soulful, organic sound that should appease fans who were disappointed with the relative tameness of his last solo effort, *Pilgrim*. Using much of the band he worked with on last year's B. B. King collaboration, *Riding with the King* (which includes Nathan East on bass and Steve Gadd on drums), Clapton turns in a collection of blues ("Got You on My Mind"), soul (Ray Charles' "Come Back Baby"), pop ("Modern Girl"), and the laid-back samba of the record's title track.

For someone who has had such an enormous impact on rock guitar, Clapton comes off as a humble man who simply makes music he enjoys. I met up with Clapton in Birmingham, England, before a concert run. Wearing worn-out jeans, tennis shoes, and a black T-shirt with "Supreme" written on it, the 56-year-old guitarist looked amazingly fit and exuded a youthful vitality—especially when he talked about blues records that turn him on, or the new music that's influencing him.

A lot of your fans will be surprised by the samba feel and jazzy tone of the album's title track.

Last year, I had a chance to see João Gilberto perform in Brazil. Someone told me that was a rare occurrence—he's very eccentric and unreliable, so you'll be lucky to see him once in your lifetime. So I thought that was a blessing. He played for a long time—maybe three hours—and he didn't speak or acknowledge the audience at all. He just sat on a stool with his lyrics all over the floor and performed so perfectly that it was frightening. Seeing him had a profound effect on me, so I think "Reptile" represents where I want to go next.

Playing over a samba groove didn't feel strange to you?

There's something about flamenco and samba music that has a blues feel to me. That makes it easy for me to slip into.

What guitar did you cut that track with?

I used a Gibson L-5. I just love that tone. The sound and phrasing on "Reptile" comes a bit from Gilberto and a bit from B. B. King—that woolly tone he'll occasionally use. I wanted that guitar to personify the

LEE DICKSON ON CLAPTON'S GEAR

Lee Dickson has been Clapton's guitar tech since 1979. Here, he details his employer's various gear evolutions. —Darrin Fox

"Eric recorded Reptile with the same setup he has been using the past few years—his signature Strats plugged into a copy of a '58 Twin Fender tweed," explains Dickson. "The stock guitars are outfitted with Fender Noiseless single-coils and a TBX tone circuit, which provides 21dB of midrange boost. The only other electric he used was a '55 Gibson L-5. For acoustics, Eric used a Martin 000-4 ECB prototype for steel-string parts, and a Herendino nylon-string—which is his favorite guitar at the moment.

"Eric's amps have been worked on by various people over the years—including the guys at the Fender Custom Shop. The last incarnation was tweaked by John Suhr. For speakers, he uses a combination of Mojotones and Eminence-designed Fender speakers.

"Live, Eric plugs his guitars into a Dunlop CryBaby, a Demeter Tremulator, and an A/B/Y box that allows him to choose the Twin, a Leslie speaker cab powered by a Marshall JCM 800, or both. I change the strings before every show with an Ernie Ball .009–.042 set. His onstage acoustic is a Martin 000-28 strung with Martin .012–.054s. He runs the Martin's stock piezo pickup into a direct box. Recently, he has felt the

album, so I put it all over the record.

Do you see yourself delving deeper into other musical styles?

Possibly. I'd like to visit more mellow and subtle musical areas. I'd really love to do a semi-jazz project. Not really jazz, but maybe standards—like when we did "Come Rain or Come Shine" on *Riding with the King*. There are a lot of standards I'd like to approach with a jazz/blues feel.

Did you expect the tremendous success of *Riding with the King*?

I knew there were a lot of people waiting for B. B. and me to do something together. But, to be honest, the record did better than I thought it would.

Did the experience of *Riding with the King* affect *Reptile*?

For both albums, the goal was to try to record as live as possible, and to have a lot of musicians playing very minimally—all performing

---

piezo sound is too harsh in the treble frequencies, so we've been using a combination of the piezo and an AKG C460 mic.

"Eric has adopted a less-is-more philosophy toward gear over the last decade or so. When I first started working for him, he was using Music Man stuff—130 heads through open-back cabs loaded with JBL K-120s. After that, there was a short period when he used Dean Markley amps. He also phased out the Leslie in favor of various chorus pedals. When he went on the road with Roger Waters for the *Pros and Cons of Hitchhiking* tour, he entered a Marshall phase and began using JCM 800s. Then there was a Soldano period. The only time Eric went crazy with effects—and it was mostly my doing—was when he had a Bradshaw rig and, later, a Pete Cornish-built rack. It was insane for him to have all that stuff, because all he used was a Dytronics Tri-Stereo chorus.

"There's nothing worse in this job than repetition, so, thankfully, Eric always has the element of surprise in his playing. He plays differently every night. Where I really saw Eric's genius was during the *From the Cradle* tour. Although I had worked for him a long time by then, I was blown away by his ability to do an Elmore James tune and sound like Elmore, and then do a Freddie King number and sound like Freddie. He would morph into the style of his heroes and *nail* them. It was incredible. To hear him play like that made the hair on the back of my neck stand up—and I used to stand there as a fan watching Cream!"

tiny parts that weave the music together like a fabric.

Do you get the same charge out of the blues now as you did when you were 15?

Yes. The blues has a strong home-base feel to me. At the moment, we only delve into the blues a few times in the live set. We do "Hoochie Coochie Man," "Five Long Years," and "Have You Ever Loved a Woman?" When we get to the second tune, I either settle in, or I don't—it depends where my head is at. Sometimes I just can't find it. The blues is really difficult because it requires complete commitment. I really have to focus myself. If I can manage to do that, it's usually the highlight of the gig.

How do you get in that head space in the studio?

You have to make the recording process a live experience. It's very rare that I'll overdub a solo—I find that very difficult. Most of the solos I record are when I'm playing with the band, and they're usually first or second takes. "Come Back Baby," for example, was a first take.

That tune brings out a lot of the Buddy Guy influence in your playing—the crazy overbending and wild phrasing.

We covered a lot of different musical areas on *Reptile*, but when I hit the blues territory, all of this pent-up emotion came out. The feelings came rushing through—almost overpowering me. I think that's how that crazier style manifests itself.

Do you still enjoy touring?

The physical price of touring is very high, but it's worth it when the band gets onstage and the musical chemistry happens. That's why I do it. When it's not right onstage, *then* you're in trouble. You're paying the price, but not getting anything back.

Do you ever hear a song from your past—say a Yardbirds or Bluesbreakers tune—and say, "Wow, where did that come from?"

Of course. I don't hear my old stuff very often though, and I don't go into my record collection and pull out my old albums. I imagine the John Mayall stuff would be quite a jump to listen to—because it was so long ago and I'm convinced that the music is pretty powerful stuff—but I don't go out of my way to research my past.

How would you describe your evolution as a player from the Yardbirds to now?

Most of my development has been the realization that I don't need to be a genius—that I can actually learn songs my own way. For example, I was sitting around one day, and I figured out an arrangement of "Somewhere Over the Rainbow." I found the chords I needed to get the tune out, and I assumed they were correct. Well, in fact, they're not—they're *my* chords, and it's my version of the song. But I think that's a legitimate way of learning—self-educated theory.

What did it take to get to that point?

I gained confidence in my own musical intuition. All the time that I knew I could play blues, I was still very insecure

> *"All the time that I knew I could play blues, I was still very insecure about my standing as a legitimate musician."*
>
> ✦ ✦ ✦ ✦ ✦ ✦

about my standing as a legitimate musician. I didn't feel I could sit and have a conversation with a jazz player about music because they were on a higher level than me. Yet I've found over the last few years that I can approach any kind of music and bring a unique point of view to it. For example, when I toured with the Legends Band—which included Joe Sample, Marcus Miller, David Sanborn, and Steve Gadd—I thought I wasn't worthy to play with them. But even though I felt I wasn't in their league, when we talked about music I realized, "Hey, I *do* know enough to stand alongside these guys and play."

Do you prefer the studio or the stage?

Ideally, the two should be almost the same thing. What I like to do when I'm recording is play like I'm onstage. However, we recorded *Pilgrim* on Pro Tools, and I found working like that too abstract. It was very difficult to master, because it was just me and my partner Simon Climie and the choices were *endless*. That record took a year and a half to make. You tend to try to attain perfection, because you feel you *can*. "River of Tears," for example, took three weeks to record, because I would redo the guitar part over and over. You don't lose any of the previous takes, so why not? That's a legitimate way to record, but, for me, it's self-defeating.

But Pro Tools does make arranging songs easier because you can move parts around.

Yeah, but it's almost like having false boobs [*laughs*]. It's not quite right, because the part doesn't really belong where it is. Working with Pro Tools is a cerebral way of making music—it's like trying to put a

ALAN DOUGLAS ON RECORDING *REPTILE*

"With Eric and his band, you have to make sure you're *always* recording," says Alan Douglas, who has engineered all of Clapton's records since *From the Cradle.* "I'm working with the best musicians on the planet, so it's a case of recording in the original sense of the word: archiving a particular moment in time and making sure it's a faithful—and hopefully glorious—representation of what was going on. When you have that much talent in the room, there are a lot of musical subtleties and interactive nuances, and you have to make sure everything is captured.

"We started the record on a Sony 3348 recorder, and then we went to the 24-bit 3348 HR. We used Pro Tools, but its main purpose was to edit arrangements—we didn't use it to comp parts. Pro Tools also makes overdubbing very fast, because you don't have to wait for the tape to rewind.

"Almost 99.9 percent of Eric's sound is in his fingers, so I used the same miking formula I always use for him—three close mics positioned on one speaker and some room mics. The close mics were an Electro-Voice RE20, a Beyer M88, and a Shure SM57. The room mics included a Brawner VM1, a Neumann M-50, and various others. There were no EQ adjustments at the board—I fine-tuned the amp tones with mic placement. By varying the balance of the three close mics, I could get whatever sound I needed. For example, if I wanted a brighter sound, I'd bring up the mic pointed directly at the speaker cone. If I wanted more midrange honk, I'd increase the level of the mic positioned off-axis to the speaker. And because the RE20 typically captures more low end, I'd go for that mic if I needed a warmer tone.

"I recorded the acoustic guitars with an old tube Schoeps microphone from the '60s. We generally placed the mic at the midpoint of the top of the neck and soundhole and added some gentle compression.

"What sets Eric apart from most guitarists is natural talent. He was born to be a great guitarist. The first time I worked with Eric he was demoing some tunes for a film, and there was no amp at the session. I was a huge fan of Eric's from his Cream days, and I remember thinking, 'You've got to get an amp—this will never work.' But I plugged him into a tube preamp, dialed up some reverb and delay, and it sounded *exactly* like Eric Clapton." —*Darrin Fox*

square peg in a round hole. Simon is a genius at that stuff. He can con-
struct a solo from a bunch of different takes, and I'll listen to it and say,
"That's really good." But in my heart, I don't quite believe it. I admire
it, but I don't believe it.

**Do you see yourself reverting to more old-school recording
techniques?**

I would like to take myself, a rhythm section, and one reel of tape,
and make an entire album in a day. That used to be possible. Cream
recorded *Disraeli Gears* over a weekend, and I recorded *Unplugged* in an
evening, so I know it can be done.

**Your tones over the past couple of years have gotten rawer
and more immediate.**

It may be a reflection of my way of looking at life—more econom-
ical and direct.

How do you cast guitars for songs?

I go for what I think is right, but I'm often wrong. In that case, I
just do an about-face. A lot of the time the best stuff is accidental. The
guys I work with in the studio know to keep the tape running, because
I play the best stuff when I don't know I'm recording and I'm just
noodling. If I get an idea and say, "Okay, roll tape," I usually don't get
it quite right.

What stage of your career would you like to revisit?

Without a doubt, I would like to go back to the beginning of the
'60s, before I was a professional. That was a time when I would wan-
der around London, hang out in pubs and clubs, and study other musicians. Local players were very influential to me.

**When you changed from Gibsons to Fenders, was your style
already changing, or did switching guitars have an effect on
your playing?**

I think the guitar dictated the way I played to a certain extent.
Because the Strat has less sustain—it's harder to bend on, and harder
to hold the bends and apply vibrato—I play more notes.

**Was it a conscious decision to get away from the
Gibson/Marshall combination?**

I didn't look at the change as "I'm done with that." It was more a
case of wanting to try something else. The Strat thing came almost
directly from hearing *Hoodoo Man Blues* by Junior Wells with Buddy
Guy. You could really hear the Strat. It was so immediate. You heard the
sound of the wood. I wanted to pursue that sound. It's funny, because

after I had gone down that road, I wanted to go back to the thick sound of a Les Paul without changing guitars. That's when I got the Fender signature model with the midrange-boost function. Now I have the best of both worlds.

You've said in the past that after you heard the Band you made the decision to leave the bombast of Cream. Did hearing them also affect how you wanted to hear the guitar?

Very much so. What I appreciated about the Band was that they were more concerned with songs and singing. They would have three- and four-part harmonies, and the guitar was put back into perspective as being accompaniment. That suited me well, because I had gotten so tired of the virtuosity—or *pseudo*-virtuosity—thing of long, boring guitar solos just because they were expected. The Band brought things back into perspective. The priority was the song.

At this time, do you consider yourself a songwriter first and a guitarist second?

Yes, I think I've reached that point. For me, it was a reverse process. I started out as solely a guitar player, then I learned how to sing, and then I learned how to write and eventually became a songwriter. Now I feel like all of those skills are equal.

Do you ever tire of playing older tunes such as "Badge" or "Sunshine of Your Love"?

Believe it or not, I still find them refreshing. The tiring thing is trying to bring new songs from *Reptile* to the stage and introduce them to an audience. You're towing a big weight, because nobody has heard them and they're not really interested. But when you go into "Badge," *everyone* knows it.

What do you play on the guitar at home?

If you hand me a guitar, I'll play the blues. That's the place I automatically go.

8.
"IF I GET CAUGHT UP IN EGO, I'LL LOSE EVERYTHING"

✦ ✦ ✦ ✦ ✦ ✦

FEBRUARY 2003

*It's more than a tad facile to call Eric Clapton the "Greta Garbo" of the gui-
tar, but, like the reclusive 1920s/1930s screen idol, he rarely talks to the press.
For our June 2001 cover story upon the release of* Reptile, *for example, we had
to fly associate editor Darrin Fox to a group roundtable for European journal-
ists held in Birmingham, England. Before that, our most recent interview was
November 1994.*

This year, to promote his new live album, One More Car, One More
Rider, *Clapton opted to film an electronic press kit with* Rolling Stone *senior
editor David Wild. Apparently, this will be his only word on the subject. While
not as musically in depth as a full cowabunga* GP *interview, the discussion did
reveal some interesting tidbits about Clapton's career plans, his dependence on
his band, his "schmaltzy" taste, and his legacy. Here are some excerpts from
Clapton and Wild's chat.* —Michael Molenda

What's the story behind the title of the live album?

Well, I have a kind of longing for the days of my youth, you know,
and I used to love fun fairs. One would come through my hometown
about three times a year, and, at the end of the evening, the rides would
get shorter and shorter. So, at the bumper cars, through this really
scratchy microphone you'd hear, "One more car, one more ride." And
the title is also kind of a full-cycle thing, because I'm starting to think this
will probably be my last album—or last live album, anyway. So it's the
end of the evening—the last go-around. I'll probably go out in dribs and
drabs, but I don't think I can do big tours anymore. So the title sums that
up for me, and it becomes part of my own history, too.

How did you choose the material for the tour?

It's funny, because, with my repertoire, I tend to go back to the old

Clapton in a publicity shot for 2005's *Back Home* album.

chestnuts. Like "Badge," for example. It has big guitar riffs and quirky lyrics, and I think I have a weakness of character around presentation where I think I need epic stuff. I will always choose things that are tried and tested. And if a song is new, then the band has to be able to bring it to life.

Do you have any secrets for keeping your older material sounding fresh?

I depend entirely on the band—that's where I launch from to get any kind of inspiration. The most important thing I can do is listen to what they're doing, and see if I need to bring a fresh attitude to the music.

You really became a soul singer on this last tour. How do you feel about your vocals?

I'm okay with my singing. The easiest thing to embrace about it is that I know it comes from the heart. I can sing from my feelings very easily, and that might be due to what I learned from playing the guitar. I'm not a technician vocally—or on the guitar—but what I've always been able to do is express.

A lot of the album is culled from the Los Angeles Forum performance. What are some of your memories of that gig?

By the time we got to that show, we had been touring Europe for about eight months. And when we got to America, I was finally able to use [organist/keyboardist] Billy Preston for the first time, and the whole thing just took off for me. I don't know what Billy has got—it's indefinable—but he attracts the band like a pot of honey. I mean, what a good lead musician needs—or what *I* need, anyway—is a band that can play on its own, so when the soloist stops playing, the music is still grooving. With someone like Billy, that's what happens. I can step in, or step out, and it's still going on. He's an incredible focal point, and he has absolute perfect taste in what to do.

On this particular collection, the songs are very eclectic. They range from sambas to traditional blues to "Somewhere Over the Rainbow."

When I was a kid, I used to laugh at people who'd go on talent shows and say they wanted to be "all-around entertainers." Well, I never did. You know, I don't consider myself an entertainer at all, but I *do* like to stretch the musical boundaries as much as it feels comfortable. And I've always believed that just about anything that has ever been written can be put into a blues framework. That's why I was interested in seeing how "Somewhere Over the Rainbow" could be approached. I'm a real schmaltzy taste guy, and I love songs like that—show songs from *Carousel*

CLAPTON'S 2004 CREW

Guitars: Fender Eric Clapton Stratocasters (custom painted by Crash and other underground artists), '55 Gibson L-5, Martin 000-28EC.

Amps: Dennis Cornell Eric Clapton Custom 80 2x12 combo (with Tone Tubby hemp-cone speakers), Fender Custom Shop Twin (modified by John Suhr).

Effects: Dytronics CS-5 Tri-Stereo chorus, Jim Dunlop BB-535 CryBaby, Leslie speaker (powered by a Marshall or Fender Tone Master), Avalon direct box.

Strings: Ernie Ball (.010–.046), Martin 80/20 Bronze (.012–.054).

and *South Pacific*—and I don't want them to be untouchable. I mean, Johnny Guitar Watson did a version of "Embraceable You" that's one of the most soulful things you'll ever hear.

Is it moving to you, as you go around the world, that these songs communicate beyond language?

I count myself to be very fortunate that I'm in a creative process that is easily understood on a very deep level. It's a gift that I can make music, and also that I can tune in as a listener. The music doesn't even need lyrics—it doesn't even have to be a *song*. I mean, when I was first listening to rock and roll, I didn't know what the lyrics were, and I never really cared that much. It was the *sound* that would get me. And the fact that I can be a part of that tree—well, what more can anyone ask for?

At this point, what drives you to make music?

The *love* of it is the most powerful thing, and that will never die. And I'm always looking to hear something I haven't heard before.

What has been your most rewarding musical experience to date?

I have to look at the rewards in terms of who I get to meet, because my music was inspired by heroes, and my heroes were the great blues guys. So the first person who comes to mind is B. B. King, and then Buddy Guy, and then it goes on and on. Maybe it was working with B. B. on *Riding with the King*. As we made that album, he kind of accepted me as, you know, a colleague. And that, I think, is the most anyone can aspire to in this business—to stop being in awe of someone and just be with them like they're a peer.

What do you make of the current state of music?

I pretty much don't care about the charts and stuff like that. It's all very transient—you can be in one day, and then gone in a year's time. My principle is to avoid all of that, and to concentrate on what I can give and get from the music itself.

As someone who is routinely called a guitar god, do you think it's dangerous to be called an idol?

It's a choice. I can choose whether or not to employ it in any way, or let it affect the way I behave around other people. Whatever your standing in life, the most important thing is behaving in ways that *help* other people. It's the same with music. I am a servant of the music, and that makes me *your* servant, really. I have the responsibility to do the best I can with the gifts I have. And if I get caught up in ego, I'll lose everything. It'll burn. And that's a guarantee.

9

"I RESPOND TO THE WAY ROBERT JOHNSON DEALT WITH FEAR AND LONELINESS AND SADNESS, AND HOW HE EXPRESSED THOSE THINGS IN SUCH A BEAUTIFUL WAY"

✦ ✦ ✦ ✦ ✦ ✦

BY BARRY CLEVELAND
MAY 2004

During *Guitar Player*'s early years, a seemingly endless controversy raged among readers as to whether Clapton, Page, Beck, or Hendrix was the greatest guitarist. Slowhand's advocates pointed to his visionary work with the Yardbirds, John Mayall's Bluesbreakers, Cream, and Blind Faith when making their case. But when their man veered off into less guitar-god-like territory with Delaney and Bonnie—and then appeared incognito with Derek and the Dominos—more than a few guitar fans expressed varying degrees of trepidation. Those feelings turned to a sense of betrayal in some as Clapton continued his forays into what many perceived as crass commercialism. At one point, in the '70s, he hardly played guitar at all during live performances

But as much as Clapton believed in the musical validity of his more commercial work, he would periodically "return to the blues" as an act of penance for his possibly errant ways, with his hero Robert Johnson in the role of chief confessor.

"I think of Johnson's music as a landmark that I navigate by whenever I feel myself going adrift," Clapton relates in the liner notes for *Me and Mr. Johnson*, his new album of Johnson covers. "I have always trust-

> *"When I listen to Johnson's music, it makes me think about parallels to my own life."*
>
> ✦ ✦ ✦ ✦ ✦ ✦

ed its purity, and I always will."

Ironically, Robert Johnson was by no means a blues "purist." Johnson was a seasoned professional who kept abreast of current trends during the mid-'30s Depression years, and he was capable of playing in styles as far afield of blues as Tin Pan Alley tunes and even polka music. Out of Johnson's vast repertoire, his record company chose to release those songs that were potential hits in the blues styles proven commercially successful by artists such as Leroy Carr, Peetie Wheatstraw, and Robert Johnson's own hero, Lonnie Johnson. The big epiphany here is that Johnson— the revered King of the Delta Blues singers—was as stylistically adventurous as Clapton has been, and just as commercially savvy. One wonders if Johnson would have suffered the same criticism from guitar zealots as Clapton has endured had the entire Johnson repertoire been recorded and released?

Nonetheless, Clapton is not about to let such considerations interfere with his faith in Johnson—a faith to which he bears witness each time he sings "Cross Road Blues," "Rambling on my Mind," "If I Had Possession Over Judgment Day," and other selections from the Johnson hymnal.

Skeptical readers might reasonably ask whether anyone would care about another collection of Robert Johnson covers were it the work of someone else. After all, Peter Green's excellent *Robert Johnson Songbook* passed almost completely under the popular radar back in 1998. But art either speaks for itself or it doesn't, and while *Me and Mr. Johnson* may be something less than the Voice of God, it is chockablock with gutsy, soulful, and sophisticated ensemble guitar playing, and it is certainly Clapton's most spiritually substantial offering in a very long time.

You've often stated that the whole "Clapton is God" movement

"I RESPOND TO THE WAY ROBERT JOHNSON DEALT WITH
FEAR AND LONELINESS AND SADNESS…"

The elder statesman of modern electric blues—Clapton riffing away in 2010.

back in the early '60s was a silly romanticization. Is it possible that you are romanticizing and mythologizing Robert Johnson in a similar way?

I was originally attracted to Robert Johnson's myth and the legend—the darkness and risk. But, on a much deeper level, I was responding to the way he dealt with fear and loneliness and sadness, and how he expressed those things in such a beautiful way. I look at his music and the legend as two separate entities. The music itself has its own life, so even if Johnson was alive today, and had settled down and become, say, a banker, my appreciation for his work would be absolutely unaffected by that. The recordings are amazing and real, and everything else is peripheral.

When I listen to Johnson's music, it makes me think about parallels to my own life. What happens is I resonate with what I'm hearing, and that's the reason I listen to any music. For example, if it's jazz, I'll resonate more to Clifford Brown than to Miles Davis. I don't know why. It's something in what is being transmitted from the human being in a totally subconscious way.

You mentioned jazz. Is Louis Armstrong someone who was an influence on you?

Yes, he was a huge influence.

Your phrasing shares many characteristics with his.

That's a tremendous compliment. Wynton Marsalis has pointed out how people who thought Armstrong's style had deteriorated in his later years were missing the point, and that, in fact, what he'd developed was the importance of nuance. I actually began my career by playing banjo and guitar in a New Orleans–style jazz band, and we played a lot of the early Hot Five and Hot Seven stuff. So yeah, Armstrong plays exactly the way I'd love to play.

There's some wonderful interplay between Doyle Bramhall II, Andy Fairweather Low, and yourself on the new record. Why did you choose to have three guitarists playing together live in the studio?

The first time I noticed how efficient that method could be, and the quality it could provide, was on *Riding with the King*. I was reminded of an Aretha Franklin session I observed at Atlantic Studios back in the '60s, with Joe South, Bobby Hinton, and the Womacks all playing guitars together. They each played very little, but the parts fit together into a single fabric, which is what I was going for on *Me and Mr. Johnson*.

83

"I RESPOND TO THE WAY ROBERT JOHNSON DEALT WITH
FEAR AND LONELINESS AND SADNESS..."

Given what the songs on *Me and Mr. Johnson* mean to you personally, how did you approach the task of arranging them?

One method was to simply take the lyric and throw everything else away. Rather than play the original version for the other guys, I'd just tell them what key it was in and count it off. That way, I was the only one who knew what was going on, and they played completely from feeling, responding to the songs as they heard me singing them.

In other cases, I felt we needed to respect the original arrangements, so we took the songs apart and analyzed them. For example, Andy is an incredible country-blues scholar, and when we were doing "Little Queen of Spades" and "Me and the Devil," he took the record home and listened through headphones to find out exactly what time signatures the intros were in, what Johnson was doing underneath the vocal in the IV-chord section, etc. Besides contributing to the accuracy of the arrangements, that process made me realize that, even though I thought I had become a good listener, I could be quite wrong on some things.

Did any of you play in open tunings as Johnson did on the original versions?

On some of the songs, all three of us played in open tunings, or different versions of those tunings. For most things, Doyle tunes a whole-step down anyway, and when he goes to an open tuning, he might want to have an octave thing, or two strings tuned to unison. So, on a song such as "If I Had Possession Over Judgment Day," Andy and I would be in a conventional open tuning, and Doyle would have his own version of that tuning.

You have said numerous times that the blues is a sort of musical Mecca for you, and the press periodically celebrates your "return to the blues." Where do you go in the meantime?

I don't think I go anywhere [*laughs*]. I experiment with other genres, but I don't think I ever really go very far from my calling. If you put me with a group of musicians, and we want to go into unknown territory, the starting point is usually the blues or a 12-bar. But left to my own devices, I don't sit at home and play the blues. I'll fingerpick Merle Travis style, or play some very fundamental jazz, or whatever. Nothing really has a hold over me all of the time.

In a 2001 *GP* interview, you said that you were interested in exploring mellower territory, and possibly doing some near-jazz material.

That's true. Pat Metheny has been occupying a great deal of my listening time of late, and I find his grasp of melody to be quite inspiring.

I kind of lean towards that stuff, and go as far as I can, and then I come back to what I know I can do—which is very simple.

Would it be fair to consider *Retail Therapy* [a pseudony-mous electronica record released in 1997] as an example of that kind of tentative exploration?

Yeah. I love the idea of drum and bass and jungle being combined with a solo instrument, because not many people have done that. I remember buying a collection of Jeff Beck records a few years ago, and finding that he had done exactly the same thing. It's like synchronicity. I had no idea he was doing that, but it was exactly what I thought someone ought to be doing.

Why did you choose not to put your name on the record?

Because I didn't want it to count as an album. It was just like an exercise, but I also wanted to see if it was acceptable to the underground movement on its own merits. To a certain extent it was, but, unfortu-nately, word got out that it was me, and I think the record was rejected because young people didn't want an old guy playing modern music.

In the early '70s, you began to move away from primarily gui-tar-based music to a more pop-based style, and, since that time, many of your original fans have wondered why you don't let rip with some serious guitar licks rather than playing it safe with the lighter-weight stuff. Do you feel that's a legitimate criticism?

Yeah, I do. I've grown to be quite comfortable with criticism. I used to think it was all just envy, and that the people who were laying this stuff at my door were just frustrated musicians themselves. But since I've been able to step outside of the situation, and see the criti-cism as relevant commentary, I've tried to make use of it. And when someone says, "When is he finally going to let loose and play what we know he can play," I take that as an indication that maybe I'm getting bogged down with something. So, again, I use Johnson's music as a kind of beacon to measure how far off the track I've gotten with some obsession or musical dalliance.

Do you ever find *yourself* being disappointed with another player's direction?

Sure. For example, I love the album that Pat Metheny did with Richard Bona, and I'll think, "When is he going to do an album like *that* again?" So I have my own demands and needs of other musicians.

What's a specific example of where you feel you got too far away from the blues?

85

"I RESPOND TO THE WAY ROBERT JOHNSON DEALT WITH
FEAR AND LONELINESS AND SADNESS..."

I don't know that I'm guilty of being completely lost, but if I had done another album like *Retail Therapy*, then I might have been in trouble. But I've only really ever gone so far before something brings me back. I mean, I got a lot of flack for the *Pilgrim* album—especially in the English press. They said without a doubt that this guy has lost the plot, and he doesn't know what he's doing anymore. That hurt me terribly, because me and my partner, Simon Climie, were taking quite a lot of risks by sitting down with Pro Tools and a guitar and creating a "band" with just drum loops and samples. But, ultimately, that criticism served to remind me that I'm a *musician*, and I saw that they were probably right—inasmuch as I function best making music with other musicians. So, from that point on, I was very wary of working solely with computers. I may not have taken everything I needed to know from those reviews, but they certainly woke me up to something that wasn't working.

If you had to choose one of your records to put in a time capsule—so that it would be the only thing people 1,000 years from now might know of you—which one would you choose?

What a dreadful question [*laughs*]. *461 Ocean Boulevard* and *Slowhand* were both good, but I like them all. That said, I'm always inclined to want to back my present work, because it has more of me in it—more of me *awake* in it, anyway—so my answer would be this album, or the album to come. You see, there's another album in the works, and the Robert Johnson album evolved as sort of a safety clause.

Will that be an album of original compositions?

Partly. A couple of years ago, while trying to determine which musical direction I wanted to go in, I recorded a wide variety of material. Along with my original compositions, I also recorded some old blues songs including Robert Johnson's "Traveling Riverside Blues." I sat with those recordings for six months to see which were the strongest, and the Robert Johnson song won hands down. So I decided that whenever we got into a bind working on my "actual" record, we'd just do another Johnson song to see if we could compile a second complete album, as well. As it turned out, the Johnson stuff was quick, easy, and wonderful to do, and the other stuff was laborious—as is often the case with self-written songs. We ended up finishing the Johnson album in three or four weeks.

So it was basically serendipity that the album came to be, rather than it being a calculated move?

Yes—except that I have a feeling that it was subtly planned by me, albeit not consciously [*laughs*].

Jeff Beck said that when Hendrix appeared on the scene, he had to go back and rethink everything he was doing. Did Jimi have a similar effect on you?

He did. Although when I was with Cream, I had fantasies of incorporating all of that Buddy Guy–like showman stuff into my act. But when Jimi showed up and did it all for real, it burst my bubble. I realized then that I had to look at Cream as a band, and forget about my little solo odyssey. What was even more of a shock was that Hendrix was part of America coming to England to take over, while we were all going to America trying to take it by storm. Cream was cutting *Disraeli Gears* at Atlantic Studios in New York while he was cutting *Are You Experienced* in London. Then, when we came back to England with that album, no one wanted to know, and I was pissed for a little while.

Speaking of *Disraeli Gears*, the tone you got on that record was very different than on other records. In one studio shot from those sessions, you're playing a three-pickup Les Paul through a Marshall. Is that how you got the sound, or were you also using a wah pedal as a filter?

I was full-tilt on the wah pedal for a year-and-a-half. Also, the Gibson thing was really sort of exaggerated for me. I used the bridge pickup, but with the tone control all the way off, so it was all just bottom end, and then I played on the high strings, getting a really fat tone and feeding back. I just played like that all the time. Even with power chords, there was never any variation in my tone.

It was much later that I came to the Stratocaster, and I think that was because of Jimi. He could get more tonal variation out of that instrument than I ever thought possible. I knew about the Buddy Holly, thin-bridge-pickup sound, but I didn't know that it was possible to get the Strat to sound really big, or get it to feed back in tune—which was very easy with a Les Paul. And then, when I started playing around with the Strat, I realized it was nice to be able to play clean, too.

A lot of your early work was accompanied by drug use, but you haven't used drugs in quite a long time, and you founded a drug rehabilitation clinic to aid those who have had difficulties with abuse. Do you feel there is any legitimate use for drugs in music? Bob Marley, for example, believed they enhanced his relationship to music.

87

"I RESPOND TO THE WAY ROBERT JOHNSON DEALT WITH
FEAR AND LONELINESS AND SADNESS..."

I would be very loath to promote or demote, because, in England, there's a huge controversy surrounding the benefits of medicinal marijuana use by people suffering from diseases such as MS. You get sort of a 50/50 consensus on that, because, on the one hand, there's very strong evidence that prolonged use can cause psychosis, and I've seen that while doing voluntary work in treatment centers. And yet, other long-time users claim to get great benefits, such as a loss of pain. The question of Marley is a tricky one, because his use of marijuana was part of his religion. He wouldn't have even questioned it. It was simply his birthright to do so. I would question whether it was actually beneficial to the music.

What, if anything, do you feel drugs did for your music?

In my experience, drugs provided a kind of spiritual short circuitry. They quickly took me to places that I probably ought to have taken the time to work towards in other ways. But when the drugs had worn off, I hadn't made any of the progress that I'd thought I'd made. So I'm afraid the answer would have to be that I don't think there is a valid place for drugs in *any* aspect of one's life.

As you mentioned the word "spiritual," I'd like to address the spiritual—and, in some cases, religious—thread which runs through your work. Do you consider yourself a religious person, and, if so, how does religion inform your music?

I can go along with just about every religious concept there is, and I see value in all of them, but I don't believe I fit into any of them. What I've learned works best for me is to have a belief in something that I can divine for myself. That something can have any identity—like what they call a "higher power" in the 12-step programs—and it can change identity, too. As long as I don't make it *myself*, it's okay.

Given the iconic stature and popular success you've achieved, some guitarists feel you've become bigger than the blues. What's your take?

I hope not! The blues is a strange thing to talk about. I've always thought it was rather funny and ironic when I'd see footage of interviewers actually asking people like John Lee Hooker what the blues is. I've heard those old guys say some really funny things—either profound or ridiculous. My way of putting it is that it's a set of rules imbued with deep emotion. But, of course, that doesn't really describe anything at all. The blues is a strange phenomenon, and I'm certainly not bigger than it.

·BECK·

10.
"MY MEDIA IS TO PUT SOUNDS ACROSS"

✦ ✦ ✦ ✦ ✦ ✦

BY JOHN SHARKEY
OCTOBER 1968

Will you give us a little background on your earlier years?

I was born in 1944, and educated in a private school in England until I was 11 years old. Then I went on to a junior art school.

It seems that a lot of English guitarists started in art school. Is this the thing to do now?

It wasn't normal to go to art school when I went, but since Mick Jagger and Eric Clapton went, everyone is becoming an instant art student. I used to go there because they had good meals, and then I dropped out at 18, and took up the guitar, earning about $9 a night.

Did you have any musical training?

Yes, I did have some. My mother used to force me to play piano about two hours a day, but that was good because it made me realize I was musically sound, and that I was playing material not my own. My other training consisted of stretching rubber bands over tobacco cans and making horrible noises.

Who do you think influenced your guitar playing the most?

I think the biggest influence was rock and roll records.

How did you happen to join up with the Yardbirds?

Well, Giorgio Gomelsky appeared on the scene when I was playing at a club, and after the set we talked about a job he had for me with a new group. I said, "No, go away you nasty little man," and, after that, I joined the group and George became my manager. The group turned out to be the Yardbirds. I thought, "Well, this is interesting," because I had heard so much about them. I did my first job with them at the Marquee Club, and about blew the place apart. I decided to stay on,

and about two weeks later, we had a number-one record. But that first night with
them was something else. I had four days
to learn their tunes. They gave me their
album, *I'm a Man*. After that it was like
rags to riches.

**What were your feelings about the
Yardbirds?**

Well, when I joined the Yardbirds I got
the impression they just wanted my playing
to enhance their group as much as possible. Right. So I just worked on the whole
act until we got it down so great that we
started bringing in bits of destruction to
illustrate a point. Like an action painting—
we all sort of threw our guitars at it.

**How long were you with the
Yardbirds?**

I stayed with them about two years.

**As one of the first guitarists to use
feedback, fuzz tone, and the destruction routine, what do you think will be
the next thing for you?**

I think I contributed my fair share to
the business, right? So move on and make
way for Eric, Jimi, and the rest. The next
album is going to be much further ahead,
but not too far, because the Yardbirds *were*
too far ahead of their times. Like now,
groups all over the country are playing like
the Yardbirds were playing. Maybe a bit better—more articulate and musically more
sound—but it is still the same formula.

**In general, how do you think
groups are going, like the Mothers, for
instance.**

People are hip to material and general
construction of the group and the whole
thing. Then it was just—"Wow, there's a

Beck practicing in his room at San Francisco's Holiday Lodge Hotel while on tour with the Jeff Beck Group, December 6, 1968.

rock and roll group onstage. He is doing this, and he is doing that." It was *all* dazzling. But now, people have gotten hip to everybody, and they just enjoy the music.

What do you think about a group like the Mothers?

They are all right. There are so many different things you can get from their concerts. If you are a musician, you can sit and ignore all the rest of it. If you are a freak, you can dig the appearance. But I think they are putting down the American way too much.

What do you think is happening musically?

I think the quality of music is going up constantly. Guitar playing is at its all-time high.

What kind of instruments do you have and what do you think of them?

I've got a Telecaster and I like it. I use super-light-gauge Ernie Ball strings, and a 200-watt Marshall amp with four cabinets. But this instrument thing is out of hand. If Eric Clapton sold his guitar and bought a $10 guitar, the kids would do the same.

Do you feel the number of people in your group is right?

Yes, I have a lead guitarist, a bass, a drummer, and a lead singer—four in all—and it works out fine.

What do you think of the classical thing?

I actually studied it, but I wouldn't dare interfere with it now because it would louse up my own style at the moment.

How are your records coming along?

Well, the first album was the most difficult stumbling block for the group. In that one, we decided not to use the fuzz tone so much. But this second album will be the one to show the excellence of the group.

Do you record loud, through the board, or what?

We record as naturally as possible. You can only be as good as the engineer that is doing it. We recorded this last album in three days with EMI in England. We had a good engineer, and I feel we got the sound we wanted.

Do you listen to other guitar players?

I listen to them all. I like to hear all I can, but Hooker is my favorite. He plays so fast you think he is playing with his fingers. He is really unbelievable.

With your own playing, what do you feel will be your greatest change?

Well, I've been in a stage of stagnation waiting to see what direction guitarists are going to take. Eric has made a name for himself in England, and so has Jimi Hendrix, so my addition only seems to make things worse. I sort of stayed at a level—this semi-blues bit. Now, I know exactly what this thing is, and I am about ready to develop my new thing.

Can you give us a hint as to the direction you will be taking?

It's making the noises people like to hear. My media is to put sounds across.

Who do you listen to, to get this sound?

I listen to everything, everybody, and anything. I get my impressions off everyone. I have a little trouble with Scottish bagpipe music, but the rest I can take.

How about the sitar sound?

I have decided to wait when it comes to Indian music. That is a sound that has to be studied for years. I have listened to Ravi Shankar, and I respect him. He says it takes seven years, at least, to master the basics of the sitar. This music is short and sweet, and it really doesn't last but a few years.

Do you find it easier to work individually or within a group?

When I was with the Yardbirds, they used to get certain things out of me, but now it is like giving a little child a piece of ground to play in—a huge 20-mile field—and say, "Play." He has all that space to play, and he'll probably just sit down and do nothing. You know what I mean? But when you are restricted, you want to get out. When I was with the Yardbirds, I was restricted so badly that I used to be like a naughty boy and play all these weird things all the time. Now, I've got my own band, and it's like being in my own field—there's so much to do that it is really difficult. So I don't know what is best—being in a group and being uptight, or playing out of place on my own.

How do you start working out your songs?

We start a song with a good beat—whatever goes on top of that either destroys or makes the number.

Do you like to get into the group-type thing?

In our group it's a question of lead singer. Everything is on one person at a time. I don't believe people are capable of taking on two things at one time yet. I think that the lead or soloist doesn't want to be missed—he doesn't want to be cheated out of anything—so our formula is to play solid things with the sound all together, and then the lead vocalist can sing his head off. But, in between this singing, I want to get those guitar bits in.

How do you go about getting the right material?

We have a very temperamental group here in that it is very talented. They are working for me, because I am the person who started the group. I find it terribly difficult to choose material that everyone is going to immediately agree to. When you are a creative group like the Yardbirds were, it is not so difficult, because you can all improvise. When it comes right down to one person saying, "Well, we'll do this," it really bombs out. So we try to compromise and decide on the tunes we think we can do best.

In closing, I would like to ask you what you think has been the best thing to happen to your group since you started?

The best thing was probably the Fillmore East show. I felt we really settled something there.

11.
"EMOTION RULES EVERYTHING I DO"

✦ ✦ ✦ ✦ ✦ ✦

BY STEVE ROSEN
DECEMBER 1973

Among guitarists, Jeff Beck has few peers. Bubbly, elusive, humoresque guitar work has been his trademark since his first performances with the Yardbirds over half a dozen years ago. Currently playing with ex–Vanilla Fudge/Cactus rhythm section Carmine Appice and Tim Bogert, the thin-figured Beck is only one of a small handful of early-wave British guitarists who have continued to produce music that satisfies both creatively and technically.

A contemporary of Beck, Jimmy Page has failed to recreate the magic he performed as guitarist for the Yardbirds. Led Zeppelin started off as nothing more than a grandiose reproduction of Beck's past work with Rod Stewart (witness Zeppelin's first album), and although "Pagey's" playing on that debut album would make any guitarist's fingernails fall off, that disc was, still in all, highly unoriginal. And even the most fanatical Eric Clapton patron wouldn't quibble over the fact that after his short-lived brilliance with Cream, he ran an uphill race.

Jeff Beck was in Los Angeles for a series of concerts with his new trio, and during a two-hour interview made false the rumors that he eats reporters for breakfast. At once fascinating and amiable, the legendary guitarist became acquainted with a vodka and tonic while talking about his playing, his amplifiers, his guitars, and his feelings about the music scene.

What's the first guitar that you ever got hold of?

A friend of mine had a guitar, a beaten-up old acoustic thing. It had about one string, but that's all I needed because I couldn't use any more. One string was plenty for me to grapple with. Then, that broke, and where were we going to get another one from? I didn't know—I took bits of old piano wire and stuck it on.

You made your own guitar?

Yeah. I made a guitar. The first one I made was out of a piece of cigar box, and then I progressed on that. I cut the front and back out of plywood, made steamed-round sides, and glued it all together. My old man threw it out in the garden because I had a row with him—busted it. I had so little money, and that was the thing I wanted to do so much. I'd go down to the music shop, wait until the place was pretty packed out, and then I whip one of these pickups right out of the shop. It sold for about two pounds, this pickup—that's about six dollars. Oh boy, I couldn't have cared if I'd got thrown in jail for six months—I had my pickup. And there was a little hole cut in the guitar that had been waiting for that pickup for about eight months. And it fitted perfectly because I had already got the dimensions from a plan, and it just slipped in there with two screws and, boy, I was the king! I used to deliberately carry my guitar around without a case so everyone could see what it looked like. I used to ride a bike with it—stick it on my back. I could see then that it just wasn't a fly-by-night thing, because the expressions on people's faces when they saw this weird guitar—that was something. It wasn't something boring like a violin or a sax in a very stock-looking case. It was bright yellow with these wires and knobs on it. People just freaked out. I got my first gig at a fairground somewhere, and boogied around there with that. I was playing Eddie Cochran stuff, but nobody was into it.

Did you ever have any training or lessons?

Not on the guitar. Well, I went for one lesson on a Spanish guitar. Because there were rumors going around my school that you couldn't possibly play any guitar—any electric guitar—unless you had proper classical training. And I was a bit thick then, and I said, "Right, okay, where do we start?" I went straight up to the guy, and he knew less than I did. I said, "Now listen here, if I'm gonna get on, I just better leave and go home." He didn't even have the barre chords right. I'd ready-up before my first lesson—I'd swatted out. I'd learned a few shapes and stuff, and I was expecting this man to teach me everything in a couple of minutes. And he said, "Right, now practice this. No playing, just practice putting your finger across the neck." And I went like that, and I said, "Right, where do we go now?" He said, "Well, that's it. I want you to go away and practice that for a week." And I said, "Well, I at least want to hit the strings once." No way.

You used a Telecaster as the first guitar you played with the Yardbirds?

Yeah. There was a group called the Walker Brothers. There was John and Scott and Gary Walker, and it was John Walker who had an Esquire that I really fell in love with. He sold it to me for $75, and because it had a blonde neck and a black scratch plate, it was just one of the most sought-after guitars in England. All the guitar freaks would go, "Hey," and they'd all been putting on the black scratch plates, but it didn't have the blonde neck to go with it. And I had the blonde neck. I was the cat's whiskers again. I'd been playing this Esquire, and had just come to grips with it, and I gave my other Telecaster to Pagey. He used to play that. He had it painted all psychedelic, and he has a silver scratch plate on it.

Were you using any fuzzes or boosters with the Yardbirds?

I used to use a fuzz box—no other attachments.

What kind of amps were you using then?

I had a Vox AC30 for the greater part of the time I was with that group. When we came over here, we realized that one AC30 was not going to be adequate. Mind you, in some of the places we played, sticking with the AC30 might have been the best move. Because the louder the guitar, the less you heard of the drums and everything else. So at least it was balanced—the guitar sound was in context with the rest of the sound of the group. But then we found the supporting groups had banks and banks of amplifiers—three Vox Super Beatles hooked together, you know. I had that once at a big festival, and it made the front page of the paper. This crazy lunatic had 400 watts of amps hooked together! That was at the Richmond Jazz Festival.

What was your first experience with feedback?

Well, that was unavoidable, because playing in small clubs you always get feedback because of bad sound systems. All the amps were underpowered and screwed up full volume, so they were always whistling. My amp was always whistling! And I'd kick it and bash it and a couple of tubes would break, and I'd be playing largely on an amp with just one output tube still working. It would feed back, so I decided to use it rather than fight it. It was hopeless to try and play a chord, because it would just go "*rrrr*." So when I progressed on to a bigger amp, and I didn't get feedback, I kind of missed it. I turned the volume to 10, hit a note, and there wasn't any distortion—it was too clean. It was horrible. So the ideal thing was to get the beauty of the feedback, but *controllable* feedback.

Had Eric Clapton been using feedback?

No. I never heard him.

So when you smashed guitars, it was more out of frustration or anger than a theatrical thing?

Yeah. The amp had blown up, or my guitar was out of tune, or Keith [Relf, Yardbirds singer] was coughing and spluttering onstage. He used to use a respiratory spray, and right in the blues solo, he'd give this "*sssss, sssss, sssss*" with his respiratory thing, you know. There's nothing more frustrating than going on with so much to say, and so much on your mind, and not being able to put it out. There's only one way out—break that guitar!

How many guitars did you break with the Yardbirds?

I never broke any. You can't break Fenders unless you swing them around full blast. I used to just give angry little jabs at the speaker, and if it went up in a cloud of smoke, then I was happy. But if it just stayed there stubbornly and was still crackling at me, I'd give it some stick.

When you formed the first Jeff Beck Group, you changed to a Les Paul?

Yeah—that was from hearing Eric with the Bluesbreakers. The difference was the amazing quality of the instrument. You know, the Fenders are so cheap in feel. You pick up a Les Paul, and it's heavy and it really means something. It means business. And then I found that I was doing things I never dreamed I could.

What type of things?

Well, just general things like chords. Chords were a bit of a pain in the ass because, well, the Fender was nice, because you could grip it like a weapon and really chunk out the chords. But when you came to the more subtle stuff, it wasn't there. There was just no sustain. You kind of fluffed up a few runs. But on the Les Paul you couldn't. You'd fluff because you'd attempt something really hard, but you knew damn well that with a little bit of practice you'd get it. And then, after a while, I got so used to the Les Paul that there was no turning back. I picked up the Fender and thought, "How the hell did I ever play this?"

Do you find that when you use a Stratocaster it tends to go out of tune when you use the tremolo bar?

It depends how you've got it strung up. If you've got good, really settled-in strings that are strong, then it'll stay in tune. If you've got a very cheap brand of strings that stretch all over, you're going to put it out of tune in no time.

What kind of strings are you using?

I don't know—we just buy them by the gross.

When did you start using Marshalls?

Well, I didn't really care what I plugged into, so long as I could be heard. I wasn't after a lot of volume. I used to ask other groups and roadies what trouble they had with amps blowing up every five minutes and things, and the unanimous vote seemed to be to use Marshalls.

What kind of amplifiers do you use now?

I'm using Univox speaker cabinets and Sunn tops.

"[In my own group,] I had so much freedom that I didn't know what to do with it. . . . Now . . . I'm not going any- place."

✦ ✦ ✦ ✦ ✦ ✦

Did you use any boosters with the Jeff Beck Group?

No, there weren't any boosters around. I used a ToneBender.

When did you first start playing slide?

In the Yardbirds, on an Elmore James thing we used to do called "I Done Wrong." That was fun to play. But I never tuned a guitar to a chord.

Was there any reason?

It meant changing over to another guitar, and I thought that looked terrible onstage—watching a guy change guitars. You know, I just liked to stand there after a number and look cool. I mean, I didn't want to have to do all this sort of toiletry.

Do you think that since leaving the Yardbirds and forming your own groups that you are able to play more freely?

Yeah, but I had so much freedom that I didn't know what to do with it. The other members of the Yardbirds would always have ideas, and that's probably where I did the most creative playing—the most inventive. Now I'm just perfecting my technique. I'm not going anyplace.

Have you ever consciously tried to do any theatrics onstage?

I never wanted to work something out before. I thought, "While I'm playing, I've got to move, so let's see if I can roll it all into one without actually working at it." And I used to sort of do little steps and stuff like that—stuff that wouldn't bother me while I was playing. I'd have a little tiny part of my brain working on the stage act, but 99.5 percent would be working on the guitar playing.

Does it bother you, or do you find it a compliment, that many people consider you the greatest rock guitarist to ever play? Do you feel that you constantly have to be creative and inventive?

Well, it's nice to be on the move, but I don't worry. I've got a little bit of time behind me—six years of playing in front of people—and I've got that amount of time to look at. It's not as if I've just broken in last week and I've got to worry. The more time I've got behind me, the better I can judge my own progression—or *digression* or whatever.

Do you consider yourself a flash guitarist?

Oh, absolutely. Why not? Well, I don't try to baffle people. If chicks are going to stand there, and go, "Huh?," and look at each other, then I'm wasting my time. I want to play notes and stuff and chord construction that they'll understand. If you hit a heavy discord, it may be painful for somebody to listen to, so I've tried to kind of incorporate dazzling playing, and, at the same time, make it commercial. I can understand Mahavishnu because they've done what I wanted to do, really. John McLaughlin is far more technically knowledgeable. I mean, I don't know half of what he knows. I don't know chords. I just never had to worry about those kind of chords because they weren't usable. McLaughlin wouldn't come and watch *me*, let me tell you.

So when you started playing you never realized that it would mushroom into what it is now?

No. God, no. I had no idea.

If you could have seen it happening, would you have still stayed in it?

Yeah. I would have worked my balls off. I would have got it right. I wouldn't have wasted my time. But, who knows, I might be wasting my time doing something now. Something might be passing us both by. If the press would give me a chance, I might come up with something new. They might not realize it, but I play from emotion. I've never consciously tried to be a flash. Emotion rules everything I do.

12.

"THERE'S NO SENSE RESTRICTING YOURSELF IN MUSIC—IT'S SUPPOSED TO GIVE YOU FREEDOM"

✦ ✦ ✦ ✦ ✦ ✦

BY LOWELL CAUFFIEL
NOVEMBER 1975

Jeff Beck is not ready to let his guitar playing rest on its own laurels. He has already made weighty contributions with a legendary stint in the Yardbirds in the '60s, as well as later endeavors in various groups he has formed. Those heralded accomplishments, however, are only so much history. Beck, now in his early 30s, has gone through what one of his associates appropriately called a "musical rebirth."

After a lark with Tim Bogert and Carmine Appice in 1973, the British guitarist retreated to a reclusive lifestyle at his home in rural England. This year, he re-emerged on the music scene with an album entitled *Blow by Blow*. A guitar-dominated disc, it shot to the top of the sales charts in a matter of weeks—quite a feat for an all-instrumental album. But beyond its high listenability, the album displayed new directions for Beck, who has moved into a mode some call "jazz-rock." Beck's unmistakable style remains, but jazz leads and more involved rhythms and chording also grace his latest vinyl effort.

With the album's success, Beck and a new band (Max Middleton on keyboards, Bernard Purdie on drums, and Wilbur Bascomb on bass) made a tour of the United States on a double bill with another musical innovator, John McLaughlin and his Mahavishnu Orchestra. In Detroit, Beck agreed to talk about the increasingly popular jazz-rock fusion, and the movement of his guitar playing towards that style. Relaxing in his dressing room, he was friendly and attentive, although, earlier, he had

given three encores—one where McLaughlin had joined him for a jam—
and had a second, sold-out concert to do later the same evening.

**Did you move towards jazz for the sake of expression, or because
it was more of a technical challenge?**

Both. It really wasn't too much of a challenge, because if anything
gets the better of me, I leave it. But it was nice to hear myself play something else than basic rock.

Were there any particular records that led you in that direction?

I'm not a record freak. If I get a tape, I'll play it in the car while I'm
driving someplace. But I don't sit down and religiously listen to records.
I just buy a handful of tapes that knock me out—things like Billy
Cobham, Stanley Clarke, and all the great rock and rollers. I call Billy
Cobham a "rock and roller" because he's so forceful. Rock is an energy
to me. It's more complex now than it was, but it's rock just the same.

**But the licks you are playing, they are nothing like the clichés
on your 1968 album *Truth*.**

No, no. That's gone. It's finished. Everybody has been doing them—
like Humble Pie, you know. Mick Ronson tries to do it. Jimmy Page does
it still, and he gets away with it—he makes a living at it.

**Do you think audiences—especially the older ones—are get-
ting sick of most rock sounds?**

They're not getting sick of it, but they need to be led some other
place. They need to be given the opportunity to get into some other
things. I suppose I could get a group and go out there and clean up by
singing about rot, and playing "I Ain't Superstitious" by turning it into
nostalgia. But *that* is nothing new. I'd rather have people start shouting
with "Cause We've Ended as Lovers"—something that has some class.
Because it's written by Stevie Wonder, that gives it immediate class.

**From the technical end, have you been listening to one musi-
cian in particular that influenced your guitar playing?**

Yes. I listened to Jan Hammer—the Moog player from the previous
Mahavishnu Orchestra. He also played with Billy Cobham on *Spectrum*.
That gave me a new, exciting look into the future. He plays the Moog a
lot like a guitar, and his sounds went straight into me. So I started playing like him. I mean, I didn't sound like him, but his phrases influenced
me immensely.

Do you play a lot of scales?

No. I play the notes I think I want to hear. I don't practice a scale.

"THERE'S NO SENSE RESTRICTING YOURSELF IN MUSIC—IT'S
SUPPOSED TO GIVE YOU FREEDOM"

Beck with Tim Bogert (lower left) and Carmine Appice in the short-lived Beck, Bogert & Appice project.

That's very hard—very depressing. In fact, it's exactly the opposite: I like to play easy things that *sound* hard.

On _Blow by Blow_, though, in some cuts you run up the neck in rapid-fire notes—jazz style. Were you capable of doing that, let's say, five years ago?

Oh yeah. But it was so out of place in the music I was doing then. I would sound like I was showing off all the time. When you have an intricate rhythm section, it fits in.

Does it help to learn how to read music?

It doesn't help me at all. After all, nobody is following the little dots. The audience isn't going to clap because you've hit every little dot. They're going to clap because they like what they hear. That's the way I look at it—it's far away from the standard set of rules laid down by the concert pianists. If they don't play their pieces absolutely by the book, they boo you off. You know, even if they miss the last note in the concert [*laughs*]. That's too heavy for me.

You're still improvising a lot, then?

Oh, yeah—just jazzing around. There's no sense restricting yourself in music. It's supposed to be there to give you freedom.

Have you been jamming with anyone during the layoff you've had since Beck, Bogert & Appice?

I don't jam. I'm a country boy, and there are always things to do with the house, garden, cars. When I'm finished doing what I have to do, I play to relax. I don't get up at breakfast time and practice.

You're not a six-hour-a-day man, then?

No. I think that's a good way to be great, but then you fizzle out—you peak too soon. I want to peak out just before I die, you know [*laughs*].

Has playing with Max Middleton, who's quite jazz-influenced in his keyboard work, helped your musical growth?

Very true. When I want to put something into practice, I always call Max up, because he can get the right piano, and play just what I have in mind. His backing is so fantastic that it makes a simple lick sound great. He encourages me in everything I want to do. He's incredibly enthusiastic.

Did he draw you out?

He draws out something in me that I've been afraid would be there which is, like, *taste*.

Nothing wrong with that.

No, but it could put me out of a job, you know [*laughs*].

On the song "Diamond Dust," there's orchestration. Are there any difficulties working with strings?

I hated it when I first heard it, because I was so used to listening to the track without it. Like you go into the studio fresh the next morning, and you think, "Ahh, that's a nice track. Leave it alone." Then you overdub, and you hear people messing around with the mix, and you get used to it, and then when you finally hear the strings on it you think, "Oh, my God!" But it's too easy to kick the stuff off. You have to live with it awhile. I take my recordings home and listen to them so that I know I'm giving them a fair chance. If, after a month or so, if I hate what I've done, I take it off.

Have you made any equipment changes?

I'm still using the same wattage output—200 watts with two Fender speaker cabinets and two Marshall tops. I have the amp miked, though. I used to use Sunn amps. The Marshall tops give you the right sort of gritty sound. The Sunn is a bit too clean. The Fender speakers are a bit more reliable than the Marshall speakers, but the Marshall top is better, I think.

You used your 1954 Les Paul Standard on the album and tour, but also some Stratocasters. I thought you had given up on Stratocasters?

No. I don't know. It's just a good stage guitar, although it's technically a bitch to get a hold of and play. But it comes over well, and it slices through the atmosphere with the highs.

What accessories are you using?

An overdrive booster and a wah-wah. The boost is just a preamp—it's not a fuzz box—that gives you instant power, sustain, and distortion.

What is the principle behind that bag and tube you use that makes your guitar sound like it's talking?

It's a signal from the guitar that comes up the tube. When I hit the note, it will come up the tube into my mouth. Then, you can "play" the sound into your mouth through the tube, and make the sound do what you want just by moving your mouth. That was invented about 40 years ago in "Sparky's Magic Wand"—a kid's record they used to play. This kid used to go for piano lessons, and he had a dream where his piano came to life, and started talking to him. It was a voice by a piano chord going, "Spaaaarky." It was great, and that's where the idea came from.

If you could make a generalization, what would you call the music you're making now?

It crosses the gap between white rock and Mahavishnu, or jazz-rock. It bridges a lot of gaps. It's more digestible—the rhythms are easier to understand than Mahavishnu's—but it's still on the fringe.

There are many guitarists who are in rock and roll ruts. What advice would you have to get out of that—to help someone expand into different musical veins?

That would make it too easy for them if I told you, wouldn't it? I've spent half my life trying to get out of ruts. You've just got to do what you do best. Get a band you really like playing with, and just go. If you're in a depression, it's a personal thing. Pull yourself out of the personal depression, and start playing. If everything is jumping around you, you jump with it. The music usually reflects what's going on in your personal life.

13.
"A SOLO SHOULD *DO* SOMETHING—IT SHOULDN'T JUST BE THERE AS A COSMETIC"

✦ ✦ ✦ ✦ ✦ ✦

BY JAS OBRECHT
OCTOBER 1980

Jeff Beck is one of the greatest guitarists to have emerged from rock and roll. Led Zeppelin's Jimmy Page said in *Guitar Player*: "When he's on, he's probably the best there is."

Beginning with his first major recorded part—the unforgettable sitar-flavored hook that propelled the Yardbirds' "Heart Full of Soul" to the top of the charts in 1965—Beck has remained constant to his self-proclaimed goal of expanding the electric guitar's boundaries. Over the years, he has led blues-based rock bands (introducing Rod Stewart and Ron Wood to the world in the process), fronted a power trio, and carved some of the first inroads towards what is now known as jazz-rock fusion. He has never compromised or sold out, remaining a law unto himself. And although he has recorded several albums that are now considered by many to be classics—*Truth, Beck-Ola, Blow by Blow,* and *Wired,* to name a few—there is surprisingly little similarity among them. Not only has he successfully changed styles, but, rarer still, he has become an archetype guitarist for most styles he chooses.

Because of his sonic innovations and ability to arrange tunes to best showcase his talents, Beck has garnered little of the "he-can't-play-the-way-he-used-to" criticism that has plagued other '60s axemen. His style blends snatches of early Les Paul, the best elements of rock and blues guitar, slide, subtle Eastern influences, lines derived from keyboards, and bits of everything he's heard—all performed with an elasticity, craziness, and flash that's unique to him. A true showman, Jeff is capable of ear-splitting feedback followed by surprising subtlety, wild theatrics, and solos that begin seemingly off-balance and out-of-key before being woven together in intricate, beautifully constructed climaxes. While his styles may have evolved, the unmistakable Beck fire and ingenuity remain.

Jeff Beck was born in Surrey, England, on June 24, 1944. He attended private schools until he was 11, and then enrolled in Wimbledon Art School. As a child, he practiced piano with his mother for a couple of hours a day.

"My other training," he adds, "consisted of stretching rubber bands over tobacco cans and making horrible noises."

Early Les Paul recordings and broadcasts from the Near East that came over the family radio fired his desire to become a musician. When the family budget couldn't be stretched to include the cost of an electric guitar, he pounded together his own out of pieces of wood, homemade frets, and a pickup swiped from a nearby music store.

As he described in his December '73 *Guitar Player* cover story: "I used to deliberately carry my guitar around without a case so everyone could see what it looked like. I used to stick it on my back and ride a bicycle. I could see then it wasn't a fly-by-night thing, because the expressions on people's faces when they saw this weird guitar was something. It was bright yellow with these wires and knobs on it. People just freaked out."

At 18, Jeff dropped out of school and began earning nine dollars a night as a guitarist. By 1964, he was steadily gigging on Eel Pie Island with a local band called the Tridents. In December, Eric Clapton quit the Yardbirds—a London-based band that was pioneering heavy-metal music while translating high-energy blues into hard rock—during the recording of their single "For Your Love." Keith Relf, lead singer for the group, offered the position of lead guitarist to Jimmy Page, who, at that time, was a busy session player. Page declined, and recommended Beck in his stead.

Although his playing was heavily blues-based when he joined the Yardbirds, Jeff began to change when he toured America for the first time, and saw that B. B. King and other bluesmen were beginning to get booked at the Fillmores and other rock-oriented venues. His task of bringing blues guitar to white audiences done, he delved into rock, vowing to "expand it, experiment with it, and do new things to it." Beck came into his own as a guitarist, and by the time his 20-month stint with the band was up, he had come to epitomize the rising breed of psychedelic guitar heroes. A dandy in ruffled sleeves and jewelry, he blistered audiences with loud volume and a progressive style incorporating feedback, distortion, tasteful fuzz, power chords, Eastern motifs, slide parts, and theatrics such as soloing with the guitar held over his head or behind his back. (Several sources report that while in London, Jimi Hendrix studied Beck's techniques, and later used some of them in his own act.)

By the end of 1965, Beck had appeared on two albums released in the U.S. *For Your Love* featured him on "My Girl Sloopy," the slide-tinged "I Ain't Done Wrong," and a blues tune called "I'm Not Talking." *Having a Rave Up* included the hits "Heart Full of Soul," "I'm a Man," and "Train Kept A-Rolling." In May '66, *The Yardbirds* was released in England, and a modified version was distributed in the U.S. as *Over Sideways Down*. To relieve building tension within the band, Jimmy Page came in on bass in mid-1966, and then switched to guitar so that he and Beck could both play lead. In September and October, the Yardbirds toured with the Rolling Stones, and then flew to the U.S. During this tour, Beck reportedly suffered a breakdown, and after smashing his favorite guitar onstage, he returned home to pursue a solo career. Unfortunately, of the Page-Beck Yardbirds collaborations, only "Happenings Ten Years Time Ago," "Psycho Daisies," and "Stroll On" remain. The guitarists also appeared together in the film *Blow Up*, playing double lead on "Stroll On."

By the summer of 1967, Beck was one of the first British rock superstars who owed his celebrity to instrumental prowess. He embarked on a brief solo career, churning out the singles "Hi Ho Silver Lining," "Beck's Bolero," and an instrumental version of "Love Is Blue." Later in the year, he organized the first Jeff Beck Group with Rod Stewart and Ronnie Wood. The three men continued as a unit for more than two years while various drummers—notably Aynsley Dunbar and Mickey Waller—came and went. Their first album, *Truth*, to this day remains one of Jeff's most critically acclaimed efforts. Pianist Nicky Hopkins, who sat in on *Truth*, joined the lineup in October 1968, and appeared on the follow-up, *Beck-Ola*. This incarnation of the Jeff Beck Group toured the U.S. in 1968, receiving accolades in the press for their high-powered sound and command of the blues. Mounting personal conflicts, however, caused the group to collapse in July '69. By then, Beck already had plans for forming a band with bassist Tim Bogert and drummer Carmine Appice, but this failed when Jeff fractured his skull in a car crash in December.

In April 1971, Jeff formed another edition of the Jeff Beck Group with singer Bob Tench, bassist Clive Chaman, pianist Max Middleton, and drummer Cozy Powell. They released two albums—*Rough And*

Ready and the Steve Cropper-produced *Jeff Beck Group*—both of which hinted at Beck's movement towards a more jazz-oriented vein. By early '73, Jeff had trimmed his lineup down to the three-piece Beck, Bogert & Appice. Immediately viewed as a supergroup, they failed to live up to expectations. One album came out in the U.S., *Beck, Bogert & Appice*, while another, *Live in Japan 1973*, was released only in the Far East. To this day, Beck seems to harbor few fond memories of this lineup.

After the demise of the trio in April '74, Beck retired to his 80-acre estate in the English countryside. In October, he recorded *Blow by Blow* with former Beatles producer George Martin. The album proved to be full of stunning instrument virtuosity as Jeff explored, among other things, the role his guitar could play in the framework of a large orchestra. In his November '75 *GP* cover story he described his new musical direction: "It crosses the gap between white rock and Mahavishnu or jazz-rock. It bridges a lot of gaps." The album shot to the top of the charts, and Jeff toured the U.S. on a double bill with the Mahavishnu Orchestra in 1975.

During the recording of *Blow by Blow* Jeff became influenced by keyboard synthesist Jan Hammer, and he enlisted his support for his next Martin-produced LP, *Wired*, in June '76. As with *Blow by Blow*, Beck's emphasis was again on technique and harmonic variety in a strongly rhythmic jazz-rock environment. The album reached number 16 in the U.S. charts, and was voted best guitar album in that year's *Guitar Player* readership poll (*Blow by Blow* had also won the year before). Jeff joined Hammer and his group to tour Australia and the U.S. In March 1977, this lineup recorded the Hammer-produced *Live* LP, which featured material from both previous albums.

In November 1978, Jeff formed an ad hoc group with bassist Stanley Clarke (with whom he has appeared on three albums), keyboardist Tony Hymas, and drummer Simon Phillips to tour Japan. Afterwards, Jeff enlisted bassist Mo Foster and Hammer to record *There and Back* with Hymas and Phillips. Released earlier this summer, the album represents a more metallic brand of fusion and a further refinement of Beck's distinctive style.

Aside from playing guitar, Jeff's main pastime is tinkering with automobiles. The following interview was conducted while he was in San Jose, California, to attend a hot rod show.

Given the broad scope of your early musical environment, why did you choose the guitar as your instrument?

"A SOLO SHOULD DO SOMETHING—IT SHOULDN'T JUST
BE THERE AS A COSMETIC"

Beck rehearsing for a
televised performance
on *The Midnight
Special*, May 2, 1975.

A lot of time has gone by since I made the choice. I remember messing around on a violin and not wanting to use the bow. I couldn't stand the thought of bowing instead of touching the strings—that's something from a child's age, you know. There was a frustration because the bow was getting in the way. And when you're a kid, I suppose you just want to get at the strings and pull them—some sort of built-in, natural thing. It was more fun, and I was more accurate pulling the string than bowing it. But, at the same time, having said that, the bow sound was better than the noise you'd make with your finger.

Do you feel the guitar is an unlimited instrument?

For me, it's definitely limited. It seems to be limited for a lot of other players, too, judging by what I've heard on radio rock shows. They all sound like they've reached about where they're going with it. No experimentation seems to be happening on general terms. Obviously, like backroom boys are doing other things, but it's not really getting on record, is it? The stock sound is still there—the Gibson Les Pauls cranked up and loud Fender Strats. You get a few nice pedal effects going on the records, but it's not really much to make you sit back and think, "Wow! What's that?" And if you do, nine times out of ten it's a synthesizer that's making the noise rather than the guitar.

How has your relationship with the guitar changed over the last couple of years?

Well, I just ignore what's going on around me, really. I have to, because living where I live, I haven't got a hotline to anybody telling me what's going on. But I still think that, poetically, the guitar is as limited as you want to make it. Tonally it's limited. If you've got a good ear, you can tell what's been done to the guitar, what circuits it's going though. You can tell how much the pure note is being doctored up just by listening to a record. You don't even have to be there when the guy is doing it.

Have you learned a lot since *Blow by Blow*?

I've learned a lot, and I haven't learned a lot. I've learned that people are ready for anything, but I've also learned that it's difficult to continue once you've got someone's attention. All right, so that album *Blow by Blow* was a major change in my life, really, but that was an accident. The album was sort of put together naturally. You couldn't force out another album like that, so it's difficult to make a follow-up simply because one tends to start thinking, "Well, if they liked that, they'd like this. Maybe I should do another one like that," and so and so. The tendency would be to choose the most popular number and enlarge on that, but I don't work like that. You know, like with the old Motown things, if they had a number-one hit with a star, then the star would probably turn out three records very similar in approach. They'd play it safe, and get an identity going, but that's exactly what I'm not into.

At the time you recorded *Blow by Blow*, had rock gotten too stale for you?

I reckon you're right. That's probably what it was. It's still pretty stale. I mean, aren't you tired of all the big-sounding heavy metal and crashing around? It's just so *standard*.

Do you listen to other forms of music?

I only listen to things that catch my ear, and that's not very often. I like to use the influence, but not get too heavily buried in it. It's too easy to get marched off somewhere by somebody. You get swept away by them, and, before you know it, you're copying them. It's not like I'm turning out albums by the dozen—far from it—but when I do one, it seems to be tugging more in my direction and where *I* want to be, rather than if I was a hot property on the road all the time and turning out more albums. I think it works out better this way because nobody wants to keep hearing the same name—"Beck, Beck, Beck," or whoever it is. It's an instant death once you start turning out loads of great albums, because you're so near the pinnacle of your career, and then you can only go down. It doesn't matter how big you get. It's just that, once that point is reached, you can only go down. I don't like that side of it. I like to just turn out an album when I think I've got enough decent material. If people are around to buy it, then that's all I want.

Do you have to be in a certain state of consciousness to play your best?

Yeah. There's no doubt about that.

Do you know what that state is?

No, I don't [*laughs*]. Even after you've played something, and everyone is really into it, and then you're playing it back, and the whole studio is buzzing, you *still* don't realize what it was that made you play like that. You're enjoying what's happening at that particular time when people are listening to it.

Are your emotions tied in with the way you play?

It's purely emotional. I can sort of switch on "automatic" and play, but it sounds terrible. I've got to be wound up, and in the right mood.

Have there been times when you've played better in a room by yourself than you ever could on vinyl?

Yeah. I can play unbelievably in a room on my own. But then, I have to know the door's locked and no one is listening.

Why is that?

Because there are going to be mistakes and horrible goofs and things, but it's good fun. It's great therapy, you know, to just lock yourself away. You don't have to play at ear-shattering volume, but just loud enough to get the spirit of the stage thing going on your own. That's when you start really finding some nice, interesting things.

Do you use the guitar much to play yourself in and out of moods?

Yeah. But if one gets down that much, picking the guitar up won't really help much, because if you happen to play a phrase that you don't like, you're worse.

Are you very self-critical?

They tell me that—and I must be, because things take a long time for me to get them out. It's because I think over-indulgence in anything is wrong—whether it's practicing 50 hours a day or eating too much food. There's a balance with me, as there should be with everything and everybody. I've tried to keep it so that I don't lose my technique, such as it is, and I'm able to execute the ideas that come out.

How do you do that? By practicing a lot?

No. I don't think I want to practice too much because that depresses me. I get good speed, but then I start playing nonsense because I'm not thinking. A good layoff makes me think a lot. It helps me get both things together—the creativity and the speed.

Do hooks come to you when you don't have a guitar in your hands?

Yeah.

How do you remember them?

You don't, really. Something gets stored in the back of your mind, and then you hope that something might come out—maybe in a different form.

Have your views on soloing changed through the years?

Playing with Jan Hammer sort of knocked all the soloing out of me. I mean, a three-week tour, exchanging solos with a person like Jan can take you to your limit on soloing. So I've got no particular desire to play ten-minute solos. Those were never valid anyway. In my book—*never*. It was just a cheap way of building up a tension in the audience. I remember that in the days of Ten Years After and several other groups, the people were clapping in a sense of relief of tension when you'd finish the solo—not because it was amazing or anything. That's what I saw. Maybe some nights there was a valid long solo. Once one group got away with it, a lot of other groups started following by doing ten-minute rubbish solos, and started to make people clap, and that's wrong because it's misleading the people. They don't know what's going on, and they can only hear so much.

In the framework of your music, what do you think a solo should do?

It should do something—it shouldn't just be there as a cosmetic. It should have some aim, take the tune somewhere. I'm not saying I can do it, but I try and take the tune somewhere. You know, you never get people saying any more, "Ah, listen to this guitar solo! Wait until this part comes!" They talk over it. When the first few bars of the tune come over the speakers, they say, "Oh yeah, right." And then they'll just party over it. In the old days—'68—you actually used to listen for things, like in Sly Stone's records there would be some noise, or some little solo, or even a triad or a jab on the keyboard, and you'd say, "Wow! Listen to this bit!" You would carry the whole thing out somewhere else. An album was just one piece of flat music going along.

You've used the guitar in dialogue throughout most of your career—even back in the first Jeff Beck Group when you traded solos with Rod Stewart's voice. Has this been an attempt to get out of the routine of having to do extended solos?

No. It just comes naturally. It sounds corny, but it's just sort of like putting icing on a cake, or holding a conversation with somebody. Really, that's all you're doing. You're saying something through the guitar, or whatever it is you're playing. I just try to say it as clearly as possible, because there are no prizes for speaking double-Dutch. Nobody can understand you. There's nothing worse than a boring sermon that you know already, or that you don't know and aren't interested in. It's as simple as that, really.

What influence has Jan Hammer had on your playing?

He's just a master of melody. His chords are *his* chords—if anyone else plays those chords, you say, "Hey, those are Jan Hammer's chords!" I mean, they're obviously not his—nobody can say that they've invented a chord, because they are already there. You discover them. But he plays in a certain way that is unmistakably him. To my ears—I don't expect anybody else to dial in on it so readily—his soloing is just so picturesque.

He's never flashy—flamboyant, I suppose, but never flashy. Even on his wild solos, he's still creative. He still finishes off all the notes in the right places, and he never makes a mistake unless it's something like counting the number of bars where you're supposed to change—maybe he'll forget. But when he knows the number—look out! We played "Freeway Jam" about 50 times on the road—I've got a lot of tapes of the tunes we used to play—and not once did he ever play the same solo.

Does that make you play the same?

No. The fun time for me is listening to those tapes, and hearing the way I was altering as he would alter—neither of us copying each other. Like if there was a flurry of runs that he would do, I would take over. And if I did a flurry of runs, he would take over, and it would just melt into one. That's music to me.

Have there been other people with whom you've shared this kind of musical relationship?

Not really. Not on such an electric level. Rod and I used to bounce off each other because that was just a simple blues-based rock band. I had a little bit of it with Max Middleton on a very low key. What was good about Jan's thing was that whatever shortcomings it had, it still had energy and life in it. And it was only the primary stages of what could have been something really good, but it was redundant from the start, because he had his band, and he wanted to make himself a star with that band without having me in it. But he helped me become interested in rock music again, and I helped him get to where he wanted to go. At least he was able to play big, huge arenas with me where he wouldn't have on his own. So I've done my bit there.

Did you have a special goal in mind when you recorded *There and Back*?

No. I just wanted to get a collection of really good melodies, and see if they were suitable for my guitar style. There were a million melodies that I could do that wouldn't be suitable. It had to be right.

Did you process your guitar signal and Jan's synthesizer signal the same way? At some points, the tones and attacks are almost indistinguishable.

Oh, great! That's a compliment. No. I suppose it's a similarity in approach, but only mentally. I haven't got anything like the same setup as Jan has. Plus his setup is purely electronic, and mine is guitar. But there is a certain attack on bending the notes and certain basic understandings of the way the tone is. There was no concerted effort on any part to sound the same, or to dial in any trick thing and make it sound the same.

How did you work out the material for the album?

I ripped myself apart, and I ripped Tony Hymas apart. I tried to get him to understand where I was at, because Tony came in as an emergency keyboard player back in '78, when we had a tour of Japan lined up and had a problem with another keyboard player. And Tony picked it up so quickly, and he had such a good ear, and his musical training and understanding was so superb, I couldn't see any reason why it wouldn't be a good idea to start schooling him in my way. It sounds insulting to say "school him" when he knows more about music than I do, but that doesn't mean that what I'm doing is not valid. In the first two weeks, he had already begun to see what I wanted without me saying anything.

Did most of the music evolve through your playing together?

Yeah.

Was any of it written down?

Tony writes everything down. He scribbles on the backs of pieces of paper. And then, when we run through it, I say, "Well, right here, I can't get along with this framework I've got to solo over. Let's take this chord out of there and put it somewhere else." It's just custom building music between us. Of course, if it's his song to start with, whatever happens to it, it's still his song.

Did the album come out the way you had planned?

No. It never does that, because what you hear in your mind is always miles louder, or miles more wild than could be physically possible to get on record. And, sometimes, the disappointment when you actually get the goods coming through the speakers is so great that it might turn out worse than if you hadn't conceived it at all. In other words, things turn out better by accident, sometimes, but you can't organize accidents! On the album, I just didn't play as good as I know I can. I know I can play better than that. It's just when you're looking for something, you have to take what's best at that time.

What were you looking for?

Oh, I don't know. You're really hitting some $100,000 questions! You know, you have to sort of forget abut impressing anybody and tailor-making your music for a market—that's what I try and forget about, because, otherwise, you'll go crazy. There's enough work to do without worrying about that. Making music is a lot of fun when you're getting somewhere. But when you're getting stuck in a rut for a few hours, it's horrible. Horrible.

Do you have ways of getting out of it? Can you walk away and come back later?

Yeah. I didn't used to. It's difficult to walk away when you've got ten guys sitting around—like engineers and roadies—and everyone has set aside their time in that day to help you. Although, sometimes, walking out would be the best thing to do, you can't, and that's when the trouble starts. You're under pressure then. From that time on, you're under obligation to get through the session. And then you're paying the bill, and you think, "Aw, how long can this go on? It's costing me 300 bucks a minute." That depresses you, because when you want to take five and think about things, you think, "Well, if there's no progress being made, who's paying the bill? *I'm* paying the bill!" And then you wait for somebody to come up with something positive. Once they lead, then you can tail them for a while. It's a laborious thing, though. You know, they say making movies is boring, but—Jesus Christ—at least you could be outside and talking to somebody. But if somebody is trying to get a sound, or trying to get something going on a technical level in the studio, you've got to be quiet. You sit there reading the same newspaper over and over again. Then, if you go out and have a meal, it's ten-to-one that ten seconds after you've gone up the road, they'll fix whatever it was they were working on, and you'll just be holding them up. I hate recording like that, so I've got a little studio at home, but I never use it.

Is the music you play for pleasure the same as what you record?

No. Isn't it funny! I'd really like to do that, but it never seems to work out that way. There's a free feeling about the stuff I play for myself. Obviously, there are some wrong notes and things, but the freedom in the unrecorded stuff is really what should go on record. But it's always over-indulgence, or self-indulgence.

Do you run in spurts as far as composing goes? There have been times when your records featured a lot of your compositions, and, other times, little of your original material gets on vinyl.

I've reached the point where I need to be led somewhere on a melody level—not so much on the technique or guitar-trickery level. The stuff pours out of me when I've got the right tune. I can't help it—it just pours out! But if the tune isn't right, then I've got to push it a bit. If it's totally wrong, I've got to drag it.

Do you find it easier to work within the context of a group where each member contributes?

It usually works out better that way. But, at the same time, when you're playing live in a small room, there are all of the live frequencies there, and this sometimes blocks from your mind the essence of the tune. You don't notice this until they have gone home, and you're listening to the tune turned down low on a little tape machine. Then you really hear the essence of it, and how strong or how weak it is. There may be some great playing on it, and the whole thing may be tight, but the guts of the thing just may not come across. It's amazing when you reduce it down to a small speaker, and find out how little there is. And yet, when you were playing live, it sounded amazing because the sound was whitewashing a bit.

Most people are probably exposed to new records for the first time through home or car radios with small speakers.

That's right. Your ear has to be caught, and you have to want to turn it up, because it sounds so good at any low level. That's why all these powerhouse rock bands sound so diabolical. They sound great live. I'll jump up and down, and have a good time in a big hall, or in a great-sounding room. If the group is playing nice and loud—like the Who—I jump up and down. But I can't jump up and down for the Who on record. "My Generation" is still the best thing the Who ever did. I can jump up and down to that.

How equipment-conscious are you?

I'm not really worried about it. It's amazing—I've still got basically the same Marshall amp that I had with Rod Stewart. It's the same chassis, same valves. One or two things may have blown up, but it's basically the same thing. In fact, some of the valves—the tubes—have rusted into their sockets, and you can't take them out!

Have you kept certain guitars over the years?

Yeah—the ones that haven't been stolen! I've hung on to every guitar. I never sell guitars, really. In fact, one time I remember Max Middleton saying, "You've only got one guitar, and you've lost that." I used to have just one Strat because all the others had been ripped off. I had other guitars at different times, but they were all stolen, and I wound up with one guitar. Then I lost that somewhere, and thought, "Wow, I'm supposed to be a guitarist, and I haven't got an instrument." This was back in 1972 or 1973. And then, all of a sudden, I looked around my front room the other day, and I've got about 70 guitars.

Did you buy them?

No. Ibanez designed one for me, and they keep sending me these experimental models. They don't take the same one away and modify it—they just build another one and send it. So I've got hundreds of Japanese men standing outside my front door with these black cases [*laughs*]! The Japanese are fantastic—so efficient and ready to please. And they can build you anything you want. They'll do that here, too, but the Japanese are fantastic. So I've got a lot of Ibanez guitars at home. I still collect a few Fenders.

Do you go for the older, pre-CBS Fenders?

They're obviously the ones you would go for. Any guitar that feels right and sounds good is okay by me.

Do you shop for these guitars?

Never. I love guitars, but it's funny—I would never take the trouble to make an effort and go out and look for one. Even if I knew it was down the street, I wouldn't—unless, like, the concert was going to suffer because I didn't have a good guitar. Then I might go down and look. I'm not a guitar collector fanatic.

What do you look for in a guitar?

I've got *my* guitar. It's a '50s Strat. It's just terrible, but it looks at me, and challenges me every day, and I challenge it back. It has the vibrato, and it's difficult to play. It goes out of tune and all that, but when you use it properly, it sings to you. I've had it for two years.

Do you have any special devices or methods for keeping it in tune while using the vibrato bar?

I don't use any special bridge or tailpiece. I like the way Fender makes them. I've got it pretty much sewn up now by putting a very light graphite on the bridge and the nut. When the strings rock backwards and forwards and slide lengthwise along the neck, you minimize the chance of a string hangup over the nut—which is the killer. This can leave you sharp or flat, according to where you've left the bar, or how you've bent the strings.

Have your Strats been modified?

No, but I do little things to them. I kept breaking first and second strings every single night, and I wouldn't have it—I just thought there was something wrong here. The string was chafing backwards and forwards inside the tremolo setup where it comes out through the block. So I just took a piece of piping—plastic stripped off a piece of wire—and slid the outer casing down the string, and put it behind the bridge so that the string was resting on plastic. I never break a string now unless I really, really wind it up.

How do you set your action?

It's pretty high. It has to be, because if you have it too low on a Strat, it plunks like a banjo.

Do you still use Gibson Les Pauls?

Not really. You just wind up sounding like someone else with a Les Paul. I think I can sound more like me with a Strat. In fact, I think my Strat was the only guitar I used on the new album.

Do you do your own work on your guitars?

If the guitar is at my house and I want it desperately to be some other way, I'll work on it. But if it's in the warehouse where my boys can get at it, then I'll ask them to do it. But I'll have to be there for anything that involves the actual touch of the thing. If it's something like routine wiring, my boys do that.

Do you consistently use any particular brand of strings?

No. I just get a bulk of strings—like two gross—and run through them. But I'm not really that fussy about strings. I start off with a soft gauge—really thin ones—if I haven't been playing in a long time. Within a few days, though, when the tips of my fingers are conditioned, I'm back on the heavy ones.

Do you use any effects?

I've got a booster—a modified yellow box made by Ibanez. This gives me the same sound on the guitar, but louder. I don't like to have the tone changed too much, because, hey, the guitar sounds great clean! You want it to sustain and sound the same, but with a little more volume to it. And I have a Tycobrahe Paraflanger. They only made a few, and I've got two of the only ones left. They're amazing.

How much do you think equipment really matters to you musically?

It doesn't really matter. Sometimes, you might pick up someone else's guitar and play a lot more inspired on that because it's just nice. And yet, having just said that, if you play it long enough, and then go back on your own guitar, you might be inspired by *that*. It's change—variety—that keeps the thing from kicking over.

Do you play much acoustic guitar?

No. They're a pain in the ass! You wind up sounding like some folksinger. I mean, John McLaughlin can play it better than anybody I've ever heard, so I'll leave it up to him. I'll never be like that, so I just sort of sit around and enjoy what he does on it.

Do you experiment much with guitar synthesizers?

No. I've got one, and I can make it sound like the world is going to come to an end, but they're too unreliable. I used this one I've got—a Roland GS/GR 500—when we were in Spain. The equipment was set up in a bullring that they turned into a concert arena, and the sun was 110 degrees at lunchtime. Nobody covered up the synthesizer, and it was beating down on the control board. And I'll tell you what—that night, when it cooled off, all sorts of things were happening inside it.

Do you think there is much of a future in guitar synthesizers?

Only if they can keep the technique of playing like a guitar. Now, if you have to alter anything, a lot of guys will need a lot of time to re-adapt to it. I admire what they've done so far—it's incredible—but if anything interferes with your fluid sort of playing, then you're in trouble. Or, if anything goes wrong onstage with them—which *does* happen—then they should be ruled out.

Do you keep right on top of the latest developments in guitar equipment?

Not really. You know how it goes. You might think, "Wow, I'm the first one to use this!" But sooner or later, you'll find out that somebody had it before you. I've just recently got a Chapman Stick, but I didn't actually search for it. I saw this guy playing it in a club, and I just thought he invented it. I had no particular desire to get one, but I just happened to mention to my manager, "This guy plays this weird stick thing really well. Let's go and see him." He went tick-tick-tick up there in his head, and went and bought one for me. So it was nice. I've got to mess around with it and see if I can make any tunes.

Where do you think the guitar is headed in its evolution?

It's a bit desperate. Los Angeles makes me worried. I was there for two days, and every time I was at the hotel I'd flick through the FM radio stations, and it just sounded like the same guy's album on every station. It got to the point where if you tuned in to a really good disco record, you were better off, because there was more energy and less depression.

Are there any guitarists you feel are saying a lot with their playing?

Well, I really would like to answer that, but I don't get around enough to know. I've heard Steve Morse of the Dixie Dregs because Ken Scott [producer of *There and Back*] produced their album. He played some snatches of it, and I was very impressed.

Do you still listen to John McLaughlin?

Yeah, but I find that I still go back to the old Mahavishnu Orchestra with him—*The Inner Mounting Flame* and *Birds of Fire*. Usually, it works out that way—people play their best when there's a fusion in talent for the first time and the freshness is all there.

What do you think about when you're playing onstage?

Getting through [*laughs*]. Remembering things.

Do you usually try to avoid playing something the same way twice?

Well, it will happen. If you don't feel very well, and are really ill or something, you might fall back into old habits, but, shoot, you're only human. I've never analyzed my playing, because I don't like people taping things that aren't for real. I like to know if we're recording live. And yet, having said that, I'd rather hear myself record a live album, and not know I've done it. I still get a bit shaky when I know things are being recorded.

Do you ever listen back to what you've recorded, and find that you've done things you didn't know you were capable of?

Oh, yeah. That's neat. It's one of the neatest things about playing in this game, really. You have to keep it to yourself, though. You can't say to somebody, "Hey, listen to that!" I mean, I can play a solo on a record, and I can't even play it afterwards. It doesn't always happen, but there are some solos I can't play. In just a few hours, I could probably learn it parrot-fashion, but that's just completely what I'm *not* into. Leave that thing alone and do something else! Although it might be funny to sit down one night and work out exactly where I'm at.

Let's discuss a few of your techniques. When you're bending a string, how many fingers do you use?

Oh, I don't even know. It depends on how tired you are. One might do, but you might use two, depending on what context the bend is in. The bend might be a slow blues, in which case you want to get your whole fist around the neck. Or it might be something really quick, and then it'll be a one-finger job.

What kind of slide do you use?

Just a piece of chrome steel tubing, and I wear it on my middle finger.

Do you have any guitars set up especially for slide?

No. I like to use the same guitar for slide, and since I have a fairly high action, it usually lets me get through on the slide things I do. I hate changing guitars. It's such a hassle unbolting one, and bolting another one on. And they're always out of tune—no matter how carefully they are tuned. I've played all my life in standard tuning, too, because it would be disastrous to start twiddling around with the pegs on a Fender that has a tremolo arm to tune it up to a slide.

What kind of picks do you normally use?

I've got the most rubbish flatpicks ever. They're just dreadful. I forget what they're called now. They're horrible gray ones. The edges are all rough. But that doesn't make any difference, because I don't use picks any more unless my fingers hurt, or I've broken a nail. Usually, I use my bare fingers—all of them I can. Sometimes, I use all five. But if there's a rhythm to be played, then I use a pick for strumming the sharp chords.

Do you follow any conscious picking formulas?

No. My fingers just do what they do, and I have to follow along behind them. You are asking me questions that I ought to be able to answer, but I can't. I don't realize what I'm doing all the time.

When you're trying to learn something, do you follow the philosophy that slow is fast? In other words, learn all the notes to a passage before building up the speed?

Yeah—that's a pretty good rule of thumb.

Do you think that certain chords or keys have certain inherent moods?

Oh, yeah. Just by changing one note in a chord, you can change the whole meaning of the piece of music.

Do you find yourself coming back to certain ones more than others?

I've gotten into the situation now where Tony Hymas plays all the chords, and I hardly have to play them unless I'm backing him up—in which case, he insists I play the chords he wrote [*laughs*].

How much do you know of the technical side of music?

Nothing.

Can you read music?

I know enough to make myself understood when I don't like something. I can't read.

Do you have any systematic exercises or methods of practice?

No. I just pick up a guitar, and if I annoy myself within ten minutes, I'll put it down. If I'm not annoying myself, I'll keep going. In the winter, I play on and off all day, because usually the front door is frozen shut, and I can't get out anyway! I live in a large country house. I can't play if there's somebody else in the room. It makes me self-conscious.

Do you ever record your practice sessions to get ideas for songs?

The Japanese gave me a little tape recorder, and I used to record every phrase that came up. It just didn't seem to do anything. I would tape it and never play it back.

What's the hardest part of your repertoire?

There's a tune called "Space Boogie" [from *There and Back*] that's pretty hard. It calls for listening and counting bars. It will come naturally after a few nights on the road. That way, it will have had a public airing, and I'll understand more of what's to happen. But it has to be great—that number is a killer!

Over the years, you have been credited with pioneering many aspects of the rock guitarist's art, such as the use of feedback and fuzz. You've also been credited with pushing the sideman forward into the limelight. Some have said, in fact, that you were the first rock guitar hero. How much of this do you think is true, and how do you view your contributions?

I don't know [*long pause*]. That's a hard one to answer. All I know is that when the Yardbirds first came to America, all I ever saw was guys in blazers and ties playing stock-strung Fender Jazzmasters [*laughs*]. I suppose I did bring that freedom into the electric guitar, but that's just generalizing. My being a crazy lunatic made people think, "Wow! They might not like the music, but there's a chance. Now I don't feel embarrassed about opening up and playing." And if I've done that, then that's my job in a nutshell. Done.

Do you ever listen to Yardbirds stuff?

No. I find that a little bit too much of a blast from the past. It might upset me, or make me feel good, according to which tune it is, and who's around when I play it.

What are your favorite cuts from that era?

I liked some of the stuff we did with Sam Phillips—the old producer for Elvis Presley. "I'm a Man" [from *The Yardbirds Greatest Hits*] sounded all right. There's a kind of excitement there. It's still pretty hot, even if you play it now.

A lot of new wave bands seem to have traces of the Yardbirds in them.

Oh, yeah. They sound just like the Yardbirds, but without any depth. Maybe the Yardbirds didn't have the technique or the frilly bits that you can get now in recording, but they had some magic, some depth.

It's amazing that the three guitarists in the band—Eric Clapton, Jimmy Page, and yourself—have each had a lasting impact.

Well, maybe not me. I'll tell you what the crunch question is: "Would I swap places with anybody else?" The answer to that is "no." You know, at one time you think, "Wow, would I like to be Pete Townshend? Would I like to be so-and-so? Do they have a better job than I have?" No, I wouldn't swap places with anybody—not in the last six years.

You've worked hard to expand the boundaries of your instrument.

That's my job. That's really what I'm trying to do. I'm not trying it— I'm just doing it.

Do you ever see Clapton?

I've been seeing him recently, and I really take a whole different view on him now, because I've managed to get myself into a position where I can enjoy his playing. He no longer has anything to do with my style. You know, at one time we were blues, and he was better. I think he can play blues better than I can, because he studies it and is loyal to it. I'm not loyal. I try to hotrod it up a bit and change it. But when I heard him play at a gig near his house the other day, I was so knocked out. He was slithering around with a slide guitar, and sounding great! It was such a gas to see kids that had never heard him play in the Yardbirds or with John Mayall, and to see him blasting away at them in 1980. That was a buzz!

Do you ever hear from Page?

No. I don't ring him, and he doesn't ring me.

What was the origin of "Beck's Bolero"?

Oh Christ! That tune! Well, me and Jim Page arranged a session with Keith Moon in secret—just to see what would happen. But we had to have something to play in the studio because Keith only had a limited time. He could only give us like three hours before his roadies would start looking for him. So I went over to Jim's house a few days before the session, and he was strumming away on this 12-string Fender electric that had a really big sound. It was the sound of that Fender 12-string that really inspired the melody. And I don't care what he says—I invented that melody, such as it is. I know I'm going to get screamed at, because in some articles he says he invented it—that he wrote it. I say I invented it. This is what it was: He hit these *Amaj7* chords and the *Em7* chords, and I just started playing over the top of it. We agreed that we would go in and get Moonie to play a bolero rhythm with it. That's where it came from, and in three or four takes it was down. John Paul Jones on bass. In fact, that group could have been a new Led Zeppelin.

When one listens to some of the Yardbird cuts, you can hear where Led Zeppelin got some of its inspiration from you.

Yeah, they did. There's no doubt. Remember, when something has been deliberately or directly lifted from you, you either take it as a compliment, or your heart starts pumping, and you figure out which way the guy's going to die—whether with a pair of scissors or a gun or what!

What do you think when you hear people taking your licks?

That depends on if it's a horrible noise or not. If somebody says, "Wow! That sounds like you!" and it's a horrible noise, then I can do without it. But as long as my record sales are not being impaired, or I'm not directly being thrown off course, then it's a compliment.

Was the tune "Blues Deluxe" on *Truth* recorded live?

No, it wasn't. It was live in the studio, but it was an accurate representation of what we were playing at the time. That's why we decided to make it sound live. We just needed more ambience, and we thought, "If we do that, we might as well put some people in there, as well." All the time Hollywood movies have been tricking people, so I don't figure that one track on an album is any sin.

What was your relationship with Hendrix like?

It was a bit difficult. We could never enjoy a real close friendship because of what we did. He and I were both after the wild guitar playing. I liked Jimi best when we didn't talk guitars. Sometimes, he'd be at the Scene club in New York, and it wasn't happening, and he'd say, "Hey, come on, let's go." Then we would go to the Brass Rail, and when we'd walk in the restaurant, everyone would sort of be bugging us. Well, Jimi mostly. They'd say, "Hey, Jim, what's happening, man?" And I'd just sit and listen to all that. I'm still really sad about his not being here, because I need somebody around that I can believe in. I don't believe in anybody else.

Did your auto accident hurt your ability to play?

I had two accidents. I suppose they did. I suppose they must have slowed me a bit. That's what can happen when you get your head beaten around on a piece of concrete. You wake up, and you're glad to be alive, and you do see things a bit differently. I honestly can't say how much it affected my playing. I can't tell whether it was natural to change, or whether the crashes changed it.

What did giving up a vocalist do to your playing?

It made me dig around and think of like Booker T. and the M.G.s, and it made me wonder what in the hell could take over from a vocalist. It wasn't that difficult, because most of the vocalists we were talking to were singing rubbish anyway. The words they were singing were just the standard rock lyrics, or just jargon that only they knew about. I wanted to bring keyboards out more because of the waste of talent. Keyboard players want to do more than just go ding-ding-ding with their right hand. And with all the new inventions going on, it's only natural to want to bring that out, and wave the flag a bit, and say, "I'm part of this. I pushed him out there. I made him do this."

When *Wired* came out you were accused in the press of sacrificing too much to the keyboards. Do you think this was justified?

Maybe. I was probably quietly nervous about having made an instrumental album, and I probably subconsciously played the keyboards up in order to rule out any accusations that I might be stealing any limelight. I never try and do that.

Did you achieve the car horn sounds on *Live* with your Strat?

Yeah. It's just between fourths and fifths—slightly discordant. You just get two nails of the right hand, and as soon as you've plucked a bit by the bridge, you block the strings off with the left hand so the sound doesn't gradually die away. You let it go just long enough, and then by bending them down, it sounds like the Doppler effect—which is what you experience when, say, a fire truck comes along, and you hear the siren at a certain pitch. Then, when it goes past you, if you're stationary, the noise will die down. It's an audio illusion. That's just a funny thing, because the song was called "Freeway Jam." You know [*mimics carnival barker*], "Hey, folks, the bloke can make it sound like a car!"

Near the end of *Live*, you threw in a little signature lick from "Train Kept A-Rollin'." Do you usually do this onstage?

No, we were just pissed off at Aerosmith. I mean, I was known for playing "Train Kept A-Rollin'" with the Yardbirds, and these people would come up to me—and they weren't kids, they were 24—saying, "Hey, I like your angle on the Aerosmith tune!" The Rock and Roll Trio's 1950s version of that song with Paul Burlison on guitar is bitchin'. That song is hot!

When you look back over your whole career, which tunes are your favorite?

I like "Bolero."

Do you think you've peaked yet?

No. I don't think I've peaked because it has been so spasmodic. You know, it's hard for me to think of a peak in these short periods. If I'd been playing all the time, I could say, "Well, June 1977 was great, and then July wasn't so hot." But I can't answer that, really. It really makes me think about my career, though, when you dig out these questions.

14.

"THERE'S THIS MONSTER BATTLESHIP YOU'RE BUILDING, AND SOMEBODY IS MESSING AROUND WITH THE RUDDER, KEEL, AND DECK, AND YOU JUST WANT TO PUT THE GUNS ON IT!"

✦ ✦ ✦ ✦ ✦ ✦

BY JAS OBRECHT
NOVEMBER 1985

Jeff Beck leans forward and listens intently to a tape of guitar highlights from his new album, *Flash*. It's the second solo break in "Ambitious," one minute, forty seconds into the track.

"The parts that might sound like slide are done with a whammy bar on a Jackson Soloist," he observes. "I think the harmonic is a stray *G* string in there that rings louder. I just smashed the guitar, and hit the whammy arm. Because it's diving, you don't have to be fixed on a certain pitch."

A few seconds later, Jimmy Hall sings "Here is a wild man who thirsts for a fight," immediately followed by a strange, echoed sound.

That's just manic slide. You kind of start down low with a bottleneck, and rip it up—just whiz it up as fast as you can, and then down. It's a skating motion.

How did you get that song's metallic rhythm tone?
I believe it's just out-of-phase pickups—amp plus direct into the board.
Is there any slide in the main solo of "Ambitious"?

It was fingers and whammy. There's no slide in there, but I could see how it could sound like one. This guitar has so much movement in the whammy arm, you could almost depress an octave. It's a pink Jackson Soloist with "Tina Turner" written on it. It has a Kahler whammy, and I used it for most of the solos on the album. It's the first one Grover Jackson built me. He has now made me a couple of orange ones. The guitars are the way he gave them to me. I haven't touched them. [*Ed. Note: Grover Jackson adds, "All three have Seymour Duncan's Alnico II pickups, the middle one being a RWRP—reverse winding, reverse polarity. So on a 5-way switch, you get humbucking in the 2 and 4 positions. One orange one has a Floyd Rose, and the other has a standard Fender-type tremolo. They are all equipped with ebony fingerboards. Jeff likes his necks thin and narrow, 1 5/8" at the nut—sort of like an early-'60s Strat, but a little thinner in the back. These are standard Soloists, with the exception of one of the orange ones. He took a Magic Marker and drew an original Telecaster bass type of pickguard on the guitar, and asked us if we could make one and put it on there. Other than that, Jeff was very hard to get information out of as far as what he wanted."*]*

You end "Ambitious" with a distinctive trill—that string of hammer-ons and pull-offs.

Yeah. I trill with one finger. That's a false harmonic at the very end. I played the open *G*, and then I just lightly touched the fifth fret, I believe, and backed off the normal position of that harmonic until I got that descending whistle with the whammy bar. The whammy is my right arm. There might be one drop-in [overdub] in the trill of notes.

How did you manage to get the guitar to jump out of the mix so much?

With great difficulty [*laughs*]. Jason [Corsaro, engineer] is just a guitar freak, and he pushed and pushed until the limits of the studio equipment were reached.

What causes the fat, squealing guitar effects in the opening of "Gets Us All in the End"?

We messed around with that a bit. There is a bit of backwards guitar there. But, for most of it, I had already done some random soloing over a certain rhythm part with no chords determining what key it should be. I just *raved*. The tape ran out, and I just kept going and going and going. Then they hacked the tape. We decided which were the tasty licks, and they whacked them in the front of the song just to get that bizarre, manic sort of effect.

Beck onstage at the Tabernacle in Atlanta, Georgia, August 14, 1999.

What will you do for that in concert?

I'll do something. It may not be precise, but I can give the effect.

Are you concerned that the drum machine may eventually give cuts like "Gets Us All in the End" a dated sound?

Yeah, but we didn't cheat too much with it. We played pretty much how a drummer would play. We programmed just a straight, simple rock and roll figure. Maybe in years to come, we'll think, "Oh, God, what a dreadful drum box." But we didn't have to have a drummer hanging around the sessions all day—getting tired, and that sort of thing—when *I* was the one being worked over. I didn't want, "Hey, man, how long do you want me? Do you want me to come back tomorrow? Which drums do you want?" I didn't want that kind of pressure during this album. I wanted to concentrate strictly on the goodies—the cream of the cake.

Who runs interference so that you can do that?

Well, [producer] Arthur Baker helped me do that on "Gets Us All in the End." He was a great help. He encouraged me no end to do that experimental stuff on that track. I would never have done that if it hadn't been for Arthur. I've been around guys who go, "God, stop that row!" You know, real musicians.

About 55 seconds into "Escape," there's a very low line that sounds like a 6-string bass.

Jan Hammer used a Fairlight to sample an old Rickenbacker bass with a brand new string on it. It was either an *E* or an *A*. He sampled that one note into the Fairlight, and then he could play the whole bass line on the Fairlight polyphonically. That's the only track on the album he plays on.

Did you flatpick the chorused arpeggios that follow?

No. That's Jan on keyboard synthesizer [beginning 1:11 into the track].

Why was that used to imitate a guitar passage?

Because Jan had everything on floppy disc in the Fairlight when he brought it down to the studio.

Then, about 2:54 seconds in, you cause some phrases to pulse.

That's just smacking the whammy bar with the little-finger edge of the hand. Like a karate chop—that's exactly what it is.

Is the main theme of "Escape" layered guitars and keyboard synthesizer?

Two guitars. There might be a very round synth signal in there with Jan's guide melody, but I don't think you can really hear it—not on top of the two guitars. Jan wrote the melody.

What was the inspiration for your lyrical hook in "People Get Ready"—the notes that go *D*, low *A*, *D*, high *A*?

I heard Duane Hitchings, the keyboard player involved in the session, play a little passing ditty once or twice. It was just the first two notes. I said, "Duane, that sounds pretty hot. I'll duplicate it." But it wasn't enough—it was just a nuance. And I thought, "We'll flog that, because it's a memorable thing that you can whistle." So I hogged it, and I added the two other notes. That's only one guitar playing that. I recorded that song long before the ARMS show [1983's Action and Research into Multiple Sclerosis concert], and as I recall it, I did all the little bits in between the vocals—all three solos—and that little bit on the end with a minimum amount of overdubbing. I did the track in two-and-a-half hours. We'd had a preliminary session at Duane's house, and we had the thing mapped out. When we came to the Record Plant in L.A. the following day, we were really up for it. We did the backing track with Duane on an E-mu Emulator, me on a Jackson guitar with no amp—just a Rockman into the desk—and a drum machine that was incorporated into a keyboard synthesizer.

Why did you change keys from *D* to *E♭* midway through the song?

I just got bored with it being in the same key. I wanted Rod Stewart to get an uplift and go completely free.

What's going on in the final few seconds of "People Get Ready"?

Those are just notes hanging over on two different tracks. I checked out what I was doing on the rhythm track, and there was a nice low note hanging over. Then the second figure was done during the overdub vocal and lead guitar.

Did you cut "People Get Ready" with the same guitar that's in the video?

No. I borrowed that Telecaster from Seymour Duncan. I recorded the song with my pink Jackson.

What creates the unusual sounds in the first eight seconds of the first solo break in "Stop, Look, and Listen"?

There's whammy and some false harmonics on the whistle part. I just held one little finger loosely on the *A* string until I was getting the harmonic I wanted. As you move your finger towards the nut, the string length gets shorter, so the harmonic goes up. It just happened that chord—an open *A*—fit in, and I just walked backwards towards the nut on the *A* string. I used an Eventide Harmonizer with delay, and that created the sort of dropping sound.

A few seconds later, you play a fast trill that starts to ascend.

That's done by fingertapping with my right-hand index finger. I've done that technique a lot. In the *Blow by Blow* days and *Wired*, I used to play the whole figure with my two index fingers.

Are you aware of recent breakthroughs in tapping?

No. I know that guys are doing it because every time you hear a heavy metal record, some guy is using it, and it sounds really trick. But I like to just do it on the spur of the moment when I can't think of anything else to do [*laughs*].

"Get Workin'" and "Night After Night" are the first songs you've sung in many years. Were you comfortable doing that?

No. I hated it. I wanted to get on with the guitar parts. And Nile [Rodgers, producer] said, "Well, this is it. You're gonna be a big star. You're gonna be singing now." I thought, "Okay, great. I'll give him half-an-hour of that, and then we'll get him off it and get someone else in."

"Get Workin'" has some interesting, low-register chicken picking.

That's just slap. You block off all the strings with the palm of your hand, find the one you want, and use the first finger and thumb of the right hand to pull it. Then you bend with the left fingers, as well. That was done with the bridge pickup on a '53 Tele, with the treble rolled off.

What effect do you have going in the break in "Ecstasy"?

The bit where they melt together? There's no slide on that solo. That's half of a guitar sound, laced in with the Roland G-707 guitar synthesizer. There's a lot of acoustic guitar on that song, too.

What's the very first sound in "Night After Night"?

That's back to Jason [Corsaro] again. The old pink demon [Jackson Soloist], cleaner. It's a harmonic with whammy.

That's a pretty loud harmonic. Do you crank it up in the studio?

It gets pretty loud [*laughs*].

Some players use the whammy primarily to emphasize the end of a lick. But often—in the "Night After Night" solo, for example—you seem to integrate the whammy directly into the melody line itself.

Yeah, it's all there in my little friend [*motions to an imaginary whammy*]. Sometimes, I keep my hand on it while I play a whole line. That part you're talking about is country-style fingerpicking and whammy laced together. In one place [2:26], I play a descending trill with whammy, and then swoop up with the finger while the string is still sounding. I didn't move the whammy while I was doing that—I just slid my finger right up the string. I wanted a sneaky ending, so I dropped-in the part right after that.

Are the soaring, swooping lines in "You Know, We Know" [2:23 to 2:42] done with slide, bends, or whammy?

Just regular bends. I push the string a ways upwards, and then let it back down to normal pitch. For a big bend like that, I would probably use all three fingers—my ring backed by the index and middle. I have to do that in certain positions—especially down low—where I need more movement. I use the whammy at the end of that phrase, where I trill it.

Why doesn't "Back on the Street"—the B-side of the "People Get Ready" single—appear on *Flash*?

We needed a "quicky" to fill up the 7" single. They said, "Quick, quick, quick—we have to have something to go on the other side," and I wrote it in about ten minutes. It was done at the time of the video, when "People Get Ready" became a single release.

Why did you wait five years between solo LPs?

I don't know. I was just having fun relaxing, I suppose. Got into a habit.

Are you happy with *Flash*?

Only if it makes people happy. The solo in "Ambitious"—that's more what I think people would like to hear me do. Yeah, it's okay. It's getting there.

You seem to have the same sense of aggression you had as a Yardbird.

It's worse. Partly because I was cooped up in that studio with Nile Rodgers, and all that precision funk business. I got so frustrated, because there were very few slots that I could get in my style. With "Ambitious," I thought, "Well, God, I hope there's a slice of me at the end of this pie."

Do you often play at the outside edge of your ability?

Oh, yeah—bordering on total calamity.

Do you ever get angry in the studio?

Terribly. Especially if I see time sliding away and nothing is being done. I've got this curse about noticing *every* detail. I don't seem to, but I do. I know when someone is not pulling his weight, or that I may be wasting money. I can't afford huge, lengthy stays in the studio. I think about the old days, when we used to rush in and out—when an album only took about $500 to make. That's the way it should be. Dwelling on one subject for too long is not healthy to me.

Do you prefer to do your parts spontaneously?

Oh, yeah. I love doing that. But, unfortunately, we usually get pretty screwed up by having to sit around waiting for the thing to be born. There's this monster battleship you're trying to build, and somebody is messing around doing the rudder and the keel and the deck, and you want to put the guns on it!

Aside from vocals, is the whole track usually finished before your solo?

Yes. I often postpone it because of nerves. I haven't maybe done my homework, and then there's this sudden duty that is thrust upon me to come up with something. And that brings out the quality that I'm looking for. I don't mind failing in front of a whole lot of people if, at the end of the day's work, we get something unreal—or something that's somewhere on the right lines. I'll even abandon a session at 3:00 in the morning, as long as I know that I've got something for the next day that is a train of thought.

Will you try several passes at a solo?

Oh, God, yeah. I usually try to get it the first time, though. Each pass will be nothing like the one before. I might go on a theme—maybe a cascade of notes in one spot that might work really well—and then I'll go for it after a ten-minute break, and completely forget what I played. The next cascade of notes will be nothing like it. I very seldom engineer a solo to fit that previous part. I won't dwell on it until I get it exactly right. If it doesn't come naturally, I'll scrap the idea and move somewhere else.

Are you adverse to punching-in sections?

I have to do it sometimes.

What kind of amps did you use on Flash?

Mostly the Seymour Duncan. [*Ed. Note: Seymour adds, "Jeff uses my Convertible 100 amplifier, which has a 12" Celestion G12K-85 speaker, two separate channels, variable power, and modular preamp circuitry. Jeff has eight different modules, which allow him to play around with different kinds of settings. If he's playing quietly and wants to get a dirty sound, he can put in Hi Gain tubes. If he wants like an old Fender sound, he can put three Classics in it. He can get real distorted, bright, or bassy sounds. By changing the preamps, he gets a lot of his different tones."*]

Have you noticed any change in your soloing approach since 1980's *There and Back*?

Well, only the background music is so totally different on this album. I was almost told to go free and mad within a certain spot—which, for five years, I haven't been able to do. On *There and Back*, I was surrounded with really hot guys, and it made me a bit nervous. I always tried to sneak a session one day when they weren't looking. I prefer it like that. I prefer to work with a green engineer—a guy who's nothing more than a tea boy—who knows how to operate the board. That's because all the guys in the studios work so hard and know everybody. They've been witness to most of the musical history that has been made. They must have been present at some pretty memorable moments, you know. I always worry about that—whether I'm living up to expectations. They may go home that night, and go [*disgustedly*], "Oh, God."

What about your own expectations? What are the pressures of being considered . . .

If I've managed to reach somebody and addle their brain that evening, then the job's done [*laughs*].

Do you feel you always have to be "on"?

No. It doesn't affect me so much now like that. I don't mind not hitting a spot straightaway, because I have to work within the pace and capabilities that I've got.

Does your rough playing approach ever cause tuning problems?

Yeah. It's murder. There's something called a Trem-lok that prevents that from happening. You'll find that with a whammy bar, when one string breaks, the tension of the other strings is changed, and you're way off-key. The Trem-lok was a little peg. You'd depress the bar, and slide this little peg into position, and it would deactivate the tremolo and lock the strings. So if one broke, you'd still be in tune with the other five.

Do you use a pick?

No, but I've used them in the past. What got me off them was playing a lot of gigs. I used to mess around a lot and have fun onstage. I'd run around and tie up the bass player with sticky tape and things like that. I'd be laughing so hard that I couldn't hold the pick. I'd hit a chord, and the pick would ping out. If it was black, I'd never find it. One day, it pinged off down into the orchestra pit on this gig, and I felt like such an idiot because everybody saw it go, and I had to fake playing after that. I realized there was no way I was going to stoop down and pick it up, so I just kept playing without it. The pick was definitely on its way out.

Do you have more control without one?

Oh, yeah. There's no way I can use a pick now. The only time you might need it is when you play a stock guitar with very tight strings, and you want a real rigid, abrasive sound, or a real clean stroking motion—a sharp, choppy rhythm.

When you hold your index finger and thumb together to play fast lines, are you striking the string with your nail?

That's right. The thumb supports the finger. It gets more of an up-and-down motion. Just the side of the index fingernail is actually hitting the string.

On Tina Turner's *Private Dancer* LP, you climax your solo in "Steel Claw" with a fast flurry of notes [2:19 to 2:21]. Are those fingertaps?

No, that's a trill, I think.

Did you come up with the idea for the guitar sound in "Private Dancer"?

Yeah. I had a pair of Roland digital echoes. I did that session in about a half-hour. It was thrilling working with her.

Were you surprised when she engraved her name in your guitar?

I was. I said, "Don't worry about paying me for the session. Just sign this guitar so it will stay on there." She got out this green felt pen, and, of course, it wouldn't stay on a polished, painted guitar with grease all over it. So she said, "Do you want it to stay there for a real long time?" I said, "Yeah. Write it into the woodwork. Go with it." And she got a dagger out of her bag—we call it a flick knife, you call it a switchblade—a very evil-looking thing. First of all, she started chipping away, trying to make a nice engraved job. I said, "Never mind that. Just write your name." She just tore into it and rubbed nail polish on it.

Are you still going to use it on the road?

Maybe. It has a bit of a wobbly arm. The Kahler is too loose for me. I'll use one of the new orange ones.

On Rod Stewart's *Camouflage*, did you do the riffing through the verses of "Infatuation"?

No, I just did the solo. That album was done with the Jackson. It was the only guitar I was using at the time.

Was it challenging to work with Mick Jagger on *She's the Boss*?

It was difficult, yeah. Lovely guy, though—super.

Pete Townshend was on that album, too.

Yeah, but I didn't meet him. He did his parts after we finished in Nassau. Mick took the tapes away and had Townshend beef up some rhythm guitar. That's all.

How did you come to choose an acoustic guitar for the solo on "Just Another Night"?

Nothing else worked. All else failed, and out came the acoustic. I didn't want to be seen just sitting around doing nothing when they were saying, "It isn't working." I wanted to work for the guy, you know. Mick had flown me out to Nassau. Funny enough, he had this Gibson J-200 there. We restrung it with electric light-gauge strings, and I did a Spanish-style solo. He loved it, so we left it on there.

For the Jagger sessions, how finished were the tracks you soloed over?

We built the whole lot. There was nothing done beforehand. He had like 16 different versions—all demos—of the same tunes with different pickup bands that he'd use. I remember using the same setup again—the pink guitar—as well as an old Tele. We had a drummer and a bass player, and we just played like a live band. I also used a '53 reissue Fender Strat with a whammy bar for the solo in "Lonely at the Top."

Do you use stock tremolos on your Fender Strats?

Yep. Don't touch them. I have three springs on the back.

What's going on in your break in Mick's "Running out of Luck"?

Tele with a bottleneck and volume swells. Both pickups. [*Ed. Note: Seymour Duncan adds, "I put together the Telecaster Jeff used on this session and some of the Tina Turner stuff. It has a '54 Fender body made of real light ash, and a newer, fairly chunky Fender neck. It has a 5-way switch and two Alnico II pickups—the bridge pickup is tapped. When the lever switch is all the way back in the bridge position, you get the full output from the bridge pickup. In the 2 position (going forward), you get the full output from both pickups. In the center position, you get the rhythm pickup by itself. The 4 position gets the rhythm pickup and the tap of the bridge pickup, so you get the lower output, and it's a little bit brighter. The 5 position gets the tapped, brighter sound of the bridge pickup by itself. I used two 50k pots, which allow him to roll the volume. It has a brass bridge, which fattens up the sound a little bit. He wanted it set up not too low, so that when he hits a note softly, he gets a real clean sound. Then, when he hits it a little bit harder, he can get that attack he's famous for. As he plays a lot with his thumb on the low strings, he likes a little bit heavier string on the bottom—a .046 or .048, going up to a .009."*]

Did you play the riff through Jagger's "Lucky at Love"?

Yeah. Tele. It was just a little line that kept refraining in my mind, so

"Most of [my effects are] in a cardboard box in the corner—thrown away. If the amp is doing the right job, you don't need that stuff."

✦ ✦ ✦ ✦ ✦ ✦

I kept it in the song. The solo has barking noises—that was a go-crazy-Jeff type.

You must have some amazing home tapes.

[*Laughs*] I'd probably be locked up if they were ever heard. I go all over the place. But I'm not usually looking to get too flowery with it, or do anything finished. I'm looking for chords and progressions. I put them down on tape—like a notebook—and when I hear them, I instantly know what I've done.

Do you ever play music that makes sense to you, but that most people wouldn't understand?

Yeah, it would seem a bit odd to them. I love to be totally left alone. I can't experiment if there's anybody in the house. I make some dreadful, awful noises. It upsets *me*, so I couldn't bear to play, knowing that somebody else has eavesdropped it.

When you're playing for yourself, what percent is experimentation?

Probably 50 or 60 percent. I'll stop what I'm doing—even after spending four or five hours trying to build a track—if I come up with an amazing few notes. I'd rather scrap the entire track I'd been working on—just to get the thing on tape. I put it in the memory bank if it is worth doing.

Did parts of *Flash* happen like that?

Most of it was pretty controlled. There were producers there to take care of that. I didn't go erasing too many things. We had a reference tape running sometimes—not so much to document performances, but for sound effects.

Do you know what you're doing in musical terms?

Nah. I had a few pointers that were given to me by a piano teacher, but I have no knowledge of musical theory at all.

Do you have any other studio projects in the can?

Like something hovering about waiting to be released? No. There's loads of stuff somewhere. There's a whole BBA [Beck, Bogert & Appice] album that I've got hidden away—a studio record that was never released. It was done after our live Japanese album. There might be a few fusion tracks lying around, too.

What are your feelings about doing videos?

As long as the video doesn't upset the initial impact of the song, then it's okay. You don't want to couple your own images with a bad video. But I'd sooner just not have the video. They are such a necessary thing for bands that have to put an image across, and they can magnify that image in a big way by visual trickery. But there's too much of that gimmicky video stuff—especially in the rapping and scratching-type videos. Otherwise, there's nothing to look at. They have to have a video like that, because there's only one guy on the record, probably, who's fooling around with 15,000 layers of sound.

Do you compose?

No. I just practice a lot at home when it snows or rains or I'm tired— you know, if I can't work outside. But now and again, I get a little flurry of days when I play—usually when I'm snowbound in the winter. I get right into it in a big way. Even if a little bit of that practice stays with me, I count that as a plus. I'm hurting for a guitar right now. I haven't played one for about a week, and I'm sick [*laughs*].

Do you play much acoustic guitar?

No. I like to mess on one, but usually I put it out of the way, and it stays there. I can't get up and get it. I usually have a Tele down at my feet when I'm watching TV. I try not to practice on one with a whammy bar, so that, later, when I'm noodling with my stage guitar, I have an extra toy to play with. I use that as a leverage for inspiration, too.

Of all your instruments, which do you play the most?

An old battered '53 Tele that I've got at home. I bought that off Seymour Duncan after the ARMS tour. As a matter of fact, my road manager bought it for a friend of his, and I told him there's no way he's having it. I said, "Tell your friend you couldn't find one. I'm having this."

Are you a fan of synthesizers?

When they're played by Jan Hammer—yeah. I've got two guitar synths at home, and they sit there gathering dust. They are really not feasible in a freedom sense of the word. You can't go in, plug in, and have fun like you would with a Strat and a Marshall. There are too many pitfalls in them. I could be corrected, but I don't like the idea of having to spend millions of dollars every time some guy comes out with an improvement.

Do you have much of an effects system?

No. I rented this rack that was called something sexy—like the Bitch or the Sex Bomb—I forget the name. It had just about every gadget you could hook up in one box. The sum total of every sound linked together makes a really interesting noise, but, individually, I could strip the thing right down and have something like a digital echo or maybe a flanger—just regular effects.

What about effects at home?

Most of it is in a cardboard box in the corner—thrown away. If the amp is doing the right job, you don't need that stuff.

How do you prepare yourself to play your best onstage?

Well, usually the bands are so far between that it's like starting all over. It's the newness of it—the power again—and having the refreshing sort of feeling of a new band of guys that are really happening. When you get amongst them for the first time in a long while, there's that wraparound kind of feeling. Plus, if they are into my music, that's what brings it out of me. It's not the end result of a lot of hard work—it's the new, refreshing feeling that you are going to do some new things.

What do you expect from your band?

I like guys that I can have a common sense of humor with—usually English. That humor helps me get through a rigorous sort of tour schedule. I love American players, too.

Do you consider yourself an "English guitarist"?

Yeah. Although I'm giving back most of my inspiration—which was gained by American influences—I'm still English right through and through. I'm not Americanized in any way. I haven't become like Eric Clapton, who's steeped in the blues and has a very American style. I'm more English than he is.

What were your impressions of the ARMS shows? Did you feel competitive with Eric Clapton and Jimmy Page?

There was a little element of that there, which you've got to expect with the three of us plunking away. But it was no way intended. We weren't up there to have a battle or anything. We traded solos, and that's about as close as we came.

The nights you performed in San Francisco, it seemed that you were trying to push further than the others were willing to go.

Well, nobody was trying to hog any limelight on that show, but, at the same time, I wanted to play within the best form and spotlight that I could. I just played as well as I could for Ronnie Lane. That's all it was. I enjoyed it a lot. I can't really add much more to that one.

You once mentioned that during the show, you felt you were playing for your musicians—Jan Hammer and Simon Phillips.

Yeah. That was on the high-pressured first gigs in London—when all eyes were on us, you know. Princess Diana was there, and she put the muckers on the audience by making them very subdued. Everybody was looking at Princess Di, and it automatically made the whole atmosphere more intense when she turned up. It was like, don't swear, don't shout, don't scream, don't act like hooligans. Obviously, if she'd left, everybody would have gone nuts. The audience clapped, but there was a noticeable difference between that show and the first night when she wasn't there.

In his July '85 *Guitar Player* interview, Eric Clapton claimed that after the ARMS shows, he began to think that you were probably the finest guitarist he'd ever seen.

You can't imagine how that makes me feel. For him to say that, it really means a lot. It sort of blows me away. That is most interesting. Old Eric—he never seemed to be the slightest bit interested in my style.

Who's the most stimulating guitarist you've ever played with?

Hendrix. No doubt about it. I don't forget those things in a hurry. And Stevie Ray Vaughan was lovely to play with.

If you could go back in time and jam with anyone . . .

I'd bring Hendrix back straightaway. If I had the power to do that, he'd be here. He'd fill up a few holes that have been there.

Some players say that on their best nights, they get into a zone where they aren't even aware of what they are playing.

That's funny. Yeah, that's true. I do that sometimes [*laughs*]. Not too often with me—I usually have to do some work. But I know what they mean.

What are the advantages of not going on the road very often?

I can't speak for anybody else, but it enables me to have a good spring clean in the brain. It drives me crazy. I start getting scared on the road with what my life is all about. I'm not a true professional in that sense. I don't go, "They all want me, I've *gotta* get out there." When I see bands, I can almost guarantee that they're on the road every minute of the year. I can't do it. I've failed so many times at trying to do long tours. I need that layoff to get inspired and encouraged for the next venture, because I'll burn out on that first venture as quickly as we can dream it up. We start with high hopes, and then try to not be brought down by restrictions of this, that, or the other—like the P.A. system.

Will you tour to promote *Flash*?

Maybe. So many of my ideas usually melt by the time we actually get around to trying to do them. As you get nearer to the day when you want to pull it all together, you realize, "Oh, God, maybe it's not possible." A six-week tour will be plenty enough—on one leg, at least. I could have three different legs of the tour. You want the show to be the primo, happening event, and the record should just be a token of it—a reminder of what you've seen. But, oftentimes, the record is miles better than live.

Can you make more money on the road than with an album?

It depends on how crafty you are, and how lucky you are with the gate and the percentage deals. You need a fair-sized auditorium to make money nowadays. And the travel! Just moving from Chicago to Detroit would be like a fortune. Our 1980 tour had a very simple stage presentation, and a pretty streamlined band, but it took two or three tractor trailers. And we really cut back—apart from sharing beds. I hate the idea that one has to go away and live unnaturally and all that. But having said that, if it hadn't been for Buddy Holly coming over and playing for us in Croydon in the 1950s . . . He made the effort. I used to think the guy would just disappear into a castle somewhere in the middle of the sky, but the next night he was in Edmonton, Cook's Ferry, or whatever. I saw Buddy Holly live, and it was the best thing I've ever seen. Gene Vincent and Buddy—not together, but very close.

Did Gene have Cliff Gallup with him?

No, I wish! That was one of the crimes of the music world—that the Blue Caps were not allowed over in England. There was an exchange thing among musicians, and the musicians' union said that Gene could come, but he couldn't bring the whole band. I mean, the one thing you wanted to see! I don't know whether Cliff would have been there anyway, because he hated traveling. A very muted Cliff Gallup was interviewed in that rockabilly article you put in *Guitar Player* ["Roots of Rockabilly," Dec. '83]. He's the one guy I have to meet before I go. Just for him to tell me to "f★★k off" would be enough. I wouldn't care if he was playing "Girl from Ipanema" in a Howard Johnson's lounge—I have to meet him. I have to meet Paul Burlison, too. These are just my schoolboy heroes.

What's the special appeal of Cliff Gallup?

You can't tell from listening? God, he was the most experimental, wild, end of the . . . I mean, some of that stuff on Gene Vincent & the Blue Caps albums holds up even today. Wild, ridiculous runs all over the place.

What would you like guitarists to have learned from you?

Get a job [*laughs*]. No. I never thought about this. As long as they have seen a concert that has made them go away going, "[*clicks fingers*] *That's* what I want to do," then I'm happy. It's a healthy thing. But if someone starts picking away at my style and trying to nibble chinks out of it, I don't like that. And I do get upset about it if I hear great chunks that sound like they've been hacked out of a record of mine. It might be one refrain that's played over and over again, and then he'll do a little bit of himself, and then it'll come back to me again. I get cross with that sometimes—frustrated. All the kids in his neighborhood think he's king, you know.

Didn't you ever find yourself doing the same thing when you were young?

I was doing a lot of that, but then it was blatant copying. In the early days, I had to do copies of Hank Marvin. It was irresistible. I felt his style and tone were so nice. If you could stand up onstage in a band and entertain a crowd with it, they'd go away saying, "Hey, that group is great! They sound like the Shadows." That was all that mattered then. It wasn't to stay like that. I'd rather a guy told me he enjoyed my playing and left it at that.

How has the profession of rock guitar changed in the time you've been involved with it?

Since day one? Generally speaking, the emphasis in English pop music is not as heavily on guitar. If I heard a guitarist play a solo over there, I'd listen. When I come over to America, I don't listen, because it's *all* guitar. It becomes kind of a wall of confusion. There are so many wild guitar solos going on every record. It's scream, scream, scream.

What's your objective when you solo?

Try and get out without any trouble [*laughs*]. Slide right through it.

Is there anything you want to learn, any new techniques to be mastered?

I don't know. If people like what I've done up to know, I'll just carry on that way—bend the rules.

Can you foresee a time when you give up music?

No. I wouldn't like that. I don't like the thought of being booted out of the music business. I'm just amazed that I've still got a job. And it's all down to the people that you have in your readership.

15.

"THERE'S ALWAYS SOMETHING IN THE GUITAR THAT NEVER CEASES TO AMAZE ME—SOME SICK SOUND THAT I NEVER HEARD BEFORE"

✦ ✦ ✦ ✦ ✦ ✦

BY LISA SHARKEN
MAY 1999

Since Jeff Beck released his first solo album, *Truth*, in 1968, his output has been frustratingly meager, and a long time coming. A hardcore perfectionist who doubles as his own worst critic, Beck often takes several years between discs to create material he deems worthy, and he throws out far more music than he keeps. In fact, if it were up to him, he'd probably still be mixing *Blow by Blow*.

The fretboard wizard's latest release, *Who Else!*, is a collection of 11 instrumentals in a variety of styles, ranging from techno to blues to Irish traditional music. Beck—who is miffed that the *other* Beck has made it impossible for him to release an eponymously titled album—has spent the years since 1989's *Guitar Shop* listening, absorbing influences, and "shouting at the television." The result is an album that embraces the '90s, pays homage to the past, and looks toward the future of guitar.

Not surprisingly, *Who Else!* was a difficult album to make. In fact, it was made in two phases over two years, with two separate groups of musicians and producers. The first phase included Pino Palladino on bass with Steve Lukather co-producing, and the only track on the album from those sessions is "Psycho Sam." Phase two was co-produced by Tony Hymas—who also wrote a considerable portion of the album's

Beck working the whammy bar on one of his signature model Fender Stratocasters.

material—and features Beck's current live band: Jennifer Batten on guitar synth, Steve Alexander on drums, and Randy Hope-Taylor on bass. Guest artists include Jan Hammer and Chrissie Hynde, who supplies the vocal parts on "Space for the Papa."

Despite the difficult birth, *Who Else!* is another thrilling chapter in the career of the man hailed by many guitar greats as the greatest guitar player ever. And even if that young, hip-hop-influenced tunesmith does have a popular stranglehold on the surname, for guitarists, there is only *one* Beck.

You seem to reinvent yourself with every record. Is that a conscious effort?

No, it's just what I absorb through listening to things. It's a perpetual thing. The time between records enables me to become somebody else. I don't know whether people think that I sit around and channel surf or go to the record shop. I don't. In fact, I probably should do more searching for new stuff, but who wants to hear something fantastic? I want to hear that everyone is crap and that there's no competition.

What were some of the difficulties you encountered in putting together this record?

To go into a studio with no proper design on how you want to sound is a disaster—especially with great players. They make *anything* sound good. You need to have a captain telling you where it's going or you'll hit an iceberg. We crashed into a few icebergs on the way. Unless a miracle happens, your album is never going to get done, whereas if the material is right on, it'll finish itself a lot faster.

We never had a general picture of how the record was going to sound. I wrote one tune that was a very majestic-sounding jungle track with hypnotic, monotonous rhythms. It was a marriage of a Hendrix-type guitar over a jungle groove, but, unfortunately, it was a novelty track. It lurked about, and I wanted to make an album around that one piece because I was so proud of it, but nothing was made. So it's in the can—the trash can.

The truth of the matter is, we didn't have enough material when we started. The stuff that was coming out was so distant and unrelated. Only one track stuck out, and it was sort of like ZZ Top on speed. It wasn't until the 11th hour that I rang up Tony Hymas and asked him to write some music. I've got a boatload of stuff that will probably end up being more useful as ballast for the boat.

How long does it take you to get sounds in the studio?

Ten years! I put down the drummer and the bass player first. They're still the engine in the band, and if they're kicking my backside, I'm happy.

Is it difficult for Jeff Beck, the co-producer of the record, to be objective about the performances of Jeff Beck, the guitarist?

I know when a performance is right. I know when it's sick enough to be acceptable. If it's not twisted enough, I'm not going to use it.

I've heard it takes a long time before you consider a track a "keeper."

It takes the threat of death, or a breach of contract. If I ever went into the accounts department at the record company, I'd probably have a heart attack. They must love me because I'm six years behind in the albums I owe them.

Did you do much pre-production to prepare for the actual recording sessions?

I cut some tracks in my home studio. I have a Mackie 32•8 mixer with the usual junk—a Lexicon LXP-1, some compressors and limiters, two Tascam DA-88s, and one Neumann mic. With that mic, I don't need to go to another studio to record the guitars. They sound better at my studio than they do anywhere else. We've moved to new horizons in what we're capable of doing in the home studio. Sampling technology is incredible. Any sound you want is possible now.

What types of guitars, amps, and effects did you use on the record?

My gear was the same on almost all of the tracks. It was just my surf-green Strat through one 50-watt Marshall head and a 1960 Marshall BX cabinet loaded with 25-watt Celestion greenbacks. The Marshall is one of the new JCM 2000 Series models—the DSL50. It has two channels—one has a vintage distortion sound, and the other has a classic tone. It sounds like you're playing at a million watts with a nice, agreeable amount of distortion that can be continuously varied. I love it.

"Another Place" and "Angel (Footsteps)," were recorded with a '52 Fender Reissue Telecaster through a DigiTech Legend preamp. The Tele suited those songs perfectly. It has that liquid, creamy sort of sound, while the Strat is a little bit edgy.

I usually record dry, and add all of the outboard stuff in the mix. But for "Another Place," I played through a Lexicon LXP-1 for delay and reverb. There's a nasty hum at the very end of the track—a rogue element that crept in. At the end of the song, as the note decays, you can hear the buzz come in. But I left it.

Can you tell me more about your Strat?

It's one of the first of my signature models—the one that was engraved by Little Richard, and that's why I cherish it. It's the one that got battered onstage, and it's the one I always get handed when we play anywhere, so it has become a workhorse. But I'm going to retire it. It has two splits right down the back—the result of being thrown 60 feet into the air.

What kind of pickups are in that guitar?

They're just stock Fender single-coils.

You're not using Fender Lace-Sensors?

No.

Does it have a huge neck, as did the first production models?

No, but I've probably changed the neck because Fender sends me new necks all the time. I couldn't see the sense of having no options. Obviously, if you buy a new car, you want options. Even if you like the car, you may want a different seat or pedals. It's stupid to make a huge, tree trunk neck if some kid has small hands. But Fender told me they wanted to put out the exact same guitar that I play. So there it is. If you want to change it, then it isn't what I play. But it's whatever you want. I mean, if your guitar sounds the way you want, then make the neck fit it. Get your old man to shave it down.

What kind of frets do you prefer?

I like the Gibson Les Paul–type. I took a little bit of the Gibson tradition—that kind of big, fat fret thing—because I didn't like the thin, original Fender frets.

How do you like the action set on your guitars?

I've gone to setting it lower to get a little more speed. It's about as low as it can go before it starts to buzz. I hate that "fizzing" sound. When I have the fatter strings and I'm in good shape, training-wise, I can afford to lift the action a bit. It does sound better with high action. Hendrix's action was about an inch off the fretboard. It was really up there.

Where do you prefer pickup height to be set?

I get them as close as I can to the strings, but I set the front pickup a little bit lower because, obviously, you're getting more bass in that position. And I just set the middle pickup so that it doesn't get in the way.

Do you do your own setups?

No. I just play the thing until it literally falls to bits. If I'm having trouble with the action, I will straighten out my own necks and set up the bridges. I enjoy doing it, I just don't let people know that I know how to do it!

How much does the guitar's setup affect your performance?

If I picked up, say, Brian May's or Jennifer's guitars, I probably wouldn't be able to play them. They're all set up so personally to their taste. I need the utility of an "everyman's" setup. That never did any harm to the original rockabilly stars. When you bought a guitar in the '50s, you got what the factory made for you.

Speaking of Jennifer, what was it about her that first caught your attention?

I saw Jennifer with Michael Jackson, but I really remembered her from your magazine. I used to think that girls were just muscling in—that playing guitar was a male thing. But Jennifer is more dedicated than most people I know—including me. Bringing her into the band was definitely a bloody right choice. She's the magical difference. I can't do without her humor. It's so much fun working with her.

Is her role in the band more supportive, like a keyboard player?

It sounds a bit unkind to say that. She's a MIDI guitarist, and she seems quite happy to fulfill that function. To me, it's great to hear the sound of rocket ships, and then hear an organ. She has it down. But I know she wants to do her own thing, and there's no point in having her do half her act within the constraints of my band. But these are early days yet. We'll have to wait and see how the band evolves over time.

How were the album's live tracks recorded?

We tried to make a live album in Germany, but it didn't work out. We recorded four concerts, and when we heard the tapes, we thought it was a disaster—not because the playing was particularly rough, it just wasn't as precise as I wanted. Also, the sound was sort of crap. Everything was close-miked—which was totally wrong. It would have been all right for an intimate kind of thing, where you want to hear that dry, in-your-face sound, but that's not what I wanted.

We used a live version of "Brush with the Blues" on the album because it's a totally different animal from the big, powerful stuff we play. It's genuine—there's nothing altered. We just threw up the mics, added a little ambience, and that was it. It was recorded live in Munich at a 2,500-seat venue. "Space for the Papa" is live, too, although we fixed it up and added Chrissie Hynde's vocal. But the solo is exactly what I played live.

Does your live rig differ from the gear you use in the studio?

No—it's just the Marshall DSL50. I like to keep things simple. On the *Guitar Shop* tour with Stevie Ray Vaughan in 1989, our rigs were like

total opposites. I was using a
Fender Twin with one spare for
emergency purposes, and Stevie
just could not understand what
was going on. He had this massive
rig with about six amps linked
together, and his sound was so
rich and full.

I don't know if I'd really want
a system like that, but I do plan to
try out some new amplification. I
bet I'll wind up with the old
Marshall again. I understand it. I
know its habits and its quirkiness.
Also, there's a combination that
worked really well for the *Guitar
Shop* album—a Fender Twin and
a Princeton wired in series. If you
switched off the Princeton, a

*"The Marshall
sound is the
balls. It's the
big daddy, and
it has that
growl that no
other amp has."*

✦ ✦ ✦ ✦ ✦ ✦

throatiness in the tone disappeared, and the sound sucked without it.

What are your typical amp settings?

On the Marshall head, the gain is set at about one o'clock. The other
channel is set clean with about 10 percent distortion, and turned nearly
all the way up. That way, I've got full force on both channels. That's it.
For the tone controls, I tend to back off a little on the bass because you
don't want all that woof—it can get in the way of the drums and bass. I
set it with a lot of midrange, presence, and top end. We kill the whistle on
the guitar—if there is any—with the presence control. I have no trouble
with that, because a lot of my playing is done with all the top end rolled
off the guitar. The high frequencies are so cranked on the amp that it
sounds toppy enough already. If you were to open up the treble on my
guitar, you'd probably kill yourself!

What kind of speakers are you using?

They're stock—probably Celestions.

**On your last tour in 1995, you combined Fender Bassmans
and 50-watt Marshall Super Lead Plexis. What are the advantages
of using Fender and Marshall amps together?**

They each serve a different purpose. Let's put it like this: Buddy
Holly would not have sounded the way he did with a Marshall. He has

the crisp and sparkly thing, which is what the Fender does best. Hendrix couldn't have sounded as good with a Fender—it has diamond sparkles all over it. That crystal clarity is fine for country bands and Fleetwood Mac, but if you want to get a little bit rude and loud, you've got to have a Marshall. The Marshall sound is the balls. It's the big daddy, and it has that growl that no other amp has.

What's different about the way you approach playing solos live and in the studio?

Obviously, live, you're completely unfettered and don't care about making rattling noises. In the studio, if there's a nasty noise, you stop. I try to make the solos as nutty as possible—disregarding the punch-in and punch-out—and just playing to get ideas on tape. That's the main thing. Nine times out of ten, I'll rehearse something, and then not play it. We'll get to the punch-in, and I'll do something else.

Are most of your live solos totally improvised?

Yeah. There's no design. In fact, they happen so fast that I don't really know what I'm doing half the time. It's like trying to tell somebody about a car crash. It's all over in two-fifths of a second, and then you're talking about it for ten hours afterward. All I know is that there are certain stages during a solo where I realize whether it's going well or not. If it's not going well, then I jump in and try to rescue it.

Do you ever use Pro Tools to piece together solos?

I might try it, but the music still must exist as an organic launching pad. For example, sometimes an acceptable accident happens where I think, "I would've done that, but I didn't. *This* happened instead." In that case, using Pro Tools to move things around is merely accommodating something that's humanly possible.

What kind of slide did you use on "Space for the Papa," and which finger did you wear it on?

I used a Plexiglas tube and a capo. It gave me that metallic kind of overtone—a real smooth, almost trombone-like sound. I wear it on my middle finger, because I can play single-string solos with the slide stuck in the air.

Do you ever use open tunings when you play slide?

Not really. I've played in standard tuning for so long that I automatically sound like Muddy Waters or George Thorogood or Elmore James when I tune to an *E* chord.

In recent years, you seem to have gained more technical control over the instrument in terms of playing harmonics and microtones.

That's because I've been so impressed by Eastern music and John McLaughlin. Guys like that are sent here for a purpose—besides to piss you off—as the standard that you have to look at. They exist. They're not figments of your dreams. You can go out and buy the records, listen to them, and learn from them. That's exactly what I did. I got the Bulgarian Women's Choir CD, and I thought, "Well, maybe I should just sit and listen to this for about ten years." That CD is the most agonizingly wonderful thing. It had nothing to do with rock and roll, but it impressed me just as much. A part of my psyche moves into tears every time I hear it.

From a technical standpoint, I inadvertently discovered a way of getting microtones and such out of the Strat, and making music out of them. Up to that point, the Strat was Buddy Holly's guitar—and Cliff Gallup's of the Blue Caps—and was played very conventionally.

How do you keep the strings in tune with a standard tremolo?

What makes you think they stay in tune? Fender has come a long way in keeping the tuning problems at bay, but a new string will still always go off until you've stretched it. The roller nut on my guitar has a twin roller on the first three strings—which helps to keep those strings in check—and the tremolo is a standard spring tremolo. It's not like the Floyd Rose, which slackens them off until they're dangling on the floor. I think that's a complete waste of time. I just make sure the spring tension on the tremolo arm is exactly what I want. If that isn't right, and there isn't enough upward motion—or if it goes down and bottoms out—I'm in trouble. It's basically down to the string thickness. If the thickness of one string is off, it throws the whole thing out.

What type of strings are you using?

I use Ernie Ball strings and I'm planning to move up to a .012 on the first string. But that's brutal. I need to be on tour for about two months before that gauge is comfortable. Right now, I'm using an .011 on the first string, and a .048 or .050 on the bottom string.

You've been playing without a pick for many years now. Who did you listen to while developing your fingerpicking technique?

I listened to the '50s Merle Travis and Chet Atkins records, and although I loved that style, I never wanted to have a career where I sit on a stool and play. I just did it because I wanted to know how it was done, but I never thought I'd ever put that style into practice. I simply couldn't see the sense of wasting all of the other fingers by holding a pick between your thumb and first finger. The loss of the pick was a blessing in disguise, really.

How much abuse do your hands sustain during a gig?

Not a lot, but the first week of a tour is like murder. When you're onstage you don't notice the pain, but afterwards I see the dark red spots on the tips of my fingers. Usually they heal pretty well. If I keep practicing every day, I'm all right. When I don't, the trouble starts.

How do you maintain the nails on your picking hand?

The nails on my right hand are a little bit longer than on my left. I just keep them just long enough so that they protect the fingertips. If I cut them too short, it's a bit painful.

Has your relationship with the guitar changed over the years?

It's a battered wife. It's embarrassing. I'm sure the society for the protection of battered guitars has my picture. There's always something in the guitar that never ceases to amaze me, some sick sound that I never heard before. That's what my job is, really. It's not playing fantastic runs and trying to dazzle everybody, it's coming up with some little cheesy trick. This is rock and roll.

As an instrumentalist, you have the gift of being able to use the guitar in place of the human voice.

That seems to be what I do. So many instrumental bands sound like either a zipped-up version of the Ventures or a backing track that needs a vocal.

Many people believe you don't practice.

I practice every day—sometimes even longer than five minutes! You can practice subconsciously, you know, and if you're watching TV, it's better to have something strapped around your neck than not. But you're not gonna get in there if you don't practice. You have to sit there until you get it right.

What do you think of the state of music today?

It's a bit like a silent movie, isn't it? It's about time to move onto the talkies! I do enjoy some techno bands—especially the Prodigy. If you see the Prodigy in full flood, forget it. There are not many metal bands that can keep up with that.

Do you listen to your own work?

I don't want to hear it once it's done. Sometimes I will, but only if I'm feeling strong enough to handle it. If my ego's down, I won't put it on.

What do you think of some of the younger up-and-coming players?

Crap.

But you did play with Jonny Lang at the Grammy Awards.

He was suffering from laryngitis, so any after-hours chat or jamming was out the window because he had to go back and rest. I never really heard him play—which was a bummer. I think it's wonderful that the young guys get a "girlie" crowd. I don't mean that disrespectfully. Jonny waves the flag for the blues, which is great, because if young guys like him don't carry it on, it's going to die.

Who do you consider the most important guitarists of our time?

Eric Clapton and Jimi Hendrix, I suppose. Jimmy Page, too, although he was sort of an ambassador for riffs and mystique, rather than an innovator.

Django Reinhardt is still *the* best guitarist, and there's no question about that, ever. Stevie Ray Vaughan was great, of course. He had a large chunk of Hendrix in him, and Hendrix carried a big chunk of Buddy Guy. In 1959, Buddy was doing all of that showbiz stuff, playing around with the guitar and teasing the audience with it. T-Bone Walker used to do that, too. He used to finish off his act by playing with one hand while carrying his amp off with the other. I thought that was the coolest thing in the entire universe when I saw that.

Albert Lee is still the king of that kind of country stuff, and I don't hear enough of it. And Jennifer is going to be monstrous. I can't wait for her to get out and do her thing. But Eric has just become phenomenal. There's no one else like him with an electric guitar. Even though he sings non-rock songs these days, he's still a great influence on rock guitar. I'm proud that he's British. And, of course, Hendrix still has more of a bark even though he has been dead for nearly 30 years. It's astonishing, the interest in someone who only had an 18-month to two-year career. It's amazing.

Where do you see guitar music heading in the next decade?

Although I want music to stay pure, we're going into the 21st century and you've got to be with it—whether you like it or not. In 20 years, you won't find all these blues bands playing slightly updated and hot-rodded Muddy Waters songs. I've remained pretty much faithful to what I do on guitar—without any tricks—and whatever else changes around that, it's all right by me.

I can't really tell you more than that, except that if I don't hear something that makes me want to grab a guitar and run up onstage, I might as well go home. That's a good measuring stick. And it's the techno bands that are inspiring me to get myself going again.

16.
"I CAN'T BEAR TO LISTEN TO MY RECORDS. I HEAR ALL THE MISTAKES"

✦ ✦ ✦ ✦ ✦ ✦

BY MATT BLACKETT
DECEMBER 2000

What is it about England? The little island of gloomy weather and questionable cuisine has produced some of the greatest rock and roll of all time. With all due respect to the great music that is played all over the world, no other place has the Beatles, the Stones, Zeppelin, Black Sabbath, Queen—the list goes on. And one thing is certain: No other place has Jeff Beck.

In his 40-year career, Beck has done more to push stylistic and technical boundaries than any of his contemporaries, predecessors, or followers. Whereas many of his compatriots have been doing much the same thing for ages, Beck has reinvented himself so many times we scarcely notice anymore. He is also so unerringly brilliant that it's easy to take him for granted.

Sadly, Beck does seem taken for granted in his homeland. Clapton and Page are household words, but it's rare to find kids on the streets of London who are familiar with Beck. Yet, as I follow him through a recording studio, it's obvious he is revered in that environment. There is a hushed respect—even awe—as he walks through a room.

And Beck is literally brimming with music. Sitting in the studio cafe, he can't go more than a minute without drumming out some ridiculously funky rhythm on the table. With a guitar in his hands for a photo shoot, he plays nonstop—psychotic blues riffs, jazzy Les Paul–inspired lines, Albert Lee–style hot-rod country licks, and just about everything else. In true Beck fashion, he is still self-critical to a fault, stopping to fix what he perceives as mistakes even when playing unplugged for a photographer.

Although he is quick to joke and laugh, there is an understated power and authority about Beck. When he makes a pronouncement on music, you believe him. And while you can sometimes get the sense he might have given up the music business long ago, he seems more compelled to play guitar than ever.

Take the release of *You Had It Coming*. This is his second offering in less than two years—an unheard-of turnaround time for him. Full of slamming techno grooves, angry tones, and unfathomable beauty, *You Had It Coming* is like nothing he has ever done, and exactly what you'd expect from him. It contains plenty of his twisted, space-rock stylings, yet it also features some of his most breathtakingly emotional playing ever.

You Had It Coming producer Andy Wright joined Beck on this inter-

SEYMOUR DUNCAN ON BECK'S ESQUIRE SWAP

"When I was in England in the '70s, Jeff was recording the second Beck, Bogert & Appice album, not far from the Fender Soundhouse, where I was working at the time," says pickup maker extraordinaire Seymour Duncan. "I wanted to put a guitar together for him, because the Les Paul he played on *Truth* had gotten ripped off. I had a '59 Tele with a rosewood fingerboard. I took the rosewood board off, replaced it with a maple fingerboard, and put Gibson frets on it. That made for a pretty thick neck—kind of like his old Les Paul. The pickups were PAFs taken out of a black Gibson Flying V that had belonged to Lonnie Mack. The pickups were broken, so I rewound them by hand. I called this guitar the 'Tele-Gib.'

"I gave it to Jeff, and he ended up using it on 'Cause We've Ended as Lovers' on *Blow by Blow*. He loved it. He could easily do all the volume swells with it, and even use the tone control like a wah-wah. In fact, he dedicated that song to Roy Buchanan, who also used those techniques. For me, it was a real thrill to have this connection between my two heroes.

"About a week later, Jeff's manager, Ralph Baker, came over with a gunny sack with three Fender guitars in it: a '54 Strat, a '51 Tele, and the '54 Esquire that Jeff had played in the Yardbirds. Ralph told me, 'Jeff said to take your pick, and just fix the other two.' I was a huge fan of his tone with the Yardbirds, so I grabbed the Esquire. Jeff gave me the guitar in appreciation for the Tele-Gib—which he still has. Right now, the Esquire is on loan to the Rock and Roll Hall of Fame in Cleveland. I've been offered a lot of money for that guitar, but I would never sell it." —*Matt Blackett*

view, and the two spoke candidly about the making of the album, the creative process, and the elegance of simplicity.

Were you consciously moving in a certain direction for this record?

Beck: Not really. I just absorb sounds that I find impressive, even if they're on a record I loathe. The good bits lodge in my memory, and I think, "I'm going to have a melody like that," or "I'm going to use that drum sound, but I'm sure as hell not going to use it like that."

> *"I just absorb sounds that I find impressive, even if they're on a record I loathe."*
>
> ✦ ✦ ✦ ✦ ✦ ✦

Wright: There were certain styles that we *didn't* want to get into—like drum 'n' bass. That style has gotten really overused and has turned into a fashion statement. We didn't want to make a fashion statement.

What did you want to do?

Wright: We wanted great beats and great guitar parts. I wanted the production to have a real clarity where each part would have its own meaning and not fight with a lot of extra riffs.

Beck: Controlled mayhem was what we were looking for.

How did you record *You Had It Coming***?**

Wright: Here's the album [holds up a hard drive]—18GB! I used Digital Performer software and Pro Tools hardware. I recorded Jeff by running a Shure SM57 into a Urei 1176 compressor, then into a Past module [a replication of a vintage Neve console channel], and, finally, into the Pro Tools converters. That was the setup.

Beck: I should probably lie and say I stacked 40 Marshalls to the ceiling, but I actually kept it very simple: a Strat, a 100-watt Marshall JCM 2000, and my fingers.

Wright: As far as I'm concerned, there are a lot of people who over-think the recording process. Engineers and producers would come in while the tracks were playing back and they'd say, "Man, that's a great guitar tone! How in the world did you get that?" They'd be disappointed when we told them it was a Strat, a Marshall, and an SM57.

How did you mix?

Wright: I don't use tape until the very end. When the tracks are absolutely finished I'll put them on tape and mix. Most of the tunes had only 12 or 14 tracks, and it all sounded fabulous and fat. And we would really drive the levels—it was commonplace for the needles to be buried in the red.

Beck: It's true. I was astounded at the bad taste of the man [*laughs*].

Tell me about the first cut, "Earthquake."

Beck: That's Jennifer Batten's composition. I used my Strat through the Marshall. The intro is the bridge and middle pickups, and the main melody is the neck pickup.

Wright: We let that intro go on a bit. It builds the tension quite nicely.

Beck: Yeah, it gives a certain amount of dangerous horror to the listener.

How did you set the controls on your guitar?

Beck: My Strats are wired with a tone control for the bridge pickup. I roll the treble all the way off the bridge and middle pickups, and get all my top end from the amp. I run my neck pickup a little brighter.

Did you record any of the guitars direct?

Wright: No. I used various plug-ins after the fact—to get the sweeping EQ on the intro to "Earthquake," for example—but we didn't use any amp simulations.

Let's move on to "Roy's Toy." This song has a different sound to it.

Beck: The first sound you hear is this guy Roy's roadster. We recorded it with a pair of Neumann mics. Great sound. As for the guitar, I've got a wah pedal that's on halfway—just where it started to get palatable. I certainly didn't want to be pumping it '60s-style.

You're not known for using many pedals.

Beck: I know. I got worried when that pedal arrived. I couldn't bear to plug it in. I had to have someone else do it for me! I use that tone several times on the record, though.

How did that guitar part come about?

Beck: I was doing a solo with some tapping on the *A* string. Andy heard that section and liked it, so he stripped it out of context and used it for this song. That happened a lot on this record—I would play and Andy would use his digital scissors and snip out the great bits.

Wright: It would be unreasonable to say that Jeff played and I edited. We would go through the tracks together, looking for bits that inspired us both. The parts we settled on would be the tools for the construction of the tracks. It was a very collaborative process.

The melody is full of those whammy bar flutters. How do you do those?

Beck: I have the bar set up so that it floats—even if I just hit a note hard, it'll vibrate. If this melody was taken from a solo, I was probably doing it deliberately, hitting the bar with my knuckle. I don't recall. I didn't realize we'd be doing a postmortem on the album [*laughs*].

What's the ring modulator in the solo?

Beck: The ring modulator is one of my all-time favorite nasty sounds. We used an old Maestro—complete with all the cobwebs in it.

It's a very clean, consonant sound for a ring modulator—how did you keep it from getting creepy?

Beck: I spent time tuning it. I knew what key I was in, and if you tune it properly, and stay within certain parameters of the key, it'll go with you.

"Nadia" has a strangely beautiful melody. It sounds like it's in a major key on the way up and a minor key on the way down.

Beck: Yeah, it is.

Wright: It was written by a contemporary-dance artist in England named Nitin Sawhney. It was originally tracked with an Indian woman singing the melody. Our challenge was to reinterpret it as a guitar piece.

Beck: I fell in love with the tune the first time I heard it. This woman—singing such an incredible scale, accurately and in tune—really blew me away. And she was singing over these gluey, Western chords—*Gmaj7* and *Dmaj7*. Those aren't usually my kind of chords, but the combination made me think, "I want to try that."

Was it tough to record?

Beck: It was one of the most difficult things I've ever had to do. Everything I know technique-wise is on that track. It's a combination of bottleneck, fingers, and whammy bar—it's like balancing 16 plates on sticks! Those swoops you hear couldn't possibly be played with fingers and frets. Those were done with the bottleneck, which I wear on my middle finger. The little trills are done with fingers, and I'm also doing volume swells on the fly with my volume knob.

Wright: We didn't double many parts on the record, but we decided to double that melody at the end—just to bring it out a bit.

Of all the parts to double!

Beck: Well, we didn't double any of the rhythm riffs. Sometimes, when you double-track, a part can become very processed and pretty—too slick. You lose that raw edge. Here, we just wanted to introduce a change, but we waited until the end of the tune. I had gotten to the point where I could play the melody pretty well by then.

On "Blackbird," how do you get the super-high notes? Are you bouncing something on the strings?

Beck: I used a dinner fork, actually. Most of the normal-sounding notes are done with a bottleneck.

Did you work to make sure each part had its own sonic niche?

Wright: Well, not really. Some records where everything has its own space sound really tidy and boring to me. We didn't want that. On this record, there are all sorts of sonic destruction going on—but with *clarity*.

How did the drums figure into your plan?

Wright: I did some of the programming, but Aiden Love did most of it. I would take his beats and rearrange them like a jigsaw puzzle. There are no overtones on the drums—I didn't want them to get in the way of the guitars.

Beck: Aiden gave us some great beats that were wonderful launching pads for me to play riffs to. Very inspiring.

Are you happy with the record?

Beck: I cook sometimes, and sometimes I can't eat what I cook. I smell all of the ingredients instead of the finished meal. I have to leave it for a while before I can appreciate it for what it is. It's that way with recording for me. I can't judge it five minutes later.

Wright: I think it's superb. It was a pleasure to make. I relished all the challenges we met on this record, and I'm looking forward to the next one.

Beck: Lying bastard!

Have you ever recorded anything that approaches what you hear in your head?

Beck: I normally can't bear to listen. I hear all the mistakes. But I heard "Goodbye Porkpie Hat" [from *Wired*] at my birthday party, and I remember thinking, "Well, that's not too bad. That's pretty good."

Most of your fans can tell it's you after only one or two notes. Who can you pick out in the space of a couple of notes?

Beck: Django. Within the first flourish I know it's him. Albert Lee, too. I revel in his solos, and I know him right away. There are others: John McLaughlin—because he's the fastest and cleanest in the West—Jimi, and Earl Hooker. A lot of players just melt together, though. They all have a similar color to them. I'm not going to mention any names, but you know what I mean.

How much of your style depends on the whammy bar at this point?

Beck: Quite a lot of it. I can simulate voice sounds, Eastern things, Bulgarian tremolos—all in mid-flight, which I couldn't do any other way.

Could you do a gig on a Tele?

Beck: I'd have to rehearse, but I could do it. I still love the bare bones Tele. But why bother when this simple pivoting device with three coiled springs can give me what I want?

Your intonation seems so perfect, whether you're bending notes or playing slide. How did you learn that?

Beck: There were some painful moments, let me tell you. I've screwed up big time onstage. The more fluid I became, though, the more excited I got at the possibility of reaching those notes. But it was a hairy, seat-of-the-pants experience. I guess I got good at compensating—I'm ready to jump off the wrong note very, very quickly. And I'll make something out of it no matter what.

Do you have perfect pitch?

Beck: I think so. I mean, I might not be able to whistle you an *E*, but if you give me one note, and I'll give you all the rest.

Do you still get nervous before a gig?

Beck: Oh yeah. It's a natural reaction to doing the most exhilarating thing known other than jumping out of an airplane. Some big heads might not worry, but I think caring, sensitive people will feel a little apprehensive. You want to give the audience a good show. When I go onstage, the adrenaline rush is like coming close to death without actually being stabbed. It's like cheating death.

When are you happiest onstage?

Beck: When there's a genuine wave of good vibes from the audience. I always hope they'll go away loving it. I want them to be bathed in something they love. *That's* why I do what I do.

17.
"I'VE ALWAYS BEEN AN IMPULSIVE PLAYER, AND IF I'M NOT ON, NOTHING WILL GET DONE"

✦ ✦ ✦ ✦ ✦ ✦

BY BARRY CLEVELAND
SEPTEMBER 2003

Jeff Beck has always presented a moving target. Whether it's infusing the Yardbirds' blues-based pop with psychedelia, pioneering heavy metal with the first Jeff Beck Group, reinterpreting funk and soul with the second JBG, going full-tilt boogie with Beck, Bogert & Appice, altering the trajectory of jazz fusion, or interacting with electronica and world music, Beck has eluded categorization for more than 35 years. And he has done it without sacrificing his personal or musical integrity.

Beck's style and tone are immediately recognizable, and he plays with a sincerity and emotional directness that contrast sharply with the current focus on rock "personalities" and the increasing prevalence of instrumental mediocrity. While acknowledging a nearly complete disregard for music theory, Beck possesses an uncanny ability to *feel* his way through complex harmonic constructions, and even navigate the microtonal intervals and inflections common to Eastern European and Indian music.

On his new album, simply entitled *Jeff*, Beck teams with electronica wizards Apollo 440 and Dean Garcia, sonic iconoclast David Torn, keyboardist/composer Tony Hymas, heavy metal re-mixer Mike Barbiero, and producer/composer Andy Wright. The music ranges from bigbeat-style improvisations to full orchestral arrangements, with bits of blues, hip-hop, Sly Stone, the Beach Boys, and even Bulgarian folk music underpinning Beck's often breathtaking guitar playing.

The guitarist arrived for the interview in top shape and brimming with a childlike enthusiasm and vitality that belie his age. Despite Beck's many years grappling with the music industry, he remains remarkably unjaded, and though regarded by many as the world's greatest living guitarist, he is disarmingly modest and unassuming.

JEFF ON JEFF

"Hotrod Honeymoon"

"The main riff was played on a Strat, and the slide bit on a Tele," says Beck. "That was just a whim that I had, and I came up with the bare bones of it—a summery, Beach Boys–type thing. We brought in a Beach Boys tribute band called the Beached Boys to record the harmony vocals. Originally, we sampled the dialogue off a compilation CD of really bad hotrod movies. It sounded cool, but we didn't want to pay royalties, so we got professional voice-over artists to redo it."

"Plan B"

"That's one of the David Torn remixes, and it's almost unrecognizable from what I gave him! He left the guitar pretty much the way it was, but he put a scaffolding around it, and replaced things with his own stuff. If I played you the original you wouldn't believe it—it was more like ZZ Top. The squawking filter sound is a Snarling Dog Whine-O-Wah, and it's *great*. It's so cheesy, and it does the nastiest things. If you have your amp set too loud it'll go [*makes whirring sound*]. But who cares? It might be like a trombone going off that you didn't bargain for, so you play with that."

"Porcupine"

"The Arabic-sounding sustain on the solo is a Stratocaster and the Snarling Dogs pedal. I OD'd on that pedal, but I don't care. It's done, and I can't un-OD it. I don't go through racks of stuff. If it doesn't sound good with the clean amp sound for starters, look out. Try and get something better, *then* put your Snarling Dog in."

"Trouble Man"

"That started out as a barbaric jam. I've got this Maestro ring mod going—one of the '60s ones with a slide on either side that you use to tune it while you're

Having just completed a new record, what's your gut-level feeling about it at this point?

I'm sick and tired of it. I don't think I've ever hated anything I've done more. It's hard to reflect back to what I liked about the demos when I first started the thing over a year ago. You know, that inspiration you put on tape that first day wanes very quickly unless things really

playing. It *ripped*. Dean Garcia [bassist] brought in this loop that we played to, and I just went wild. We were going to release it as it was—just an open-ended, wild jam—but it didn't have any shape. After we got over the euphoria, we thought we'd better shape it somehow, so we edited the piece in Pro Tools."

"Bulgarian"
"That's a traditional Bulgarian song. On the original, there's an eight- or nine-part vocal harmony, and you can hardly distinguish the lead voice. We started with the idea of multitracking the guitar to emulate the sound of these girls—which would have been cool—but it sounded like a keyboard after we got through the first five tracks. It sounded like a bad synthesizer player! It was depressing, because after making all the effort required to work out the chord changes and follow the mood shifts, it didn't sound as good as we hoped it would. So I just played one line—like a voice—over a 37-piece orchestra.

"There was a lot of volume knob manipulation, because guitar is very vulnerable when playing against an orchestra. To just pick up notes after the decay of the preceding note is too clumsy, and it doesn't sit nicely with the orchestra, so I'm really conscious of the attack. I want it to sound like a voice, and not too much like a guitar. To save me embarrassment, we cut the orchestra first, so that I didn't have to follow the conductor.

"I think the guitar I played was 'Anoushka.' I have a new Strat that I keep in E♭ tuning [*tuned down a half-step from standard*] that was signed by Anoushka Shankar, which is why I call it that. I have another Strat in concert pitch that's called THX. Anoushka has fat strings—a .052 on the bottom, and an .011 or .012 on the top."

"Line Dance with Monkeys"
"Another David Torn remix that he completely redubbed. There's obvious keyboard sounds on it, but everything else is guitar."

(CONTINUED ON NEXT PAGE)

take off, and *stagnation* is the word that springs to mind [*laughs*].

How did you do the demos?

I worked with Andy Wright and a tech assistant who ran the computers. I would start playing a riff with the guitar—just trying to cut some kind of shape to a song—and then we'd put on a drum groove with a view towards overdubbing real drums and real players afterwards. Bad move. We should have got the songs, got the players, and then recorded it. It actually takes longer if you haven't got the material, and you're guessing and pinning tails on donkeys. With people, you get things done because human beings interact. And if it isn't happen-

(CONTINUED FROM PREVIOUS PAGE)

"Why Lord Oh Why"

"This is blues, but it's Tony Hymas blues with a twist—*and* a 37-piece orchestra. Originally, we'd put an absurd bunch of orchestral flurries and accents where the heavy guitar comes in, but Tony decided the guitar should do it instead. He wanted the guitar to just come in and kick ass."

"Seasons"

"That's kind of a clubby-type thing. I wanted a Brooklyn telephone operator's voice on it. We got this girl who is a television voice-over actress to come in and do it."

"Take a Ride"

"This song was played on a weird old Danelectro baritone."

"Pay Me No Mind"

"Eric Martin wrote this for me. It's a hooky thing, and I tried to get a Meters-type, New Orleans groove. The guitar is a straight-ahead Telecaster sound, and I'm also playing bass. We wanted a summery thing that was radio friendly and not too far-out."

"My Thing"

"Yet another Torn remix! I wanted to get that Sly Stone 'I Want to Take You Higher' energy. The vocalist is something else. We were having a party at my house, and as we were playing she grabbed the mic and started ranting to her then-to-be husband, 'Don't Mess With Me.' I had the recorder going, and I thought, 'This is the coolest thing [*laughs*].'" —*Barry Cleveland*

ing you've got to wait. End of day. But with a machine sitting there, the tendency is to just plow on for hours and hours, and I really hate that. I wind up hating the sound of my own guitar. This will probably be the last album I do with a mouse.

How did you hook up with David Torn?

I got his CD from a good friend in New York who collects weird music and sends me a goodie box every six months. I said to myself, "What is this *SPLaTTeRCeLL*?" And *boom*, within a minute I was sitting there riveted. I thought, "This guy's twisted, and I want twisted." I sent him a track that wasn't really cutting it, because I thought that it would work once it was "Splatterized."

Do you typically compose by working out basic guitar ideas and then come up with things that work along with them?

Yeah, yeah. I give the basic track a quick blast in my car minutes before I arrive at the studio, and just see what it does for me. There's no use in preparing hours before, because I'm not focused. The only time I can focus is when I know that within two or three hours I'm going to commit to recording. I've always been an impulsive player, and if I'm not on that day, nothing will get done. If I'm recording for someone else, it's usually a solo or some fills or something on a song that already exists—and *that's* easy.

Some of your older material, such as the pieces on *Blow by Blow* and *Wired*, was more composed.

Absolutely. They were pieces we played. We thrashed them, and we got to the point where we said, "This is great. Let's record it as soon as we know it well enough, and not get too familiar. Let's not overcook it." But that was an ancient style of recording. Then again, now you've got the White Stripes, and I can almost guarantee you they don't mess around with a song. They just go in and play it, and then have a cup of tea or something.

We just did a cover story on Jack White. You actually played with him, didn't you?

Yeah! I invited them to play on my gig at the Festival Hall, and they were fantastic. When I arrived at the rehearsal, they'd painted "Yardbirds" on the bass drum, and I thought, "That's a sweet thing. They're going to go in this show one way or the other."

He's a fantastic guy—a fantastic player—and she is just gold dust for him. The simplicity and the vital crudeness of the drums is 50 percent of what they are, and there's meaning in his lyrics and meaning in

The master—Beck lays it down at the Electric Factory, Philadelphia, Pennsylvania, April 8, 2009.

his songs. They are stripped to the bare bones of what rock and roll is about, and that is really where it *should* be at. They didn't layer sounds or have Hammond organs on that record. It's just beautifully executed music played by real players. He used an old-fashioned studio with old gear. I tried to get in there soon after, but it was chockablock.

Your career has paralleled the development of multitrack recording from 4-track up through Pro Tools. Do you feel technology has taken people closer to, or further away from, the music?

I think it takes them into murky areas. I'm feeling the pinch of it myself, because there are so many things you can do to correct and drastically alter the course of what you thought you had. Sometimes the machines tell you better, and sometimes they lead you up and down. And that enables people who haven't any talent to make great-sounding records. There's a plethora of bands that sound fantastic, and they're not really doing it. But that's the general flow of the river, isn't it? And the down side of it is that if a band goes in and tries to play old-style—mic here, mic there, count the song in, let's go—it sounds completely dead unless the guy really knows where he's putting the mics. It was bad back then in the '60s, but something was more forgiving and more flattering about tape, and the way the valve amps would react to the sound. Now it's just de-funked. You have to put the funk back in by electronic means.

There's less emphasis on basic engineering skills.
Yes! It has made me lazy. I've got a sharp note in there, I'll flat it. That's terrible.

Speaking of engineering skills, what was it like working with Joe Meek?
I never met Joe Meek.

On the recently released *Shapes of Things* CD, you're credited with playing on Screaming Lord Sutch's "Dracula's Daughter," which was recorded by Meek.
I'm supposed to have played on a Lord Sutch song called "Gutty Guitar," but I don't recall playing on "Dracula's Daughter" or meeting Joe Meek.

Do you have a home studio?
I have two Tascam DA-88s, a Mackie desk, and the usual old-fashioned outboard gear. I can do guitar overdubs there to a professional standard. It makes sense to have that in case I've got some fixing to do.

So you just do a rough stereo mix with timecode, record that on the DA-88s, and then fly the new parts back into Pro Tools?
Yeah.

What gear did you use on the new record?
I used a Line 6 POD on the demos. Some of that saw its way through to the final thing, because the sound of it was good, and I thought, "I ain't going to do that solo again!" But it was a mixture of a Marshall JCM2000 DSL head with one 4x12 cab and a Line 6 2x12 combo.

A modeling amp?

"People wonder about [recording guitars], but there's really no secret.... As long as the playing is right, ... it just happens."

✦ ✦ ✦ ✦ ✦ ✦

Yeah. I was surprised. People went, "Line 6? What's that?" And I said, "Hey, you didn't complain about the sounds." I don't remember the model, but it's a fine amp. It enabled me to experiment with a lot of different textures without changing amps or plugging other things in. I also used the onboard effects.

Care to share any great tips about recording guitars?

Yeah—casually dangle a Shure SM57 over the front of the speaker. People wonder about these things, but there's really no secret. I just use the right amount of level, the right amount of distortion, and I keep a little bit of reserve volume on the guitar. That's it. As long as the playing is right, and the inflections are right, it just happens.

What gear are you bringing on your upcoming tour?

I've got to dream up a combination that kills, and I don't know what it's going to be yet. I want a fat sound that goes right across the stage.

As your new trio includes Terry Bozzio and Tony Hymas, are you returning to the *Guitar Shop* days?

Yeah, we're going back to show people what was happening. It was so fast back in 1989–90. *Boom*—one tour, one album, and a quick rehash for the Santana tour. People who never had a chance to see us will have another opportunity, and we've come that much further in the maturity of our playing, so I think it's the right way to go. And you can never get enough of Terry.

What was the reason it didn't go further back then?

Frustration with how long it took to get the album done in the first place. We didn't really want to go back in the studio after having such fun on the road. And Tony was always first and foremost a jazz and experimental type of player, and I don't think he wanted to commit to much more time.

Is it true that you don't have formal musical training?

Well, I had a few piano lessons. I knew where middle *C* was.

How do you conceptualize music for yourself?

I just listen to the sound as closely as I can—what's coming back at me—and feed off what I'm doing with the least possible interference. If I like the sound of a long note with reverb on it, I'll steer it where I want it to go, and then see what it says to me. It's *immediate* feedback from what I'm putting in.

So even when you're blowing over jazz changes you're still just playing from the heart?

Straight! I wouldn't want to know if there's a flatted fifth. I mean, I know what the chords are when I listen back. I know there's a raised fourth, a flatted fifth, a squashed ninth [*laughs*]. But I'm not bothered, as long as it sounds good. I was sitting next to Steve Kindler from the Mahavishnu Orchestra—bless his heart—on a plane while touring with Jan Hammer. I was feeling really humiliated by the talent around me, and he said, "You don't have to worry about the bars, you know exactly by instinct. We're all jealous of the fact that you don't know." I felt ten feet tall. I said, "Hey folks, I don't know any chords." I know the *sound* of a chord, and I know Django's chords—I can pick them out playing—but I just don't know what they're called. I don't want to be hampered by that. If I'm not *immediately* inspired to play, and I can't apply that inspiration directly to a piece, then something's wrong. Either I'm not the right guy for the gig, or I need to practice.

Did playing on the new Yardbirds CD—*Birdland*—bring back any feelings or thoughts?

Sure it did. The thing I found admirable was that they were still keen—and this was before they'd even had any offer from a label. But I didn't want to get it *too* authentic. It was nice to see them on a social level, as well, even though they threw me out of the band 35 years ago [*laughs*].

There's the famous story about recording "Beck's Bolero" in 1967 with Jimmy Page, John Paul Jones, and Keith Moon. Do you think about what might have happened if that band had come together?

There's no use thinking about what could have been. It was a real letdown when Keith said, "I'm staying with the Who," because the feeling when he kicked in was just so incredible that me and Jim Page thought we wouldn't even need to ask him to join the band. It was just *understood*. Then he put his dark glasses on and said, "I'll see you." And that was that. Obviously, the Who were doing well, and you've got to be pretty brave to jump out of a major band into something unknown. I think he just wanted to tell Pete that he wasn't going to be dictated to by the Who anymore. We gave him a good time that afternoon, and that's what it was supposed to be—a day of fun.

After all these years . . .

Still sounds good, doesn't it?

Jimi Hendrix acknowledged being inspired by your playing and your performance style during your Yardbirds days.

That's amazing.

And what he did with the Experience was, in some ways, an intensification and extension of Beck's Yardbirds. How did that affect you at the time?

It was a horrible time, really. Not because of *him*, but because of the fact that he swept us all aside and put us in a bin. I think that was more the case for us than for the public at large, who were happy to have us all. But I know how it felt having a girl ring up and ask, "Did you hear Jimi Hendrix?" I was having trouble with relationships and getting by on little money. It was rough all the time. I knew when I was beat, and I sat back for a year asking myself if I had anything left in me. I had a car tape player as soon as they were available, and I used to cruise around in a Corvette just listening and trying to focus on stuff—trying to figure out what I should do next to stay in the business.

I wanted to be friends with Jimi on a less flippant level, which was difficult to do. We had the perfect opportunity while driving to a jam in upstate New York. The real Jimi was coming out as he was driving, and I thought, "This is probably the greatest moment of my life." And then—lo and behold—just as I had become friends with him, the guy went and died. And the cruel part is when you read the papers and there's nothing you can do about it. It's too late. You've got to live for the moment and enjoy every minute of it.

Do you ever speculate as to what he might be doing now had he lived?

I don't want to think about it. The last thing he did was the Isle of Wight festival, and that was sad. He may have shaped himself up, but his style and personality were a new sort of blueprint for how rock stars were going to be dead pretty quickly from drugs. He was one of the first of that type. It's hard to say what he would be doing if he'd lived. It's like Eddie Cochran—what the hell would *he* be doing? If Gene Vincent was anything to go by, not much. Vincent was doing such terrible stuff towards the end of his career that you would not believe it was the same person. We all change.

Eddie Cochran doing Vegas or something.

Oh my God! Or "Over the Rainbow."

Ouch! You were talking about how it was hard seeing others succeed when you weren't making much money. Several times you have gotten to the edge of greater success, and then, for some reason, not gone ahead. Do you fear success?

Probably. The biggest incident of that type was not playing

DAVID TORN ON REMIXING MR. BECK

Twice chosen as "Best Experimental Guitarist" in GP's Readers Polls, David Torn has collaborated with artists as far-ranging as Don Cherry, Jan Garbarek, Mark Isham, Andy Summers, David Bowie, and k. d. lang. He has also contributed to numerous film soundtracks, as well as releasing seven albums under his own name, and two as SPLaTTeRCeLL. —Barry Cleveland

"I got the first track, 'Plan B,' in May," says Torn. "Jeff said he didn't like it, and that I could mix it as is, make it all funny, rewrite it, or do whatever I wanted. He loved the results, so he sent me two more. It's an amazing thing to listen to a Jeff Beck track that has already been written and edited, and then get the multitrack and listen to 30 wild, alternate guitar takes that weren't used. You go through the first 27, and they all change from bar to bar, and some are better than others, and then you get to tracks 28 through 30, and suddenly it's like, 'What the hell was that? How was it done, and how could it *possibly* sound that good?'

"On 'Line Dance with Monkeys,' I pretty much erased everything that had been recorded before—except for a couple of Jeff's riffs. I tried very hard to keep the solos completely contiguous as they were played. After removing the rest of the parts, I began going through a lot of outtakes, and I found these melodies that were so good it was like finding buried treasure. Those are what I wound up using as the melodic content.

"On 'My Thing,' there's this spontaneous chord run that I just loved. It was in a section that was only four bars long, and the phrase wasn't iterated again, so I made the section 16 bars long and did a pretty nasty little cut-up, making the phrase run in the opposite direction on the second or third iteration.

"Here's a guy who's 59 years old, and he's still *kicking* it like a beast. And it's not a calculated kick, it's a guy reacting to a drummer or a bass line. He's one of the only guitar players who really has the sound of the *whole* electric guitar in his hands. It was like that in 1968, and it's like that in 2003."

Woodstock [*with the Jeff Beck Group*]. We were still breaking ground and doing our homework in bars and small venues, and even without the bad vibes in the band, I didn't think we could have pulled it off. I just didn't think we were big-stage material, and I couldn't bear to be preserved on film playing out of my depth, and having Rod [Stewart] hating the sight of me on screen. Screw that! And I just had to follow my instinct and say, "Right, well I ain't doing that." And obviously Ronnie [Wood] and Rod had got some scheme up their sleeves in case I buggered off, and in hindsight they did the right thing [*laughs*].

Given your point about Hendrix and other stars dying as a result of the excesses of the rock and roll lifestyle, could it be that your instinct to pull back was as much an instinctive sense of self-preservation as it was a fear of success?

Yeah. I think it was. Woodstock was going to be on film, and we weren't ready for that. We'd never even had a really big P.A. We had two stupid columns on either side of the stage. We were essentially a blues band—an experimental, heavy, heavy blues band.

But well received . . .

Very well received. We were on the way, but I didn't feel we had the record to do it. And we didn't really have any stage presence—other than the goofing about that me and Woody did. And I just thought, "Next year. *Maybe*." Ron and Rod thought that I deliberately screwed it up, but I didn't. The same goes with other periods. Maybe that's the reason I'm still here.

That's the thing. You have done great work for more than three decades and are considered by many to be the world's greatest rock guitarist, while at the same time managing to lead a relatively normal life.

That's by staying out of it. Get off the bus when you're not really going anywhere. Maybe it's genetics or finally getting some of my mum's wisdom. She would always say, "Don't get on your high horse, and don't ever think you're great." And I'd say, "Ah, shut up. I *want* to be great." But gradually her words got bigger and bigger. You crash into a wall, get hurt, and you say, "Mum, you were right."

18.

"I DON'T WANT TO IMPRESS THE WORLD—REACHING PEOPLE IS THE MAGIC THING NOW"

✦ ✦ ✦ ✦ ✦ ✦

BY ART THOMPSON
JUNE 2010

There's a nomadic spirit in Jeff Beck's personality that causes his muse, and often his physical being, to push on to new frontiers even when the place he's at would seem to be the perfect altar for him to preach the gospel of godly guitar. From his Yardbirds era and onward, Beck has had the habit of changing direction or even completely disappearing just when the planets seemed perfectly aligned in his favor. But genius rarely follows a road map, and Beck's willingness to risk short-term gain in order to make lasting musical statements says a lot about his integrity and why he's still out there creating vital and exciting music while many of his peers from the British Invasion generation haven't been able to top what they did in the '60s and '70s.

Most recently, and after a fairly long hiatus following the release of his last album, which was simply titled *Jeff*, the Guv'nor surfaced like a submarine-fired missile to wow the crowd at the 2007 Crossroads Guitar Festival. And it wasn't just his awesome playing that created the huge buzz; a good deal of the clamor was due to Beck's sly enlisting of a very talented, and also very teenage looking, bassist named Tal Wilkenfeld to play alongside veteran rock drummer Vinnie Colaiuta and keyboardist Jason Rebello. The performances that followed—including the 25th Anniversary Concert of the Rock and Roll Hall of Fame at New York's Madison Square Garden—were heralded as Beck's best ever. In 2009, Beck was inducted for a second time into the Rock and Roll Hall of Fame, and he released the platinum-selling *Live at Ronnie Scott's* DVD, which also garnered him a Grammy nomination for his instrumental rendition of the Beatles tune "A Day in the Life."

Of course, after all this success, what could Jeff Beck do for an encore other than completely rearrange the furniture by launching a new album titled *Emotion & Commotion*, which finds him fronting a 64-piece orchestra on several tunes, including "Over the Rainbow," Puccini's aria "Nessun Dorma," and an instrumental redux of Jeff Buckley's performance of "Corpus Christi." Beck was clearly savoring the surprise factor when he said, "I think this album will shock people when they hear it. It's not what they expect of me." During my interview with him at the Sunset Marquis hotel in Hollywood, Beck described the new album this way: "It's Spector-esque, if you pardon the expression. It leans more towards a pop-rock sort of album than would have been the case if we'd done a classical album, which would have had to be bowtie and put-on-me-tux proper. But it's not like a drum and bass record that people can talk over and drink over. In a lot of clubs, there's not one person listening to you, it's just one big background noise. I wanted at least an album that could be listened to and be really plugged into. Maybe after a long day, you'll go sit there and listen to it. It's got just enough tweak to get you going, but it'll lull you as well."

Produced by Trevor Horn and Steve Lipson, and recorded last year at Sarm Studios in London, *Emotion & Commotion* showcases some of Beck's most beautiful playing ever—his soaring tones and fluid vibrato making even such a mournful orchestral tune as "Elegy for Dunkirk" (from the film *Atonement*) something to behold. Like a great opera singer, Beck delivers every note such intense feeling that you may not even care that there isn't an abundance of ripping lead work here. Asked whether he purposely reduced the notes-to-bar ratio in order to reveal some deeper elements in his playing, Beck answered, "Absolutely. I wanted the beauty to be there without the embellishment. I didn't want any showing off. In fact, I just found it so foreign to try to jump when it wasn't necessary to jump. The songs we're talking about didn't require any shredding, though they'll probably end up that way if it becomes a regular format with the orchestra. When we were making the record, I just kept saying to myself, 'don't get too cheeky.'"

Still, *Emotion & Commotion* doesn't entirely ignore the needs of those who simply crave a dose of Beck's fiery guitar playing, which comes to the fore on the songs "Hammerhead," "There's No Other

Me" (featuring the Colaiuta/Wilkenfeld rhythm section), and "I Put a Spell on You" (sung by Joss Stone), where Beck knocks off a killer blues solo backed by Clive Deamer on drums and Pino Palladino on bass.

At the end of the day, *Emotion & Commotion* stands as an honest and completely uncontrived statement from one of the most singularly unique guitarists on the planet. It speaks to the inner workings of someone who, despite having some serious misgivings about the process of making records (more on this later), obviously loves creating the aural equivalent of fine art and is unencumbered by the need to satisfy anyone but himself and his loyal fans. So as surprising as *Emotion & Commotion* is on a certain level, it hardly seems all that unusual for Beck, who has a history of turning loose elements into sonic marvels. As he himself put it: "Making this album gave me a similar feeling with somebody else doing the orchestration and making stuff happen the way George Martin did on *Blow by Blow*. When we started that album we had very little material as well. After the event, I started to realize how close it was."

What are the benefits and downsides of going into the studio without having the music fully prepared?

The benefit is that you are thrust in. In some ways it's better to not be too prepared. The biggest pitfall there is that you are going to sound over-rehearsed and too contrived. It's a weird process to try and remember the chain of events that lead up to how we did this, but my manager is very forceful, and he has a way of persuading me to go in unprepared. "Oh, it'll be great," he goes. And the first two weeks was miserable. Not that the other players weren't good, but they were unsuited to the sort of thing I was looking for. It wasn't until I came away that I realized I'd lost two really good players who just weren't on the same wavelength with me. But you live and learn. It was folly to go in with a bassist and drummer that I'd never heard of. It was weird for me that Tal and Vinnie weren't there—we should have gone in with a band situation. Of course, there was the stuff with just me and the orchestra, which didn't require any bass or drums at all.

Why didn't you want to use the bassist and drummer you'd been playing with for that last two years?

Well, to get them over to England for three or four tracks just didn't make sense. So we ended up doing it without them. But then we had to fly Tal over to do the bass part. And to repair some of the drum parts that were not that great, we actually sent the producer over to the States to record Vinnie. So it kind of ended up costing more in the long run, but at least they're on the album, and they did a great job on the tracks.

How does the high expectation that people have of you affect your creativity?

I'm more than overwhelmed by it, but the thing is that pressure is not the most desirable feeling. Even though it's all very complimentary, I go in the studio with this feeling that I've got to not let these people down. And then, down comes the big concrete boom on the head. And if it's a bad day or a non-productive day, I start thinking, "I can't do this." The secret, of course, is not to worry about it and just go in and make the nicest sounds you can make. And if those sounds move people, then let it go. But I don't want to think about how to impress the world. I've done enough of that, and I think reaching people is the magic thing now.

What have you been listening to for inspiration?

Lately, I've just been listening to opera singers and other great singers. Not so much blues, because they're all about embellishment, and it's all in the throat—but someone like Pavarotti, who has just the most passionate and full-sounding voice. In fact, we were going to put Puccini's "O Mio Babbino Caro" [from the opera *Gianni Schicchi*] on the album—it's just a fantastic song. But that's too classical, and I wanted to save it for a classic album that will hopefully be done with the London Philharmonic.

What was the reason for doing an album now that features orchestral pieces but isn't full-blown classical?

I had always wanted to see what it would sound like playing with a really classy string section. I'd previously made an attempt at doing a classical album. I wrote a list of about 12 tracks from composers that I loved—from Puccini to Ravel to Mahler—and they were beautiful songs that lent themselves to single-note melody. And then I did Gustav Mahler's Symphony No. 5 with the New York Philharmonic. The result was quite stunning, really, so I took it along to EMI Classics and they fell in love with it. They asked, "Where's the rest of it?" And I told them, "This is it—this is the bait we're throwing out." So they said they'd be interested if I could do 11 more tracks like that. They gave me half a dozen fabulous CDs to listen to, and that's as far as it ever went. But I did love the sound and the emotion of surrounding my guitar with all that instrumentation.

How do you interpret a classical piece in order to make it more guitar-centric?

I learn the melody completely off path and I play it like a blues, or as bluesy as I can. I use artistic license up to a point, but I can't stand listening to people do covers of great songs who think they can write better than the original composer. If the melody was worth having in the first place, then leave it alone. If you play it with all the feeling but without any embellishments, then sometimes you can slip around a little bit. But with a great piece you just don't. If the melody was crafted well enough to go with the chords, then the job's done.

What's the biggest challenge of arranging a song to play with an orchestra?

First of all, can I pull it off live? You need to make sure the song can be played live; otherwise you're going to get yourself into a big ditch and never get out of it—especially if you've got Olympic leaps all over the place and stuff like that. It's got to be played in the way the blues would be played. It has to feel that natural.

Your tones on this album are beautiful. What amps did you use?

I've found that my best friend is the straight-ahead amplifier with very little effect pedal. If distortion is needed, I'll use a much smaller amplifier and overload that rather than use a pedal to alter the circuitry. When you go through a pedal you're going through some guy's circuit before it gets to the amp. I want the amplifier to get the most honest and direct signal from the pickup. That way, you get the tonal advantage of the guitar and the fingers. I've adhered to that, and I think you can hear it on the album without any B.S., except for a couple places where I used a ring modulator—like for two bars on the Joss Stone track "There's No Other Me." You know, Jimi Hendrix didn't use too much of that either. He used one effects pedal and a Crybaby wah-wah, and he just cranked the hell out of his amplifiers.

Why did you switch to Marshall plexi reissues, which have less gain than the JCM2000s you had been using?

I was looking for purity of tone so it wouldn't jar with the orchestra. I couldn't hear a shred tone like Steve Vai gets, or even Brian May or Billy Gibbons, who have these very fat, distorted guitar tones. I just couldn't really see that working, so I tried to get the sound of my guitar as natural and organic as it could be. Like on "Over the Rainbow" or "Elegy for Dunkirk," those are just right honest performances with just me and the orchestra.

You still get a lot of sustain on those tracks, so is that the Marshall turned way up?

No, it was a Fender Champ. I joked once about making an entire album with a Champ, and I just about did that this time. In a couple of places there's a 50-watt Marshall with a 4x12 speaker cabinet, and I think that's on "Lilac Wine" and "Corpus Christi." Those songs were done in the studio live with a mic placed several feet away. But when we got into the overdubs I just ended up with a Champ. Mine is a 1950s model with that brown rag across the front, the tweed, you know? It sounds amazing, really, and you don't need volume. Some people can't do without lots of volume to get their tone, but I think if you can't get it without four million watts, something's wrong. Because a mic doesn't read volume, it reads *tone*. You've got all the level in the world at your disposal in the console, and the remixing and the rest of it to compensate for lack of power. But the tone is the thing, and that's something that came from Scotty Moore, who once told me, "Get some better tone and you're there—volume you don't need."

Can the small-amp/less-volume concept work for live playing?

By using the P.A. to act in the way it was designed—which is play at low level and use all the distortion and whatever else you need, but make sure you don't come out louder than the side-fill monitors or the front wedges—you can blow the house down, and I've done it. I've done a whole tour with a Fender Twin when Stevie Ray Vaughan was going through about four billion watts with a rig that looked like an amp shop. He asked me, "What the hell are you using? Are your amps under the stage?" I said, "Nope, that's it right there." [*Laughs.*] But we spent quite a lot of time dialing in the sound and getting rid of the squeaks and squeals. We'd raise the level and then tweak it a little bit, and then we'd raise it a little more. You can't believe what you can get out of a little 10- or 20-watt amp. I think Billy Gibbons is on that route as well, as he plays though some blown-up little thing now. You have to work in symphony with the amp for what sounds best, and it depends on what you're playing. If it's power chords, then you'd probably use a slightly bigger amp; otherwise it'll shred down into a narrow bandwidth. Most of the time, though, you can get away with a couple of Champs—one clean, one distorted—and use the clean one to get more definition.

What has led you to being more concerned about volume?

The louder the stuff is onstage, probably the worse it's going to end up sounding. Your hearing goes, your pitch goes, and you can't really hear any depth of field. If you have to question whether it's too loud, then it is too loud. The power has to be there, but without the level. But if you're going to be loud, get the speakers away from you. Lately, I've been putting one 4x12 facing backwards, just so that the P.A. guy doesn't go around the bend with too much volume. I've also seen Pete Townshend with a stack of Fenders facing each other like a sandwich, so the audience only gets the back of it. Sounded great to me, but I haven't gone that far. On a big stage, I might put four Marshalls up there, like two big stacks, and have them right at the back just to see what they

"The louder the stuff is onstage, probably the worse it's going to end up sounding. Your hearing goes, your pitch goes . . ."

✦ ✦ ✦ ✦ ✦ ✦

sound like wide open. But they'd have to be damn deep in the stage so there's not too much spillover. I'll try that on this tour, but I've got a feeling that the little Champ will win out because the orchestra and the Champ are going to sound in proportion. I played with this powerful band that had 18 pieces, and I thought I'd need a Marshall for it, but I didn't; I needed a Pignose. Even though the trumpets and the horns were blasting away, the difference in character of the guitar with that concentrated trebly sound just cut right through.

Did you use anything other than a Strat on this album?

I went through about five different guitars, and they all got put back on the rack. We did one song with a Gretsch and some with Guild even, but they just didn't sound like me. I picked the Strat back up and, *boom*, there I am again. So why go against it?

Since you play with your fingers, do you use heavier gauge strings?

My guitar is strung pretty lightly now because I haven't played live for a while. But, by mid tour, I'll go to a .012 on the first and a .052 on the bass. It's self-torture, but you've got to have that. The great Jimi Hendrix picked up my guitar once and he said, "What are these rubber bands doing here? You'll never get tone out of that." I was really disappointed because I thought I had found what I was comfortable with. But he was right; there was no guts in there. And there was no effort. The half of playing blues is you have to suffer the pain of the wire digging into your fingers. And the more you play, the harder your fingers get and the fatter your strings can get.

What were you playing when Hendrix said that to you?

A Les Paul, which is kind of a sissy guitar compared to a Strat anyway. The Les Paul is heavier, but because of that bulk you can do bends on it more easily. Also, the Les Paul's lack of a vibrato arm means you're not wrestling against the spring-loaded bridge all the time. The Strat is the ultimate because it's like having a miniature pedal steel within it. Once you get familiar with where the bends are and where they meld down into a fourth or whatever, you can do all kinds of pedal-steel-like things, which I think are cool. Some of the things that sound the most difficult are the easiest for me.

Despite having your Strat set up with a floating vibrato, you don't ever seem to touch the tuners, let alone switch guitars during a show. How do you stay in tune?

Sometimes it'll go out if it's a wild gig like Crossroads where there's like 40,000 people and I go shredding all over the stage. But unless those situations happen, the guitar stays pretty much in tune. The strings are pre-stretched to start, and they're stretched to almost the breaking point before I go on. Then they're retuned and retuned. So far, I've been lucky. I've broken a few, but it's more likely a flaw in the string somewhere around the bridge area that causes it to break rather then me playing it. But I do drive them pretty hard. Also, the roller nut that I designed seems to work pretty well—especially for the top three strings, which stay in tune really well. It has a double roller system, so the strings go over two rollers, and for some reason they don't hitch up. Because you get a lot of lateral movement when you depress the tremolo arm— the string actually moves *across* the nut—and sometimes it doesn't come all the way back, and then you're in trouble.

The way you use the vibrato on "Over the Rainbow" it sounds like you were actually trying to mimic the warble in Judy Garland's voice.

That's what I tried to do. It started out as a bit of tongue-in-cheek thing, but when I got halfway through, the whole place was soaked in tears. Vinnie is a tough guy, but even he was going, "Jeff, stop, I can't bear it!"

The melody you came up with for "Elegy for Dunkirk" has even more of a tearjerker.

That's probably the deepest thing I've ever done. I picked that melody out from the original score. I haven't seen the film *Atonement*, but I'm pretty sure I know what I'm going to see, as it's the end of the Dunkirk landing. When I heard it, I thought first of all that it was an ensemble piece for the violins and cellos. But I picked out the melody and made it a really nice piece. I altered it by putting my guitar voices in a different spot, though. I played it up an octave to get away from the down-in-the-dumps kind of thing. It's still a bit dirgey, though—a pretty sad thing.

Were there any concerns about putting "Corpus Christi" as the first song on the album?

Because you're expecting shred and it doesn't happen? That one and "Lilac Wine" sort of set the mood for the album. When I heard Jeff Buckley's versions of those songs, I was touched because they're so gorgeous. "Corpus Christi" is a traditional tune from the sixteenth century, and my dear friend and wife said to me, "That melody is the most beautiful thing I've ever heard. Please do it."

Did you originally intend "Hammerhead" to be a tribute to Jan Hammer?

That's an interesting story. About a year ago I was sitting around a campfire with Dave Gilmour and I said to him, "If we do the Royal Albert Hall, why don't you come and play?" Well, he kept me to it, and so at the gig I suggested we do the song "Jerusalem," which is very English sounding. He said, "Why don't we do 'Hi Ho Silver Lining'— it'll bring the house down?" I told him, "Not on your life." So he goes, "What if I sang it?" So I said to Jason [Rebello], "Look, we're going to do 'Silver Lining,' but I don't want to do that stomping, ching-ching-ching rhythm thing." So he said, "Right, leave it to me." He knows how much I love Jan Hammer—and Jason's a huge fan too—so he came up with a very Hammer-esque sort of riff for it. And that's the riff we played at the Royal Albert Hall concert, which made it sound much more modern. We salvaged the riff from that song and then Jason rewrote the melody to get away from "Hi Ho Silver Lining." The whole song was very inspired by Jan, and that's why I called it "Hammerhead."

What kind of wah did you use on the intro to that song?

It's the Snarling Dogs Super Bawl, which is not really an annoying wah-wah. It just opens an envelope in a very subtle way, and the sweep is not going to take your head off in full treble like a Crybaby will. I use the wah to take the top off the guitar—most of the top anyway—so you've got a voice appearing. You see, I'm trying to be a singer.

On "Never Alone" are those actual voices that you hear in the backing tracks?

I wanted to do some close harmonies on that song. One of my favorite close-harmony groups is the Mystery Voices of Bulgaria, who I've loved for like 15 or 20 years. Their harmonies are just above all reach of understanding. So I said to Jason, "Why don't you throw some really good voice samples on a pad and let's listen to how I sound with voices only." And it was much more interesting than a cheesy string pad or a Fender Rhodes pad. Soon as you get into these individual voices played with these complex chord shapes, your head starts going places, and that's the result. The riff is powerful and you've got 30 strings playing the riff along with these amazing big chords. The voices just ring better than any other instrument, but, because of their lightness, you can put the levels up and they don't rob too many frequencies.

Was it your idea to run the '50s standard "Lilac Wine" and the operatic aria "Nessun Dorma" together almost as a single piece?

No, Steve Lipson did that. I can't praise him enough. I mean he put up with me for three and a half months, and I think he wondered what the hell he had gotten involved with after a couple of weeks because I tend to loathe everything.

Why do you think that is?

I hate making that commitment and then going home and not feeling like I'd actually done anything. And the money clock's going by and it's like, "Oh God." This is all a load of crap anyway because everything is phony, the whole thing—you've got another chance at the solo. In the early days, the rockabilly acts used to learn the stuff and go in and count it off—"one, two, three." That's what I like. I'll never get that out of my blood.

But you could make records that way if you wanted to, right?

It's a question of being forced or cajoled into it by the fact that recording techniques now are different. Everything is safe and you've got choices. They can pitch correct your voice and put your instrument through virtual this, that, and the other plug-ins. And it's all there. What amp do you want? All right, *bonk*, and up it comes, and it's a bitch of an old Marshall. There's too much assistance and not enough hard-edged, c'mon, what have you got? There's a microphone, you've got the amplifier, there's the take, go and play. And that's what I really like, and I miss that. That way you're on your toes right away and you know that you're going to succeed or fail. And if you don't succeed you go back and try again. The way I'm describing is that Pro Tools draws you to a place that you don't want to be and it makes you stay there because it actually gives you something that you shouldn't have, which is a sort of flattery. The fact that you were sounding like crap a minute ago and now you don't. So I don't like that. And I tried to make this album sound like we could play it, and I'm damn sure we can play it. It's always in the back of my mind: "How are we going to do this?"

I understand that "There's No Other Me" had to be altered in the studio because you knew you couldn't pull it off live?

Yes. Jason wrote the two parts for that song and he wanted me to play the long sustaining notes that make the basis of the melody, and, in-between those lines, I was supposed to shred. The problem was that we couldn't really perform it because of the overlap—I'd have to stop playing the long notes in order to play a solo. So Joss Stone was around and she's fantastic, so I said, "Look, just come in, you can't lose—we've got a track that's smoking, and it's wide open for you." So she sat there and about an hour later she'd written these lyrics. And what a performance! I was sitting down watching her because I didn't want to get in the way, and she had a backless dress on. And I'm telling you, that was the most erotic, beautiful sight I've ever seen. The muscles she was using, and everything about her breathing—it was just an amazing sight. I wish I had filmed it. I can't wait to play it now, which, unfortunately, means we're going to have to carry her on the road.

Your performance on the *Live at Ronnie Scott's* DVD is quite outstanding. Was it pressurizing for you to perform on camera in a small room with a bunch of heavyweight players in the audience?

Slightly, especially when you've got a couple of really beautiful Asian girls looking up your nose, and their drinks are about an inch away from your feet. [*Laughs.*] It's a pretty compact little place, and I didn't eat for four days during that—literally, not a thing. I get closer to who I am when I'm not eating. Food is distancing for me. You've got to be starving and really miserable, and then you play well.

◆ PAGE ◆

19.

"MY VOCATION IS MORE IN COMPOSITION THAN IN ANYTHING ELSE— ORCHESTRATING THE GUITAR LIKE AN ARMY"

✦ ✦ ✦ ✦ ✦ ✦

BY STEVE ROSEN
JULY 1977

Conducting an interview with Jimmy Page, lead guitarist and producer/arranger for England's notorious hard-rock band Led Zeppelin, amounts very nearly to constructing a mini-history of Britledish rock and roll. Perhaps one of Zeppelin's more outstanding characteristics is its endurance, intact (no personnel changes since its inception) through an extremely tumultuous decade involving not only rock, but popular music in general. Since 1969, the group's four members—Page, bass player John Paul Jones, vocalist Robert Plant, and drummer John Bonham—have produced eight albums (two are doubles) of original and often revolutionary compositions with a heavy metal sound. For as long as the band has been an entity, their records—coupled with several well-planned and highly publicized European and American tours—have exerted a profound and acutely recognizable influence on rock groups and guitar players on both sides of the Atlantic. Page's carefully calculated guitar frenzy, engineered through the use of distortion, surrounds Plant's expressive vocals to create a tension and excitement rarely matched by Zeppelin's numerous emulators.

But the prodigious contributions of James Patrick Page, born in 1945 in Middlesex, England, date back to well before the formation of his present band. His work as a session guitarist earned him so lengthy a credit list (some sources cite Jimmy as having been on 50 to 90 percent of the records released in England during 1963–65) that he himself is no longer sure of each and every cut on which he played. Even without the exact number of his vinyl encounters known, the range of his interaction as musician and sometime producer with the landmark groups and individuals of soft and hard rock is impressive and diverse: the Who, Them, various members of the Rolling Stones, Donovan, and Jackie DeShannon, to name a few. In the mid '60s, Page joined one of the best-known British rock bands, the Yardbirds, leading to a legendary collaboration with rock/jazz guitarist Jeff Beck. When the Yardbirds disbanded in 1968, Page was ready to start his own group. According to Jimmy, at the initial meeting of Led Zeppelin, the sound of success was already bellowing through the amps, and the musicians' four-week introductory period resulted in *Led Zeppelin*, their first of many gold-record-winning LPs.

Let's try to begin at the beginning. When you first started playing, what was going on musically?

I got really stimulated by hearing early rock and roll, and knowing that something was going on that was being suppressed by the media—which it really was at the time. You had to stick by the radio, and listen to overseas radio to even hear good rock records—Little Richard and things like that. The record that made me want to play guitar was "Baby, Let's Play House" by Elvis Presley. I just sort of heard two guitars and bass and thought, "Yeah, I want to be part of this." There was just so much vitality and energy coming out of it.

When did you get your first guitar?

When I was about 14. It was all a matter of trying to pick up tips and stuff. There weren't many method books, really—apart from jazz, which had no bearing on rock and roll whatsoever at that time. But that first guitar was a Grazioso, which was like a copy of a Stratocaster. Then I got a real Stratocaster, and then one of those Gibson "Black Beauties"—which stayed with me for a long time until some thieving magpie took it to his nest. That's the guitar I did all the '60s sessions on.

Were your parents musical?

No, not at all. But they didn't mind me getting into it. I think they were quite relieved to see something being done instead of art work, which they thought was a loser's game.

What music did you play when you first started?

Early days—Page (far right) with Carter-Lewis
and the Southerners in London, 1963.

I wasn't really playing anything properly. I just knew a few bits of
solos and things—not much. I just kept getting records and learning
that way. It was the obvious influences at the beginning: Scotty Moore,
James Burton, Cliff Gallup—he was Gene Vincent's guitarist—Johnny
Weeks, and those seemed to be the most sustaining influences until I
began to hear blues guitarists Elmore James, B. B. King, and people like
that. Basically, that was the start—a mixture of rock and blues. Then I
stretched out a lot more, and I started doing studio work. I had to
branch out, and I did. I might do three sessions a day—a film session in
the morning, and then there'd be something like a rock band, and then
maybe a folk session in the evening. I didn't know *what* was coming! But
it was a really good disciplinary area to work in—the studio. And it also
gave me a chance to develop on all of the different styles.

Do you remember the first band you were in?

Just friends and things. I played in a lot of different small bands around, but nothing you could ever get any records of.

What kind of music were you playing with Neil Christian and the Crusaders?

This was before the Stones happened, so we were doing Chuck Berry, Gene Vincent, and Bo Diddley things mainly. At the time, public taste was more engineered towards Top 10 records, so it was a bit of a struggle. But there'd always be a small section of the audience into what we were doing.

Wasn't there a break in your music career at this point?

Yes. I stopped playing and went to art college for about two years while concentrating more on blues playing on my own. And then from art college to the Marquee Club in London. I used to go up and jam on a Thursday night with the interlude band. One night somebody came up and said, "Would you like to play on a record?" I said, "Yeah, why not?" It did quite well, and that was it after that. I can't remember the title of it now. From that point, I started suddenly getting all this studio work. There was a cross-roads—is it an art career or is it going to be music? Well, anyway, I had to stop going to the art college because I was really getting into music. Big Jim Sullivan—who was really brilliant—and I were the only guitarists doing those sessions. Then a point came where Stax Records started influencing music to have more brass and orchestral stuff. The guitar started to take a back trend with

The Yardbirds tearing it up at Holte Hallen, Copenhagen, Denmark, April 15, 1967.

just the occasional riff. I didn't realize how rusty I was going to get until a rock and roll session turned up from France, and I could hardly play. I thought it was time to get out, and I did.

You just stopped playing?

For a while, I just worked on my stuff alone, and then I went to a Yardbirds concert at Oxford, and they were all walking around in their penguin suits. Keith Relf got really drunk, and was saying "F**k you" right into the mic, and falling into the drums. I thought it was a great anarchistic night, and I went back into the dressing room and said,

"What a brilliant show!" There was this great argument going on. Bassist Paul Samwell-Smith said, "Well, I'm leaving the group, and if I was you, Keith, I'd do the very same thing." So he left the group, and Keith didn't. But they were stuck, you see, because they had commitments and dates, so I said, "I'll play the bass if you like." And then it worked out that we did the dual lead-guitar thing as soon as [former rhythm guitarist] Chris Dreja could get it together with the bass, which happened, though not for long. But then came the question of discipline. If you're going to do dual lead-guitar riffs and patterns, then you've got to be playing the same things. Jeff Beck had discipline occasionally, but he was an inconsistent player in that when he's on, he's probably the best there is, but at that time, and for a period afterwards, he had no respect whatsoever for audiences.

Were you playing acoustic guitar during your session period?

Yes. I had to do it on studio work. And you come to grips with it very quickly, too—very quickly, because it's what is expected. There was a lot of busking in the earlier days, but, as I say, I had to come to grips with it, and it was a good schooling.

You were also using the Les Paul for those sessions?

The Gibson Les Paul Custom—the "Black Beauty." I was one of the first people in England to have one, but I didn't know that then. I just saw it on the wall, had a go with it, and it was good. I traded a Gretsch Chet Atkins I'd had before for the Les Paul.

What kinds of amplifiers were you using for session work?

A small Supro, which I used until someone—I don't know who— smashed it up for me. I'm going to try to get another one. It's like a Harmony amp, I think, and all of *Led Zeppelin* was done on that.

What do you remember most about your early days with the Yardbirds?

One thing is it was chaotic in recording. I mean we did one tune, and didn't really know what it was. We had Ian Stewart from the Stones on piano, and we'd just finished the take, and without even hearing it [producer] Mickie Most said, "Next." I said, "I've never worked like this in my life," and he said, "Don't worry about it." It was all done very quickly, as it sounds. It was things like that that really led to the general state of mind and depression of Relf and [drummer] Jim McCarty that broke the group up. I tried to keep it together, but there was no chance. They just wouldn't have it. In fact, Relf said the magic of the band disappeared when Clapton left. I was really keen on doing anything, though—probably because of having had all that studio work and variety beforehand. So it didn't matter what way they wanted to go. They were definitely talented people, but they couldn't really see the woods for the trees at that time.

You thought the best period of the Yardbirds was when Beck was with them?

I did. Giorgio Gomelsky [the Yardbirds' manager and producer] was good for him, because he got him thinking and attempting new things. That's when they started all sorts of departures. Apparently [co-producer] Simon Napier-Bell sang the guitar riff of "Over Under Sideways Down" to Jeff to demonstrate what he wanted, but I don't know whether that's true or not. I never spoke to him about it. I know the idea of the record was to sort of emulate the sound of the old "Rock Around the Clock"–type record—that bass and backbeat thing. But it wouldn't be evident at all. Every now and again he'd say, "Let's make a record around such and such," and no one would ever know what the example was at the end of the song.

Can you describe some of your musical interaction with Beck during the Yardbirds period?

Sometimes it worked really great, and sometimes it didn't. There were a lot of harmonies that I don't think anyone else had really done—not like we did. The Stones were the only ones who got into two guitars going at the same time from old Muddy Waters records. But we were more into solos, rather than a rhythm thing. The point is, you've got to have the parts worked out, and I'd find that I was doing what I was supposed to, while something totally different would be coming from Jeff. That was all right for the areas of improvisation, but there were other parts where it just did not work. You've got to understand that Beck and I came from the same sort of roots. If you've got things you enjoy, then you want to do them—to the horrifying point where we'd done *Led Zeppelin* with "You Shook Me," and then I heard *he'd* done "You Shook Me" on *Truth*. I was terrified, because I thought they'd be the same. But I hadn't even known he'd done it, and he hadn't known that we had.

Did Beck play bass on "Over Under Sideways Down"?

No. In fact, for that LP, they just got him in to do the solos, because they'd had a lot of trouble with him. But then when I joined the band, he supposedly wasn't going to walk off anymore. Well, he did a couple of times. It's strange. If he'd had a bad day, he'd take it out on

> *"I don't think anybody con-sciously nicked [using feedback] from anybody else—it was just going on."*
>
> ✦ ✦ ✦ ✦ ✦ ✦

the audience. I don't know whether he's the same now—his playing sounds far more consistent on records. You see, on the "Beck's Bolero" thing [from *Truth*], I was working with that. The track was done, and then the producer just disappeared. He was never seen again. He simply didn't come back. Napier-Bell—he just sort of left me and Jeff to it. Jeff was playing, and I was in the box [recording booth]. And even though he says he wrote it, I wrote it. I'm playing the electric 12-string on it. Beck is doing the slide bits, and I'm basically playing around the chords. The idea was built around Maurice Ravel's "Bolero." It has a lot of drama to it—it came off right. It was a good lineup, too, with Keith Moon and everything.

Wasn't that band going to be Led Zeppelin?

It was. Yeah. Not Led Zeppelin as a name—the name came afterwards. But it was said afterwards that's what it could have been called. Because Moony wanted to get out of the Who, and so did John Entwistle, but when it came down to getting hold of a singer, it was either going to be Steve Winwood or Steve Marriott. Finally, it came down to Marriott. He was contacted, and the reply came back from his manager's office: "How would you like to have a group with no fingers, boys?" Or words to that effect. So the group was dropped because of Marriott's commitment to the Small Faces, but I think it would have been the first of all those bands like the Cream and everything. Instead, it didn't happen—apart from the "Bolero." That's the closest it got. John Paul Jones is on that, too, and so is Nicky Hopkins.

You only recorded a few songs with Beck on record?

Yeah. "Happenings Ten Years Time Ago," "Stroll On," "Train Kept A-Rollin'," and "Psycho Daisies," "Bolero," and a few other things that were earlier than the Yardbirds. Unreleased songs, such as "Louie Louie," and things like that. Really good, though—really great.

Were you using any boosters with the Yardbirds to get all those sounds?

Fuzz tone—which I'd virtually regurgitated from what I heard on "2000 Pound Bee" by the Ventures. They had a fuzz tone. It was nothing like the one this guy, Roger Mayer, made for me. He worked for the British Navy in the electronics division. He did all the fuzz pedals for Jimi Hendrix later—all those octave doublers and things like that. He made this one for me, but that was during the studio period, you see. I think Jeff had one then, but I was the one who got the effect going again. That accounted for quite a lot of the boost, and that sort of sustain in the music.

You were also doing all sorts of things with feedback?

You know "I Need You" by the Kinks? I think I did that bit there in the beginning. I don't know who really did feedback first—it just sort of happened. I don't think anybody consciously nicked it from anybody else—it was just going on. But Pete Townshend obviously was the one—through the music of his group—who made the use of feedback more his style, and so it's related to him. Whereas, the other players—like Jeff and myself—were playing more single notes and things than chords.

You used a Danelectro with the Yardbirds?

Yes, but not with Beck. I did use it in the latter days. I used it onstage for "White Summer." I used a special tuning for that. The low *E*-string was tuned down to *B*, and then it went *A, D, G, A, D*. It's like a modal tuning—a sitar tuning, in fact.

Was "Black Mountain Side" on *Led Zeppelin* an extension of that?

I wasn't totally original on that. It had been done in the folk clubs a lot. Annie Briggs was the first one I heard do that riff. I was playing it as well, and then there was Bert Jansch's version. He's the one who crystallized all the acoustic playing as far as I'm concerned. Those first few albums of his were absolutely brilliant. And the tuning on "Black Mountain Side" is the same as "White Summer." It's taken a bit of battering, that Danelectro guitar, I'm afraid.

Do those songs work well now on the Danelectro?

I played them on that guitar before, so I'd thought I'd do it again. But I might change it around to something else, because my whole amp situation is different from what it used to be. Now it's Marshall, and then it was Vox heads and different cabinets. A kind of a hodge-podge, but it worked.

You used a Vox 12-string with the Yardbirds?

That's right. I can't remember the titles now. The Mickie Most things—some of the B-sides. I remember there was one with an electric 12-string solo on the end of it that was all right. I don't have copies of them now, and I don't know what they're called. I've got *Little Games*, but that's about it.

You were using Vox amps with the Yardbirds?

AC30s. They've held up consistently well. Even the new ones are pretty good. I tried some. I got four in, tried them out, and they were all reasonably good. I was going to build up a big bank of four of them, but Bonzo's kit is so loud that they just don't come over the top of it properly.

Were the AC30s you used with the Yardbirds modified in any way?

Only by Vox. You could get ones with special treble boosters on the back—which is what I had. I didn't do that much customizing, apart from making sure all the points, soldering contacts, and things were solid.

What kind of guitar were you using on the first Led Zeppelin album?

A Telecaster. I used the Les Paul with the Yardbirds on about two numbers, and a Fender for the rest. You see, the Les Paul Custom had a central setting—a kind of out-of-phase pickup sound that Jeff couldn't get on his Les Paul, so I used mine for that sound.

Was the Telecaster the one Beck gave you?

Yes. There was work done on it, but only afterwards. I painted it. Everyone painted their guitars in those days. And I had reflective plastic sheeting underneath the pickguard that gives rainbow colors.

It sounds exactly like a Les Paul.

Yeah—well, that's the amp and everything. You see, I could get a lot of tones out of the guitar that you normally couldn't. This confusion goes back to those early sessions again with the Les Paul. Those might not sound like a Les Paul, but that's what I used. It's just different amps, mic positions, and different things. Also, if you just crank it up to the distortion point so you can sustain notes, it's bound to sound like a Les Paul. I was using the Supro amp for the first album, and still do. The "Stairway to Heaven" solo was done when I pulled out the Telecaster—which I hadn't used for a long time—plugged it into the Supro, and away it went again. That's a different sound entirely from any of the rest of the first album. It was a good versatile setup.

**What kind of acoustic guitar are you using on "Black
Mountain Side" and "Babe I'm Gonna Leave You"?**

That was a Gibson J-200 that wasn't mine. I borrowed it. It was a
beautiful guitar—really great. I've never found a guitar of that quality
anywhere since. I could play so easily on it, and get a really thick sound.
It had heavy-gauge strings on it, but it just didn't seem to feel like it.

Do you just use your fingers when playing acoustic?

Yes. I used fingerpicks once, but I find them too spiky. They're too
sharp. You can't get the tone or response that you would get, say, the way
classical players approach gut-string instruments. The way they pick, the
whole thing is the tonal response of the string. It seems important.

Can you describe your picking style?

I don't know, really. It's a cross between fingerstyle and flatpicking.
There's a guy in England called Davey Graham, and he never used any
fingerpicks or anything. He used a thumbpick every now and again, but
I prefer just a flatpick and fingers, because then it's easier to get around
from guitar to guitar. Well, it is for me, anyway. But, apparently, he has
calluses on the left hand, and all over the right, as well. He can get so
much attack on his strings, and he's really good.

**The guitar on "Communication Breakdown" sounds as if
it's coming out of a little shoebox.**

Yeah. I put it in a small room—a little, tiny vocal booth-type
thing—and miked it from a distance. You see, there's a very old recording maxim that goes: "Distance makes depth." I've used that recording
technique a hell of a lot with the band. You're always used to them
close-miking amps—just putting the microphone in front—but I'd have
a mic right out the back as well, and then balance the two, getting rid
of all the phasing problems. You shouldn't have to use EQ in the studio
if the instruments sound right. It should all be done with the micro-
phones. But everyone has gotten so carried away with EQ that they
have forgotten the whole science of microphone placement. There
aren't too many guys who know it. I'm sure Les Paul knows a lot.
Obviously, he must have been well into that—as were all those who
produced early rock records where there were only one or two mics in
the studio.

**The solo on "I Can't Quit You Babe" is interesting. There are
many pull-offs in a sort of sloppy, but amazingly inventive style.**

There are mistakes in it, but it doesn't make any difference. I'll always leave the mistakes in. I can't help it. The timing bits on the *A* and *B♭* parts are right, though it might sound wrong. The timing just *sounds* off. But there are some wrong notes. You've got to be reasonably honest about it. It's like the film soundtrack for *The Song Remains the Same*. There's no editing on that. It wasn't the best concert playing-wise at all, but it was the only one with celluloid footage, so there it was. It was all right—it was just one "as it is" performance. It wasn't one of those real magic nights, but, then again, it wasn't a terrible night. So, for all its mistakes and everything else, it's a very honest soundtrack. Rather than just trailing around through a tour with a recording mobile truck waiting for the magic night, it was just, "There you are—take it or leave it." I've got a lot of live recordings going back to 1969.

Jumping ahead to *Led Zeppelin II*, the riff in the middle of "Whole Lotta Love" is a very composed and structured phrase.

I had it worked out already—that one—before entering the studio. I had rehearsed it. And then all that other stuff—sonic wave sounds and all that—I built up in the studio using effects and things. Treatments.

How is that descending riff done?

With a metal slide and backwards echo. I think I came up with that before anybody. I know it has been used a lot now, but not at the time. I thought of it on this Mickie Most thing. In fact, some of the things that might sound a bit odd have, in fact, backwards echo involved in them, as well.

What kind of effect are you using on the beginning of "Ramble On"?

If I can remember correctly, it's like harmony feedback, and then it changes. To be more specific, most of the tracks just start off bass, drums, and guitar. Once you've done the drums and bass, you just build everything up afterwards. It's like a starting point, and you start constructing from square one.

Is the rest of the band in the studio when you put down the solos?

No. Never. I don't like anybody else in the studio when I'm putting on the guitar parts. I usually just limber up for a while, and then maybe do three solos, and take the best of the three.

Is there an electric 12-string on "Thank You"?

Yes. I think it's a Fender or Rickenbacker.

What is the effect on "Out on the Tiles"?

That's ambient sound—which is exactly what I was talking about

"MY VOCATION IS MORE IN COMPOSITION THAN IN ANYTHING
ELSE—ORCHESTRATING THE GUITAR LIKE AN ARMY"

Page in full mystical "Zoso" garb with the doubleneck Gibson he used to perform "Stairway to Heaven" live.

"The way I see recording, the whole idea is to try and capture the sound of the room live, and the emotion of the whole moment."

✦ ✦ ✦ ✦ ✦ ✦

earlier regarding close-miking and distance-miking. Getting the distance of the time lag from one end of the room to the other and putting that in, as well. The way I see recording, the whole idea is to try and capture the sound of the room live, and the emotion of the whole moment. That's the very essence of it. Consequently, you've got to capture as much of the room sound as possible.

On "Tangerine," it sounds as if you're playing a pedal steel.

I am. And there's also pedal steel on *Led Zeppelin*—on "Your Time Is Gonna Come." I had never played steel before, but I just picked it up. There are a lot of things I do first time around that I haven't done before. In fact, I hadn't touched a pedal steel from the first album to the third. It's a bit of a pinch really from the things that Chuck Berry did. But, nevertheless, it fits. The playing is more out of tune on the first album, because I hadn't got a kit to put it together.

You've also played other stringed instruments on records?

"Gallows Pole" was the first time for banjo, and "The Battle of Evermore" has a mandolin that was lying around. It wasn't mine—it was Jonesy's. I just picked it up, got the chords, and it sort of started happening. I did it more or less straight off. But, you see, that's finger-picking again. It's going back to the studio days, and developing a certain amount of technique—at least enough to be adapted and used. My fingerpicking is a sort of cross between Pete Seeger, Earl Scruggs, and total incompetence.

The fourth album was the first time you used a double-neck?

I didn't use a double-neck on that, but I had to get one afterwards to play "Stairway to Heaven." I did all those guitars on it—I just built them up. That was the beginning of my building up harmonized guitars properly. "Ten Years Gone" was an extension of that, and then "Achilles' Last Stand" is like the essential flow of it, really, because there was no time to think the things out. I had to more or less lay it down on the first track, and harmonize on the second track. It was really fast working on *Presence*—I did all the guitar overdubs on that LP in one night. The rest of the band didn't know what the hell I was going to do with it, but I wanted to give each section its own identity, and I think it came off really good. I didn't think I'd be able to do it in one night. I thought I'd have to do it in the course of three different nights to get the individual sections. But I was so into it that my mind was working properly for a change. It sort of crystallized, and everything was just pouring out. I was very happy with the guitar on that whole album as far as the maturity of the playing goes.

When you started playing the double-neck, did it require a new approach on your part?

Yes. The main thing is, there's an effect you can get where you leave the 12-string neck on and play on the 6-string neck, and you get the 12 strings vibrating in sympathy. It's like an Indian sitar, and I've worked on that a little bit. I use it on "Stairway"—not on the album, but on the film soundtrack. It's surprising—it doesn't vibrate as heavily as a sitar would, but it does add to the overall tonal quality.

You think your playing on the fourth LP is the best you've ever done?

Without a doubt. As far as consistency goes, and as far as the quality of playing on a whole album, I would say "yes." But I don't know what the best solo I've ever done is. I have no idea. My vocation is more in composition than in anything else. Building up harmonies, orchestrating the guitar like an army—a guitar army. I think that's where it's at, really, for me. I'm talking about actual orchestration in the same way you'd orchestrate a classical piece of music. Instead of using brass and violins, you treat the guitars with synthesizers or other devices—give them different treatments so that they have enough frequency range and scope and everything to keep the listener as totally committed to it as the player is. It's a difficult project, but it's one I've got to do.

Have you done anything towards this end already?

Only on these three tunes: "Stairway to Heaven," "Ten Years Gone," and "Achilles' Last Stand." I can see certain milestones along the way, like the middle section of "Four Sticks." The sound of those guitars—that's where I'm going. I've got long pieces written. I've got one really long one that's harder to play than anything. It's sort of classical, but then it goes through changes from that mood to really laid-

Page breaks out the violin bow during Led Zeppelin's debut performance at Copenhagen's Gladsaxe Teen Club, September 7, 1968. The band was booked as "the Yardbirds" and performed as "the New Yardbirds."

back rock, and then to really intensified stuff. With a few laser notes thrown in, we might be all right.

What is the amplifier setup you're using now?

Onstage? It's 100-watt Marshalls, which are customized in New York so they've got 200 watts. I've got four unstacked cabinets, and I've got a wah-wah pedal and an MXR unit. Everything else is total flash [*laughs*]. I've got a harmonizer, a Theremin, a violin bow, and an Echoplex.

Are there certain settings you use on the amp?

Depending on the acoustics of the place, the volume is up to about 3, and the rest is pretty standard.

When was the first time you used the violin bow?

The first time I recorded with it was with the Yardbirds. But the idea was put to me by a classical string player when I was doing studio work. One of us tried to bow the guitar, then we tried it between us, and it worked. At that point, I was just bowing it, but the other effects

I've obviously come up with on my own—using wah-wah, and echo. You have to put rosin on the bow, and the rosin sticks to the string and makes it vibrate.

What kinds of picks and strings do you use?

Herco heavy-gauge nylon picks and Ernie Ball Super Slinky strings.

What guitars are you using?

God, this is really hard—there are so many. My Les Paul, the usual one, and I've got a spare one if anything goes wrong. I've got a double-neck, and one of those Fender string-benders that was made for me by Gene Parsons. I've cut it back from what I was going to use on tour. I have a Martin guitar and a Gibson A-4 mandolin. The Martin is one of the cheap ones—it's not the one with the herringbone back or anything like that. It's probably a D-18. It has those nice Grover tuning machines on it. I've got a Gibson Everly Brothers that was given to me by Ronnie Wood. That's like the current favorite, but I don't take it out on the road because it's a really personal guitar. I keep it with me in the room. It's a beauty. It's fantastic. There are only a few of those around. Ron has one, and Keith Richards has one, and I've got one, as well. So it's really nice. I haven't had a chance to use it on record yet, but I will, because it has such a nice sound.

Let's see—what else have we got? I know when I come onstage it looks like a guitar shop, the way they're all standing up there. But I sold off all of my guitars before I left for America. There was a lot of old stuff hanging around that I didn't need. It's no point having things if you don't need them. When all the equipment came over here, we had done our rehearsals, and we were really on top—really in tip-top form. Then Robert caught laryngitis, and we had to postpone a lot of dates and reshuffle them, and I didn't touch a guitar for five weeks. I got a bit panicky about that—after two years on the road that's a lot to think about. And I'm still only warming up. I still can't coordinate a lot of the things I need to be doing. I'm getting by, but it's not right. I don't feel 100-percent right yet.

What year is the Les Paul you're using now?

It's a 1959. It has been repainted, but that's all gone now because it chipped off. Joe Walsh got it for me.

Do you think when you went from the Telecaster to the Les Paul that your playing changed?

Yes—I think so. It's more of a fight with a Telecaster, but there are rewards. The Gibson has a stereotyped sound maybe—I don't know. But it has beautiful sustain, and I like sustain because it relates to bowed instruments and everything—this whole area that everyone has been pushing and experimenting in. When you think about it, it's mainly sustain.

Do you use special tunings on the electric guitar?

All the time. They're my own that I've worked out, so I'd rather keep those to myself, but they're never open tunings. I have used those, but most of the things I've written have not been open tunings, so you can get more chords into them.

Did you ever meet any of those folk players you admire: Bert Jansch, John Renbourn, or any of them?

No, and the most terrifying thing of all happened about a few months ago. Jansch's playing appeared as if it was going down or something, and it turns out he has arthritis. I really think he's one of the best. He was—without any doubt—the one who crystallized so many things. As much as Hendrix had done on electric, I think he has done on acoustic. He was really way, way ahead. And for something like that to happen is such a tragedy, with a mind as brilliant as that. There you go. Another player whose physical handicap didn't stop him is Django Reinhardt. For his last LP, they pulled him out of retirement to do it. He'd been retired for years, and it's fantastic. You know the story about him in the caravan and losing fingers and such. But the record is just fantastic. He must have been playing all the time to be that good. It's horrifyingly good. Horrifying. But it's always good to hear perennial players like that—like Les Paul and people like that.

You listen to Les Paul?

Oh, yeah. You can tell Jeff Beck did too, can't you? Have you ever heard "It's Been a Long, Long Time" [a mid-1940s single by the Les Paul Trio with Bing Crosby]? You ought to hear that. He does everything on that—everything in one go. It's basically one guitar, even though they've tracked on rhythms and stuff. But, my goodness, his introductory chords and everything are fantastic. He sets the whole tone, and then he goes into this solo that is fantastic. Now that's where I heard feedback first—from Les Paul. Also, vibrato—even before B. B. King. I mean, he's the father of it all—multitracking and everything else. If it hadn't been for him, there wouldn't have been anything, really. I've traced a hell of a lot of rock and roll—little riffs and things—back to Les Paul, Chuck Berry, and Cliff Gallup.

You said that Eric Clapton was the person who synthesized the Les Paul guitar sound?

Yeah—without a doubt. When he was with the Bluesbreakers, it was just a magic combination. He got one of the Marshall amps, and away he went. It just happened. I thought he played brilliantly then— really brilliantly. That was very stirring stuff.

Do you think you were responsible for any specific guitar sounds?

This guy Nick Kent [British rock journalist] came out with this idea about how he thought the guitar parts in "Trampled Under Foot" were part of a really revolutionary sound. I hadn't realized anyone would think it was, but I can explain exactly how it's done. Again, it's sort of backwards echo and wah-wah. I don't know how responsible I was for new sounds, because there were so many good things happening around the release of the first Zeppelin album, like Hendrix and Clapton.

Were you focusing on anything in particular on the first Led Zeppelin LP with regards to certain guitar sounds?

The trouble is keeping a separation between sounds, so you don't have the same guitar effect all the time. That's where that orchestration thing comes in, and the dream has been accomplished by the computerized mixing console. The sort of struggle to achieve so many things is over. You can hear what I mean on the soundtrack for Kenneth Anger's *Lucifer Rising*. You see, I didn't play any guitar on that—apart from one point. That was all other instruments—all synthesizers. Every instrument was given a process so it didn't sound like what it really was—the voices, drones, mantras, and even tabla drums. When you've got a collage of, say, four of these sounds together, people will be drawn right in, because there will be sounds they hadn't heard before. That's basically what I'm into—collages of sound with emotional intensity and melody and all that. You know, there are so many good people around like John McLaughlin, but it's a totally different thing than what I'm doing.

Do you think he has a sustaining quality as a guitarist?

He always had that technique—right from when I first knew him when he was working in a guitar shop. I would say he was the best jazz guitarist in England then, in the traditional mode of Johnny Smith and Tal Farlow. A combination of those two is exactly what he sounded like. He was easily the best guitarist in England, and he was working in a guitar shop. I'll tell you one thing—I don't know one musician who has stuck to his guns, and who was good in the early days, who hasn't come through now with recognition from everybody.

✦ LESSONS ✦

20.
ERIC CLAPTON'S TRIPLET-BASED PENTATONIC RIFFS

✦ ✦ ✦ ✦ ✦ ✦

BY JESSE GRESS
JUNE 2006

The original British blues-rock guitar hero, Eric Clapton was referred to as "God" by many well before his 21st birthday—at least in the graffiti that decorated London circa 1965–1967. Whether or not Clapton truly is a celestial power, his transition from the Yardbirds' original guitarist to the revolutionary blues ace who powered John Mayall's Blues Breakers, Cream, Blind Faith, and Derek and the Dominos was downright biblical in the sense that it spawned perhaps the largest following of any single rock guitarist to date.

A switch to a more song-oriented approach in the early '70s has garnered Clapton massive popularity as a solo artist ever since, but his recent projects—a Cream reunion in 2005, tours with his own guitar-intensive band, and a pair of 2007 appearances with Steve Winwood—confirm that Clapton's original flame still burns brightly. Always an elegant player and a pioneer of exquisite tone, E. C. was the first to introduce the kind of smooth, repetitive triplet-based pentatonic figures in **Examples 1–4** to the blues-rock pantheon. Practice 'em until they flow like water, then append them with the trio of sweet Clapton-isms in

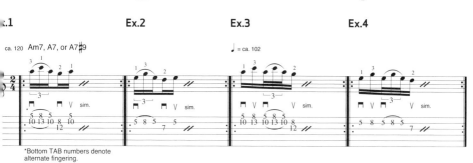

*Bottom TAB numbers denote alternate fingering.

Examples 5–7. Strive for that "Slowhand" vibrato—a study in itself—
and watch the sparks fly.

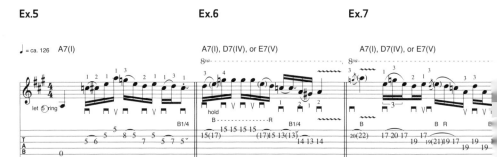

21.
JEFF BECK'S PULL-OFFS, BENDS, AND WHAMMY MAGIC

✦ ✦ ✦ ✦ ✦ ✦

BY JESSE GRESS
DECEMBER 2007

As unpredictable as they come, Jeff Beck has kept guitarists on the edge of their seats for more than four decades now, and he's not done with us yet. With his ever-expanding arsenal of techniques and his continually evolving talents at melodic interpretation, Beck shows no sign of slowing down. His mind-blowing catalog, from the Yardbirds to his current four-piece lineup (as well as numerous guest appearances on others' projects), constitutes nothing less than a university's worth of study materials.

Lose your pick (if you dare) and dig deep into the snarly pull-offs and sweet 'n' sour bendies in **Ex. 1**, the whammy-bar inflections in **Ex. 2** that leave you wondering whether you just heard a slide guitar or blues harp, and **Ex. 3**'s deliciously dissonant fingerstyle "banjo" rolls (sorry for giving this last one away, Jeff!). You'll be rewarded with goosebumps to spare.

Beck's innovative whammy work doesn't end with faux slide and harp sounds, either. You'll need a floating bar to play **Ex. 4**, which shows how the Guv'nor coaxes a tear-jerking *G* Lydian melody (actually a simple descending *D* major scale sequence à la "Dueling Banjos") from a

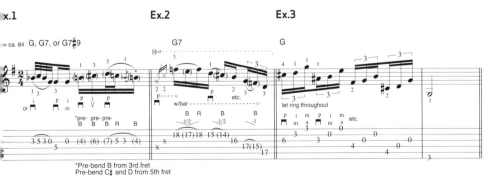

*Pre-bend B from 3rd fret
Pre-bend C♯ and D from 5th fret

single, 19th-fret *D* harmonic. Finally, **Ex. 5** offers a taste of Beck's uncannily accurate off-the-fretboard slide work—just one of many high points (no pun intended) in his live set. Mute all six strings with your fretting hand (very important), hold the slide in your plucking hand, and use it to tap and vibrate the virtual above-the-neck "fret" positions as notated. You'll be conversing with the birdies in no time.

Ex.4

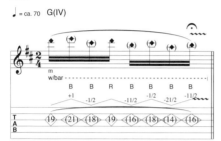

Ex.5

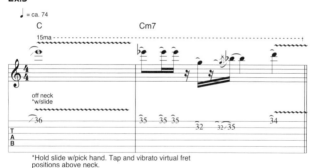

*Hold slide w/pick hand. Tap and vibrato virtual fret positions above neck.

22.
JIMMY PAGE'S ALT-TUNED DRONES AND FAUX-WHAMMY MOVES

✦ ✦ ✦ ✦ ✦ ✦

BY JESSE GRESS
NOVEMBER 2005

James Patrick Page is one clever bastard. Think what you will about the third member of the Yardbirds trinity's alleged appropriations of O.P.M. (you figure it out) during his reign with the legendary Led Zeppelin, but the wizardly guitarist—gifted with a keen producer's ear—has always had plenty of tricks of his own. For instance, Page cultivated a deep relationship with alternate tunings and used them to create lush, otherwise unobtainable musical textures on such epic Zep songs as "Kashmir" (*DADGAD*) and "The Rain Song" (*D, G, C, G, C, D*, low to high).

The deceptively simple and easy-to-play combination of simple and complex droning chord voicings that Page concocted for "The Rain Song" are presented without rhythmic reference in **Ex.1**, but after listening to the recording you should have little trouble piecing together the puzzle. (Tip: Try it on a 12-string.) In another stroke of brilliance, Page was probably the first guy to come up with the forehead-smackingly simple solution for playing whammy-style glissandi on a stop-tail Les Paul

Ex.1

by hammering-on and pulling-off notes while bending and releasing the string behind the nut with his pick hand. **Examples 2 and 3** illustrate this technique, which has since become one of rock's most enduring Spinal Tap moves.

Ex.2   **Ex.3**

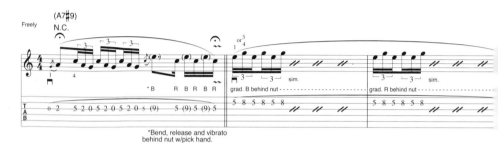

*Bend, release and vibrato
behind nut w/pick hand.